Study Guide with MacroSolve Software
Hall and Taylor's
MACROECONOMICS
Second Edition

Study Guide with MacroSolve Software
Hall and Taylor's
MACROECONOMICS
Second Edition

Stephen R. King
Rick M. McConnell
David H. Papell

W.W. Norton and Company
New York   London

IBM® is a registered trademark of the International Business Machines
Corporation.
Apple® is a registered trademark of Apple Computer, Inc.
Macintosh™ is a trademark of Apple Computer Inc.

Published simultaneously in Canada by Penguin Books Canada Ltd.
2801 John Street, Markham, Ontario L3R 1B4
Printed in the United States of America.

Second Edition

W. W. Norton & Company, Inc., 500 Fifth Avenue, New York, N.Y. 10110
W. W. Norton & Company Ltd., 37 Great Russell Street, London WC1B 3NU

ISBN 0-393-95689-X {IBM 5 1/4"}
ISBN 0-393-95783-7 {IBM 3 1/2"}
ISBN 0-393-95688-1 {MACINTOSH}

1 2 3 4 5 6 7 8 9 0

Contents

Acknowledgments

At all stages of writing the study guide and software, we have benefited greatly from the encouragement, editorial comments, and suggestions made by Drake McFeely. We are also thankful for the careful review of the problems done by Cheryl Holsey and Stephen Kerman. The feedback on the first edition that we have received from students at the University of Houston, the University of Virginia, and Stanford University has been very helpful in preparing the second edition.

Preface

The purpose of this study guide is to help you learn the material in Hall and Taylor's *Macroeconomics*, Second Edition. It isolates the major learning objectives, reviews the major terms and concepts, and provides self-tests and problem sets for every chapter in the text. Just as important, it introduces you to **MacroSolve**, a computer program for macroeconomic analysis. You can use **MacroSolve** to analyze the behavior of 19 major macroeconomic variables over the last 56 years, and to simulate with minimal effort the macroeconomic models discussed in the textbook. A word of caution before you continue, however: the study guide and the software will help you to learn the material more easily, but they are not substitutes for reading the textbook.

Each chapter in the study guide opens with a section called *Main Objectives*, which highlights the basic topics covered in the text chapter. This is followed by a section called *Key Terms and Concepts*, which reviews and explains the chapter's most important concepts. Next comes the *Self-Test*. Here, there are three types of questions: fill in the blank, true-false, and review. You will find answers to the Self-Test at the back of each chapter. Each chapter also includes a *Problem Set*, where *Worked Problems* that include step-by-step solutions precede *Review Problems* that you work yourself. Answers to the Review Problems are found at the back of each chapter. Finally, most chapters include a set of *MacroSolve Exercises* that use the enclosed software to analyze the macroeconomic questions raised in the chapter. You can also use the software to answer questions other than those offered in the text. It is easy to change key model parameters and determine the effects on other variables. Answers to the MacroSolve exercises are also found at the end of the chapter.

While every student studies differently, you might use the study guide in the following way. First, read the chapter in the textbook without worrying too much about understanding everything. Second, read the Main Objectives and Key Terms and Concepts sections in the study guide. If you come across a concept that you do not understand, go back to the text. Third, take the Self-Test as if you were taking an exam. Write down your answers, and be sure to provide an explanation for the true-false questions. Refer back to the text or to the study guide to make sure that you understand the questions that you missed. Fourth, work through the Problem Set, using the Worked Problems to learn how to solve the different types of numerical problems. Fifth, work through the MacroSolve questions. The computer will do all of the arithmetic, leaving you free to ensure that you understand the economic issues discussed in the chapter. Finally, re-read the chapter in the text to make sure that you understand it completely. You should now be well prepared to answer the questions and problems in the back of each text chapter.

Study Guide with MacroSolve Software
Hall and Taylor's
MACROECONOMICS
Second Edition

Introduction to MacroSolve

MacroSolve has been written to make learning macroeconomics easier. Many questions in macroeconomics require either the manipulation of economic times series or the algebraic solution of equations describing the economy. It is important that you know how to do both of these things. But it is also useful to be able to avoid excessive hand calculations when you are first learning the subject. MacroSolve relieves you of tis drudgery, enabling you to concentrate on understanding macroeconomic concepts.

The program can be separated into three main sections: plotting, graphing, and modeling. The plotting options enable you to plot simultaneously up to 3 of the 19 available series against time, either annually (1930–present) or quarterly (1967–present). Graphing also uses historical data, but instead of plotting the variables against time, one is graphed on the y-axis against another on the x-axis. Finally, the modeling section of MacroSolve allows you to display either graphically or numerically the effects of a wide variety of fluctuations in economic variables.

The software has been designed with both novice and experienced users in mind. For the novice, it is important to realize that there is nothing you can enter at the keyboard that will harm the computer or the program. If you make a mistake in entering something to the program, simply try it again. All mistakes can easily be remedied in this manner. For the experienced user, the menu structure has been designed to enable you to achieve quickly the results that you want, without forcing you to wade through a maze of irrelevant menus.

Now that you have a general understanding of the basic purpose of the program, you should read the instructions for either the IBM PC or Macintosh version below, depending on which one you have purchased. If you are already familiar with one version and now wish to learn the other, keep in mind that the menus, models, and theory behind the programs are identical. You will find that the only true differences are the specifics of the various selection routines and how information is presented on the screen.

Instructions for the IBM PC Version of MacroSolve

Equipment Required

The IBM version requires that you have an IBM personal computer (PC, XT, AT, Portable, or Convertible) or a compatible PC ("clone") with at least 256K of free memory. A graphics board is also highly recommended. Currently, all standard IBM monochrome and color equipment is supported. The software will work with the IBM Color Graphics Adapter, the IBM Enhanced Graphics Adapter, the Compaq monochrome display, and the Hercules or Hercules Plus high resolution monochrome graphics boards.

If you have a computer with an incompatible graphics board, or one that is not capable of displaying graphics, the graphics functions of the program will be automatically disabled. You can still see results from the models and data in tabular form, but the program will be far more useful to you if you can find a PC with a compatible graphics board.

Installing MacroSolve

You may make one copy of the diskette you have purchased, and we recommend that you do so for your personal use. Making such a copy, either to a hard disk or to a floppy diskette, is quite straightforward and is described below. If you want to move your copy of MacroSolve from one hard disk to another you must uninstall it from the first hard disk before installing the program on the new hard disk. Instructions for that process appear in the third subsection below.

Copying to a hard disk: To copy to a hard disk, put your MacroSolve diskette in drive A, and type A: followed by ENTER (or Return). At the A> prompt, type INSTALL followed by your hard disk's drive letter (generally C) and the name of a subdirectory into which you wish to install MacroSolve, for example MACRO. If that subdirectory already exists, MacroSolve will be copied to it; if it does not, the installation program will copy MacroSolve to a new subdirectory with that name.

For example, to install MacroSolve onto drive C, creating a subdirectory named MACRO, you should type

INSTALL A C MACRO

followed by ENTER.

Copying to a floppy diskette[*]: To install MacroSolve onto a floppy diskette, you will first need a formatted blank diskette. To format a new diskette, put your DOS distribution diskette in drive A, and a blank diskette into drive B. At the A> prompt, type

FORMAT/S B:

followed by ENTER. This command will copy the COMMAND.COM file to your disk in addition to formatting the disk, so that you will not need a separate start-up disk to run the program.

To install the program on this new diskette, replace the DOS diskette in drive A with the MacroSolve diskette, and type INSTALL A B followed by ENTER. When the process is complete, you will be able to run MacroSolve from the new diskette by simply typing MACRO. Moreover, MacroSolve will now start automatically if this newly installed diskette is in the A drive when you turn on your computer.

Uninstalling MacroSolve: You may want to uninstall your copy of MacroSolve, for example to move it from one hard disk to another. To uninstall MacroSolve from your hard disk, put your original MacroSolve diskette in drive A and type A: followed by ENTER. Then type UNINSTAL followed by the drive letter for your hard disk and the name of the subdirectory in which your copy of MacroSolve is installed.

For example, to remove MacroSolve from the subdirectory MACRO in drive C, type

UNINSTAL A C MACRO

followed by ENTER. All MacroSolve files will be removed, but you will still need to remove the directory using the RD command.

To remove MacroSolve from a floppy diskette, simply put the diskette with a copy installed in drive B and your original MacroSolve diskette in drive A. Type A: followed by ENTER. At the A> prompt, type UNINSTAL A B followed by ENTER.

---

[*]The presentation here assumes that you are not using an external drive. If your MacroSolve disk *is* in an external drive, replace the drive lables in what follows with the appropriate ones for your configuration.

Starting MacroSolve

Put the MacroSolve diskette into drive A of your computer, and at the A> prompt, type Macro (or MACRO, the computer does not distinguish upper from lower case entries). From there on, simply follow the instructions that the program gives you.

Colors: The program attempts to discern whether your computer's monitor is color or monochrome (Green or Amber display on a black background). The color scheme used depends on this choice. If the screen display is hard to read, you probably need to force the output to be in monochrome or color. This is done by typing MACRO followed by either color or mono; i.e., at the A> prompt from DOS, type MACRO MONO, or MACRO COLOR.

Demonstration

For a demonstration of how the program functions and a sample of its capabilities, run the program by typing MACRO DEMO. (If you want to force the program to display in color, you can type MACRO followed by both COLOR and DEMO; similarly for a monochrome demo, type MACRO MONO DEMO.)

The program will run through some of its options, and will periodically stop to show you the results of its operations. When you are ready to continue with the demonstration, press any key (for example, the SpaceBar). To exit the demonstration, press Esc ("Escape" on some keyboards).

Printing Output

Text output: If you have a printer attached to your computer, you may print nongraphics output of the program at any time pressing the Shift and PrtSc (Print Screen) keys simultaneously. Some printers will not print the vertical and horizontal lines that border the screen displays, but the numbers on the screen will print correctly.

Graphics output: If you have an Epson/IBM graphics compatible printer attached to your computer, and if you have run the DOS program GRAPHICS.COM before running MacroSolve, then graphics displays (plots, graphs, and model displays) can be printed by pressing the Shift and PrtSc keys simultaneously. If there is no printer attached, this command will be ignored. However, if there is an incompatible printer attached, you should be warned that it will print a seemingly random selection of characters. The best action that you can take at that stage is to turn off the printer. After a short wait, you can return to MacroSolve with no further ill effects. If the printed graph appears in reverse video (white lines on a black background), exit MacroSolve and re-run the graphics program, but type GRAPHICS/R rather than simply GRAPHICS. This will tell your computer to print the graphics screens properly when you re-enter MacroSolve.

MacroSolve Commands

MacroSolve commands for the IBM PC version are all entered from the keyboard using one of eight keys, all of which appear on or near the numeric keyboard of standard IBM PCs and clones. On some non-IBM computers, especially portables, the keys are located elsewhere.

The keys have the following meanings:

↑ UpArrow   Moves the cursor (highlighted rectangle on the screen) upwards.

↓ Down Arrow   Moves the cursor downwards.

←- LeftArrow   Moves the cursor to the left, or decreases a numeric value displayed in a menu.

→ RightArrow   Moves the cursor to the right, or increases a numeric value displayed in a menu.

⌐ Enter   Selects a menu entry or an option (the SpaceBar may also be used for this operation, if you prefer).

End   Exits a menu option (also exits graphics).

Home   Shows a help screen to remind you what the various menu options do.

No other key has any meaning in MacroSolve—except when the program prompts you to "Press Any Key to Continue."

Menus and Options for the IBM PC

PLOT TIME SER Menu

This option allows you to plot on the screen up to three macroeconomic time series. The time series are selected from the choices in the **Select Series** option. Once you have entered this option, you select the series by pointing at them with the cursor (which now appears inside the box with the series names in it) and pressing Enter when each desired series is highlighted. Pressing ENTER again will unselect the chosen series. A quick way to unselect all previously selected series its to use the **Unselect All** option. **ANNUAL/quartly** switches between annual data for the period 1930 to present and quarterly data for 1967 to the present. The first time you select this option, the data frequency will change from annual to quarterly. With subsequent presses, the data frequency will switch between quarterly and annual, with the currently selected data frequency capitalized. You can change the sample for which data is displayed by choosing the **Change Sample** option. The selected series can be displayed numerically using the **Tabulate Data** option, or graphically, plotted with time on the horizontal axis, using the **Start Plot** option.

GRAPH SERIES Menu

This option allows you to graph one series on the vertical axis against a second on the horizontal axis. The graph series are selected using the **Select Series** option, exactly as in the PLOT TIME SER menu. Annual and quarterly data are similarly chosen using the **ANNUAL/quartly** option. You can choose the sample for which the data is graphed by using the **Change Sample** option. The screen display is affected by the **POINTS/connect** option, which toggles between displaying the graph using points only and connecting the adjacent observations with a line. The speed with which the graph is displayed on the screen is changed by the **Slow/Fast spd.** toggle. To get an overall picture of the data, use the fast option.. The slow option will help you see more clearly what is happening in particular periods. In the slow mode, you can stop the screen display at any time by pressing a key. To see the graph on the screen, use the **Start Graph** option.

RUN THE MODEL Menu

There are a total of seven models built into the program: three static ISLM (fixed price) models and four AD/PA (aggregate demand/price adjustment) models. To select a particular model, use the **Select Model** option. This works exactly like the **Select Series** options in the PLOT TIME SER and GRAPH SERIES menus. You can change an exogenous variable (the money supply, government spending, or a price shock) in the **Change Exog Vs** option, using the cursor keys to increase or decrease these variables. You can also change some of the key model parameters in the **Change Params** option. The results for the model can be displayed in one of two ways, graphically using the **Display Model** option, or numerically using the **Tabulate Model** option.

This menu is used to change the way model results are displayed on the screen. For an AD/PA model, results are displayed in a four-quadrant diagram. The IS, LM, AD, and P curves are displayed on the left side of the screen. **Select Display** enables you to choose which variables are displayed in the two right-side windows of the screen. Series are selected in exactly the same way as in the PLOT TIME SER and GRAPH SERIES menus. The **Set Speed** option enables you to change the speed with which results are displayed on the screen. Selecting 0 (the default value) causes the program to pause after each period. **Set # Periods** changes the number of simulation periods between 2 and 20. ISLM models automatically change this to 2 periods, while AD/PA models default to 10 periods. **SIMULT/individ** toggles between displaying all windows simultaneously and concentrating on one at a time. **4 WINDOWS/islm** toggles between displaying all four windows and just displaying the ISLM diagram.

QUIT Menu

To exit the program, move the cursor to the extreme right-hand window, so that **Quit** is highlighted, and press Enter. Notice that this is the only way to exit the program other than turning the power off or rebooting. It is the only guaranteed safe manner in which to exit the program.

An Introductory Exercise on the IBM PC

If you are unfamiliar with computers, it may help you to examine the demonstration (by typing MACRO DEMO) and then try the following exercise.

First, enter the program by typing MACRO at the A> prompt that DOS gives you.

The light-colored box in the top left of the screen is the cursor (the annoying flashing cursor, with which you may be familiar, is suppressed by MacroSolve). You can practice moving it around using the cursor keys—the keys that have up, down, left, and right facing arrows on them. You can try to move the cursor anywhere, but it will only move to areas that are allowed by the program.

To plot the time series move the cursor to the top left of the screen, so that it highlights the words **Select Series** and press Enter (sometimes called "Return"). The screen changes, and now the cursor is restricted to moving in the box on the right of the screen. Notice that as you move the cursor, the series that it sits on top of is described in the box below and to the left of the cursor window.

To select the unemployment rate for plotting, move the cursor downwards until it highlights the words UNEMPLOYMENT RATE. Press Enter to select the series.

You can select the inflation rate in exactly the same manner by moving the cursor until it highlights the words INFLATION (GNP), or INFLATION (CPI) if you prefer the consumer price index measure of inflation.

Now you are finished selecting series, so press the End key (which is numbered 1 on many keyboards). This closes the selection window, and returns you to the main menu.

To plot, simply move the cursor to the second entry of the PLOT TIME SER menu so that **Start Plot** is highlighted, and press Enter. As long as your computer is equipped with a suitable graphics board, you will see a picture of the unemployment rate and the inflation rate plotted against time on the horizontal axis.

You can change the data series in exactly the same way, or you can change the data frequency from annual to quarterly by moving the cursor to the **ANNUAL/quartly** option and pressing Enter. To plot the quarterly series, move the cursor to **Start Plot**, and press Enter again.

All MacroSolve commands are entered in the same way, using the arrow keys to locate an option and the pressing Enter to select it. You can safely try any of the other options in the program; there is no better way to learn the program than to practice it. If you are not sure what a particular choice does, press the Home key for a help message.

To exit the program, move the cursor to the top right of the screen and press Enter; you will then be returned to your computer's operating system (DOS).

Instructions for the Macintosh Version of MacroSolve

Equipment Required

MacroSolve will run on any Macintosh computer with at least 512K of memory, though the MacPlus, Mac SE, and Mac II are recommended due to speed and memory requirements. Also recommended, but not required, is version 4.0 or higher of the System Folder. It can be found on the diskette at the back of this manual.

Running MacroSolve from the Diskette

You may make one copy of the diskette you purchased, and we recommend that you do so. The procedure for copying MacroSolve is discussed below under "Installing MacroSolve."

To run MacroSolve from the Macintosh disk, simply turn the machine on and insert the disk. A double-click with the mouse on the MacroSolve icon (shown below) puts you into the program, though

MacroSolve

you'll have to wait a few seconds. You'll see the title screen for a moment, and then the screen will display the available menu titles: "plot," "graph," "model," and "options." These correspond to the IBM PC menus, but are described again below.

Menus and Options for the Macintosh

MacroSolve help: If you need help when running MacroSolve, you have only to click on the first (Apple) menu. You can ask for help at any time during the program's execution. **Help MacroSolve** is the second entry of the Apple menu. After the help window appears, you will see that a list of help topics are on the left while the actual text referring to the current topic is on the right. To select a new topic, click the mouse directly on the item for which you would like more information. To scan through all topics, use the "Prev" and "Next" buttons at the bottom of the window (the current topic will change automatically). Click on the "Exit" button to remove the help window from the screen when you are finished.

Plot Menu

This menu allows you to tabulate or plot on the screen up to three macroeconomic time series. The time series are selected from the choices in the **Select Series** option. Once you have entered this option, you select a series by clicking on the box to its left. MacroSolve permits you to choose up to three series. When you have checked off the series you want, click **ok**, which returns you to the main menu. If you selected **Auto Apply** for either plot or tabulate, MacroSolve will next automatically plot and/or tabulate the series that you selected. A quick way to unselect all previously selected series is to click on the **unselect** box here.

Back in the plot menu, you have the option of selecting annual data, which give you the broad sweep back to 1930, or quarterly data, which give you a more detailed look at the record since 1967. Click on the option you want.

Your machine is now ready to display the data. For a time-series diagram, click on the **start plot** command. To see the actual numbers, you click on **tabulate data**, and when the table comes up, you can scroll through the entire series.

The last option available to you in the plot menu is **select sample**. Here you can narrow the time period for the series. For instance, if you want to focus on inflation and unemployment in the 1960s, you can enter this menu and select a sample restricted to that decade.

Graph Menu

This menu allows you to graph one of the data series against another, rather than against time. You select one series for the horizontal axis and another for the vertical one (the exercises in this study guide will specify which series goes on what axis). As with the plot menu, the first step is to select the desired series. The same nineteen series are available to you as were presented in the plot menu, but you'll have to scroll through the list to see all of them. When you see the one you want, simply click on it. A black bar will appear to indicate that this series has been selected.

Once you have selected two series, you click on **ok** to return to the main menu. Alternatively, by clicking on the box next to **graph window**, your machine will go straight to the graph when you click **ok**.

Back in the main menu, you have a number of options for your graph. Clicking on **annual** or **quarterly** selects whether the graph will trace all the way back to 1930, or whether it will produce a detailed look at the record since 1967. As with the plot menu, you can use the **set sample** option to focus on a shorter period of time than that specified in the data bank. The choice between **points** and **connect** tells MacroSolve how you want your graph displayed: as a scatter of points or with lines connecting them chronologically. Finally, you can select a **fast** or **slow** speed for the display, depending on how closely you want to study the chronological display.

Model Menu

The MacroSolve "model" menu group extends into the "options" group and offers many alternatives. You'll learn all of them with experience, but you'll find it easiest at first if you let MacroSolve make most of the choices for you. All you have to do is to change one of the variables that affects the economy. Go into the **Set exogenous** option and make a change in money supply or government spending, or simulate a price shock (or any combination of the three). Then click **ok** to return to the main menu.

To see the result, click on **display model**, and MacroSolve will give you a four-window display of the analysis: IS-LM diagram, AD/PA diagram, and a time series of each of two variables. Alternatively, you can look at the numbers themselves by selecting the **tabulate model** option.

When you get more familiar with MacroSolve, you'll want to use some of the other model options. Under **select model** you'll find a choice among seven versions of the model: three static IS-LM (fixed price) models and four AD/PA (aggregate demand/price adjustment) models. To select a particular model, use the **select model** option and click on the one you want. Under **change parameters**, you'll find six behavioral factors that affect the model's outcome; by clicking on the buttons there you can change the assumptions behind the model.

Options Menu

The menu group at the extreme right of the screen, **options**, gives you some choices about how the model will be displayed. Under the option **select display** you can specify the two variables that you want the model to display. With **set speed**, you can increase the speed with which MacroSolve carries out the display, and select whether the program should pause between each period. You can control the number of periods, between two and twenty, over which MacroSolve will carry out the analysis by selecting the **set # periods** menu. Finally, by clicking on **simultaneous** or **individual**, you tell MacroSolve to proceed through the analysis with all four screens at once or to take it one screen at a time.

When you are finished with your session on MacroSolve, you can get out of the program by selecting **quit** under the **file** menu.

Transporting MacroSolve Data and Graphs to Other Programs

Transporting either data or graphs from MacroSolve into another Macintosh program is feasible via the **Edit** menu. When you have the information on the screen that you wold like to export, simply choose **Copy Data** or **Copy Graph**, depending on the composition of what you are transferring. This information will now reside in what is known as the **Clipboard**, which is incorporated into most applications. Since it cannot hold more than one graph or set of data, however, all subsequent calls to the **Copy** command will simply overwrite whatever was previously copied. To finish the process, exit MacroSolve, open the desired destination program for the contents cf the Clipboard, and then select the **Paste** command from the **Edit** menu. The screen will now contain a picture of the last MacroSolve window that was copied.

There are two alternative ways to obtain a hard copy of your screen. If you have and Apple Imagewriter attached to your Mac, you can print the screen by pressing the **Shift**, **Option**, and **3** keys simultaneously. The printer should then print everything that you see on your screen. Or, if you want to obtain a printout on an Apple Laserwriter, you should first press **Shift**, **Option**, and **4** keys simultaneously. The first time that you do this, your Macintosh will copy the screen into a MacPaint file called **Screen0**; the next time it will copy to a file called **Screen1**; etc. These screen files can then be printed by using MacPaint.

Window Manipulation

A window, like the one shown on the next page, is simply an area on the screen created to hold and display a particular set of information. One advantage of the Macintosh over the IBM PC is that you can put more than one window on the screen at once, allowing quick alternation between windows by simply clicking inside the window itself. For example, if more than one window is currently on the screen but one is partially obscured by the others, you can click on the visible portion of the obscured window to place it and its contents in front of the other windows. Further manipulation of these windows is possible by clicking on one of the command areas we've labeled and described below the illustration.

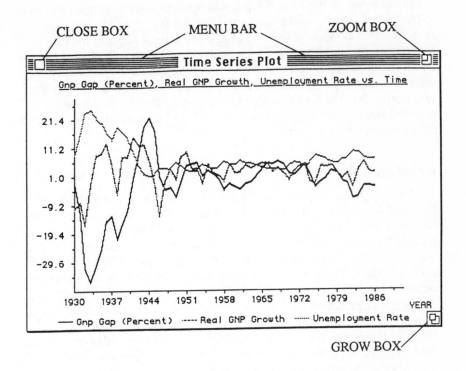

CLOSE BOX · MENU BAR · ZOOM BOX

Time Series Plot

Gnp Gap (Percent), Real GNP Growth, Unemployment Rate vs. Time

— Gnp Gap (Percent)   ----- Real GNP Growth   ······ Unemployment Rate

GROW BOX

CLOSE BOX: Removes the top (or active) window from the screen, making the next window below it the active window.

ZOOM BOX: Revises the active window so that it becomes the full size of the screen. Clicking again will return the window to its former size. As with resizing the window below, the contents of all windows containing graphics will be rescaled to best utilize the area available while still forcing information to fit in the window.

MENU BAR: By clicking anywhere in the menu bar except in the close and zoom boxes, the window can by physically dragged around the screen by moving the mouse itself. The window will be redrawn at the new location when the mouse button is released.

GROW BOX: Serves to resize a window while being anchored in the top left corner. Click and hold down the mouse button while in the box, move the mouse until the desired size is reached, and release. Again, all graphic windows will be redrawn to conform to the new window configuration.

Menu toggles: In the **Plot**, **Graph**, and **options** menus, toggles are used so that simple selections between two items can be made in one easy step. The two choices in any one toggle are separated from the other menu choices by dashed lines. The current selection will always have a check mark immediately to its left. To change a selection, simply select the other option from the menu. If you view the menu again, you will notice that the check mark now appears adjacent to the newly selected item. Selecting an item that already has a check mark next to it has no effect.

Installing MacroSolve

MacroSolve can be run either from a diskette or from a hard disk. Running MacroSolve from a hard disk is somewhat faster, but requires that you install the program to that disk. The Hard Disk Installer runs on a Macintosh with at least 512K of memory and a hard disk. It will not run on the Macintosh XL or the Apple Lisa. Once MacroSolve has been installed, it may not be moved to any other volume without first uninstalling it from the original hard disk. Moreover, you should never delete an application that has been installed to the hard disk; again, remove it with the Hard Disk Installer application. Finally, some hard disk systems have a utility which "compresses" files, making all free space contiguous (such as the HyperDrive "Optimize Disk"). This will invalidate any hard disk installations of MacroSolve. If you want to compress your hard disk, be sure to use the Hard Disk Installer to remove MacroSolve first, then compress the disk, and finally reinstall MacroSolve.

Installing MacroSolve to the hard disk: To install MacroSolve to a hard disk, insert your MacroSolve disk in the disk drive and double-click on the icon for the Hard Disk Installer (see below):

After a brief pause, the following display will appear:

```
═══════ MACLoK™ Hard Disk Install by Softguard Systems, Inc. ═══════
┌─────────Master Drive─────────┬────────Hard Disk Drive────────┐
│  HD Install Demo             │  HDInstall                    │
│                              │                               │
│  ⦿ Internal     ┌─────────┐  │            ┌─────────┐        │
│  ○ External     │  Eject  │  │            │  Drive  │        │
│                 └─────────┘  │            └─────────┘        │
├──────────────────────────────┼───────────────────────────────┤
│      ┌─────────────┐         │        ┌─────────────┐        │
│      │   Install   │         │        │   Remove    │        │
│      └─────────────┘         │        └─────────────┘        │
│  ⦿ All Files on Master Disk  │  Installations Allowed:  2    │
│  ○ Only Protected Applications│ Installations Left:     2    │
├──────────────────────────────┴───────────────────────────────┤
│  Click on Install to begin Hard Disk Install.                │
│                                          ┌─────────┐         │
│                                          │  Quit   │         │
│                                          └─────────┘         │
└──────────────────────────────────────────────────────────────┘
```

To complete the installation, simply click on **All Files on Master Disk** and then click on the **Install** button. You will see a message to that effect, and the Hard Disk Installer will exit to the Desktop, where you can double-click on the MacroSolve icon to run the program. The Hard Disk Installer will never write over any files with the same names on your hard disk without asking you first. If you really want to write over the files, click on **ok** in response to the question.

Removing MacroSolve from the hard disk: To remove MacroSolve from your hard disk, follow the same steps as above for installation, with the exception of clicking on the "Remove" button rather than clicking on "Install."

An Introductory Exercise on the Macintosh

If you are unfamiliar with the way in which Macintosh programs work, or to get some feel for using MacroSolve, you may wish to try the following exercise. Suppose that you wish to obtain a plot of the unemployment rate and the growth rate of real GNP for the years 1960 to the present. First, insert the MacroSolve distribution diskette into the disk drive in the front of your Macintosh and double-click on the MacroSolve icon to open the application.

When the menu line appears, click on the word **Plot** and while holding down the mouse button, move the mouse downward until the **Select Series** option is highlighted. Release the mouse button to enter the dialog box that enables you to actually choose the two series to plot. Once the box appears, click first on the name **Unemp Rate** and second on the name **Real GNP Growth** to select the two desired series. Then click **ok** to remove the dialog box from the screen. Remember from the instructions that you could have gotten an annual plot of the two series for the years 1930 to present by simply selecting **Automatic Apply** prior to pressing the **ok** button.

To view a plot for a reduced sample size, however, you need to incorporate one further step. This can be done by choosing **Set Sample** from the menu just as you did with **Select Series** above. When this dialog box appears, click on the right arrow of the top scroll bar and hold down the mouse button until the value in the adjacent rectangle is 1960. Again, click on the **ok** button. Now you are prepared to view the plot of the two curves (and/or see the data numerically with the **Tabulate Data** if you like). Simply choose **Start Plot** from the **Plot** menu. In seconds, your plot will appear on the screen.

With the data on your screen, you should experiment with the various window features inherent in most Macintosh applications. For example, click in the zoom box in the upper right of the menu line to re-size the window to the full extent of the screen. Then, using the grow box, decrease the size of the window. Third, try dragging the window around the screen by clicking on the menu bar and moving the mouse, releasing the button when the window has reached the desired position. Finally, when you are done experimenting, click on the close box to remove the window from the screen. These same actions will apply in all of MacroSolve's application windows.

When you wish to exit MacroSolve, choose **Quit** from the **File** menu. As you begin to use the program, keep in mind that the best way to familiarize yourself with it is through experimentation. All of the options and commands work quite like the ones which you have just completed. If you have any difficulty with MacroSolve, try the **Help MacroSolve** option in the **Apple** menu at any time during the program.

PART I

Fundamentals of Macroeconomics

CHAPTER 1   The Macroeconomy

Main Objectives

During the past 15 years fluctuations in gross national product, employment, inflation, and interest rates have been larger and more erratic than at any time since the Great Depression of the 1930s. In order to explain fluctuations in these variables, macroeconomists construct models. Chapter 1 introduces the basic properties and terminology of macroeconomic models.

Key Terms and Concepts

Macroeconomics is the study of economic fluctuations. While the long-run growth of the economy is largely determined by factors such as population growth and technological progress, this growth is irregular. The economy undergoes both **recessions**, periods of coontracting economic activity, and **recoveries**, periods of above-average economic growth following a recession. The top of a recovery is a **peak** and the bottom of a recession is a **trough**.

Real gross national product (GNP) is the most comprehensive measure of total production in the United States. It adjusts the **nominal** dollar value of goods produced for changes in prices. The **rate of inflation** is the percentage change in the average price of all goods in the economy from one year to the next.

The **employment rate** is the ratio of employed workers to the working-age population. The **unemployment rate** is the percentage of workers who are looking for work and have not yet found it. The **rate of interest** is the amount charged by lenders per dollar per year, expressed as a percent. The **money supply** consists of currency and deposits at banks.

Potential GNP (or **potential output**) is the amount of output that can be produced from the existing capital stock and labor force. Recessions and recoveries are measured by fluctuations in real GNP from its long-run, or potential, growth path. Other economic variables also fluctuate. Employment is highly correlated with GNP, and therefore falls during recessions. Inflation tends to be higher when the economy is near its peak, and lower when it is in a trough. Interest rates are procyclical; they rise during recoveries and fall during recessions.

3

Describing macroeconomic behavior in complete detail would prove unwieldy—there is too much going on. So economists construct **macro-economic models**, simplified descriptions of how consumers and firms behave and interact, to explain fluctuations. In this way, they can test their theories against observation, or note how different theories interact, without extraneous detail. We pay a great deal of attention in this course to macroeconomic models with **flexible** and **sticky prices**. Models with flexible prices assume that wages and prices adjust rapidly according to traditional supply and demand analysis. In this way, workers and machines are kept fully employed, so that the economy always operates at its long-run potential output. Models with sticky prices postulate that this adjustment takes time and explain fluctuations by bottlenecks in the adjustment process.

The model with flexible prices is illustrated in Figure 1-1. The **aggregate supply curve** is a vertical line that depicts potential output. In Chapter 6 we will see why potential output does not depend on the price level. The **aggregate demand curve**, which slopes downward, is the total amount of demand throughout the economy. In Chapter 5 we will see how the aggregate demand curve is derived. With flexible prices, changes in aggregate demand affect only the price level. They do not affect GNP.

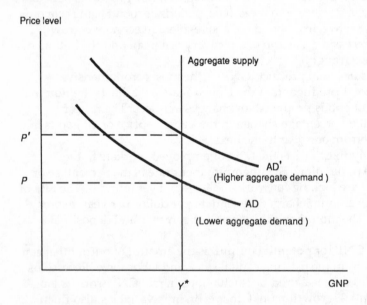

Figure 1-1

According to the model with flexible prices, real GNP can only change if potential output changes. The Great Depression of the 1930s saw real GNP fall by so much that an explanation based on a drop in potential output seemed inadequate. During the depression, John Maynard Keynes, the great British economist, created a new macro-economic model, the model with sticky prices, where shifts in aggregate demand could affect GNP. The model with sticky prices is illustrated in Figure 1-2, where the fixed price level is depicted as a horizontal line. Changes in aggregate demand affect GNP while leaving the price level unchanged.

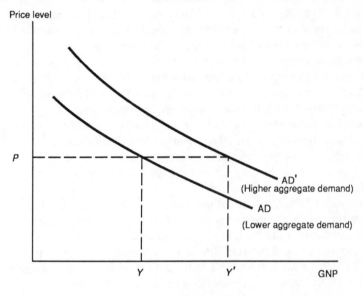

Figure 1-2

Neither the model with flexible prices nor the model with sticky prices provides a complete description of the economy. The model with sticky prices can account for short-run fluctuations in output and employment, but cannot explain inflation. The model with flexible prices can explain inflation, but not short-run fluctuations.

Price adjustment bridges the gap between the model with sticky prices and the model with flexible prices. In its simplest form, the idea of price adjustment is that when output is less than potential GNP there is pressure on prices to adjust downward. When output exceeds potential GNP, there is pressure on prices to adjust upward.

When we examine the behavior of individual firms and consumers, we will discover that expectations of the future play an important role. The theory of **rational expectations** is that firms and consumers, in forming their expectations, use whatever information is available to them in the most effective manner. While this seems innocuous, it has

5

far-reaching implications for the study of consumption, investment, and price adjustment.

One of the most important goals of macroeconomic policy-making is maintaining a steady growth of aggregate demand. There is considerable controversy, however, about how this should be accomplished. **Monetarists** such as Nobel laureate Milton Friedman, formerly of the University of Chicago and now of the Hoover Institute at Stanford University, believe that steady money growth will best stabilize the growth of aggregate demand. **Keynesians** such as Nobel laureates James Tobin of Yale University and Franco Modigliani of M.I.T. believe that changes in taxes, government spending, and the money supply should be used to offset other sources of instability in the economy.

Two major new schools of thought, both accepting the idea of rational expectations, have emerged in the last decade. **New classicals** such as Robert Lucas of the University of Chicago and Thomas Sargent of Stanford University maintain that wages and prices adjust very quickly. **New Keynesians** such as Edmund Phelps of Columbia believe that wages and prices adjust slowly. These differences in beliefs regarding the speed of wage and price adjustment, as we will see in Chapters 14 and 15, lead to very different explanations of economic fluctuations.

The remainder of the book develops a macroeconomic model that incorporates the concepts presented above. Sticky prices are assumed in the short run to explain fluctuations in output and employment. In the long run, flexible prices explain inflation and guide the economy to potential GNP. Price adjustment explains the transition from the short run to the long run. Rational expectations are assumed throughout.

Self-Test

Fill in the Blank

1. The economy is in a _____ if production and employment are falling.

2. When production and employment are increasing rapidly, the economy is in a _____.

3. During the past 15 years, fluctuations in the United States economy have been larger and more erratic than at any time since _____.

4. The _____ is the percentage change in the price level from one year to the next.

5. _____ is the most comprehensive measure of total production in the United States.

6. The nominal interest rate minus the expected rate of inflation is the_____.

7. If prices were _____ workers and machines would be fully employed.

8. Shifts in demand influence output if prices are _____.

9. If firms and consumers make the most of the information available to them, they are said to form their expectations _____.

10. _____ output is the amount of output that can be produced from the existing capital stock and labor force.

11. Real GNP adjusts the _____ dollar value of goods produced for changes in prices.

12. The money supply divided by the price level is called _____ money.

True-False

13. A peak is the bottom of a recession.

14. Economic fluctuations are regular and can be anticipated with great accuracy.

15. Interest rates are procyclical.

16. With perfectly flexible prices, shifts in demand cannot explain recessions and booms.

17. Macroeconomists are very successful at predicting interest rates.

18. The economy is in a recovery if production and employment are increasing rapidly.

19. Economic fluctuations have increased since World War II.

20. Fluctuations in employment follow closely the fluctuations in real GNP.

21. With sticky prices, output always equals potential GNP.

22. Declines in inflation usually occur during recessions.

23. The recession in the early 1980s was the largest in the last 75 years.

24. The employment rate is the ratio of employed workers to unemployed workers.

Review Questions

25. What is the long-term pattern of economic fluctuations in the United States?

26. Explain why macroeconomics are concerned about economic fluctuations.

27. What other economic variables fluctuate along with GNP?

28. What determines potential output?

29. How are the price level and output determined in the models with flexible prices and sticky prices?

30. How are economic fluctuations explained in the models with flexible prices and sticky prices?

31. Why did Keynes reject the model with flexible prices?

32. Why is the model with sticky prices inappropriate for the long run?

33. What is the difference between Keynesians and monetarists?

34. What is a simple expression of the idea of price adjustment?

35. What is meant by rational expectations?

36. What is the difference between new classicals and new Keynesians?

Problem Set

Worked Problems

1. Suppose the aggregate demand curve is given by the expression $Y = 4000 + 2000/P$, where Y is output and P is the price level. Potential output is $Y^* = \$5000$ billion.

a. Draw the aggregate demand and supply curves on a diagram with the price level P on the vertical axis and output Y on the horizontal axis.

b. What is the price level P if prices are flexible?

c. Suppose that prices are sticky and $P = 1$. What is the level of actual output? Is actual output Y above or below potential output Y^*? Is there pressure on the price level to move upward or downward?

d. Suppose that prices are sticky and $P = 3$. What is the level of output now? Is it above or below potential output? What pressure is there on prices?

a. *The aggregate supply curve is a vertical line where output = potential output = $5000 billion. The aggregate demand curve is downward sloping because output demanded is lower if prices are higher.*

b. *If prices are flexible output equals potential output. Thus 4000 + 2000/P = $5000 billion, which can only hold if P = 2.*

c. *If prices are sticky and P = 1, actual output Y = 4000 + 2000/1 = $6000 billion. Since potential output Y* = $5000 billion, actual output is above potential, putting pressure on the price level to move upward.*

d. *If prices are sticky and P = 3, actual output Y = 4000 + 2000/3 = $4667 billion. Since potential output Y* = $5000 billion, actual output is below potential, putting pressure on prices to fall.*

2. The price level was 54 in 1950, 69 in 1960, 92 in 1970, and 178 in 1980. What was the rate of inflation for the 1950s, 1960s, and 1970s? Why would models with sticky prices be more appropriate for the 1950s and 1960s than for the 1970s?

The rate of inflation was 28 percent for the 1950s, 33 percent for the 1960s, and 93 percent for the 1970s. Models with sticky prices are more appropriate for the 1950s and 1960s than for the 1970s because inflation was much lower.

Review Problems

3. Suppose the aggregate demand curve is given by the expression $Y = 5000 + 3000/P$, where Y is output and P is the price level. Potential output $Y^* = \$6500$.

a. Draw the aggregate demand and supply curves.

b. What is the price level P if prices are flexible?

c. Suppose that prices are sticky and $P = 3$. What is the level of actual output? Is actual output Y above or below potential output Y^*? Is there pressure on the price level to move upward or downward?

4. Suppose the aggregate demand curve is still given by $Y = 5000 + 3000/P$, but potential output $Y^* = \$8000$.

a. Draw the new aggregate demand and supply curves.

b. What is P if prices are flexible? Compare your answer with Problem 3b.

c. Suppose that prices are sticky and $P = 3$. What is the level of output now? Is it above or below potential output? What pressure is there on prices?

5. Suppose that the aggregate demand curve is now given by $Y = 6500 + 3000/P$, with potential output $Y^* = \$8000$.

a. Draw the aggregate demand and supply curves.

b. What is P now if prices are flexible? Compare your answer with Problem 4b.

c. Suppose that prices are sticky and $P = 2$. What is the level of output now? Is it above or below potential output? What pressure is there on prices?

6. The price level was 107.9 in 1984, 111.5 in 1985, and 114.5 in 1986. What were the rates of inflation for 1985 and 1986? If people expect the rate of inflation to be the average rate of inflation in the previous two years, what was the expected rate of inflation in 1986? If the interest rate in 1986 was 6 percent, what was the real interest rate?

MacroSolve Exercises

1. Plot, using the **PLOT SERIES** option, the GNP gap (the percentage deviation of real GNP from potential real GNP) using annual data. Identify the years when troughs and peaks occur. (It will be useful to tabulate the data to identify the exact years when these occur. Peaks occur in periods when the GNP gap is greater than the surrounding observations, and troughs occur when the GNP gap is more negative than the surrounding observations.)

a. On average, how frequent are recessions? Has this frequency increased or decreased since the Second World War? Why might the frequency have changed?

b. Are business fluctuations symmetric? In other words, is the period of decline between peaks and troughs longer or shorter than the upswing from troughs to peaks? Can you think of any reasons for this?

2. Using annual data, graph the GNP gap on the horizontal axis against the unemployment rate on the vertical axis. Is unemployment procyclical or countercyclical? In other words, when output is high relative to potential output, is the unemployment rate high (so that unemployment is procyclical) or low (countercyclical)? Explain why.

3. Plot interest rates from 1930 to 1987. Are short- and long-term interest rates generally high or low in the recession periods that you identified in question 1? (It may help to tabulate interest rates and the GNP gap to answer this question.) Why do you think that this is the case?

4. Plot both the real interest rate and the inflation rate on the same screen using quarterly data from 1967 to 1987. When the inflation rate changes, do the real and nominal interest rates generally move in the same direction or in opposite directions? Why?

5. Do the real interest rate and the GNP gap generally move in the same direction or opposite direction? Can you think of any explanations for this?

Answers to the Self-Test

1. Recession
2. Recovery
3. The Great Depression of the 1930s
4. Inflation rate
5. Real gross national product
6. Real interest rate
7. Flexible
8. Sticky
9. Rationally
10. Potential
11. Nominal
12. Real
13. False. A peak is the top of a recovery.

14. False. They are irregular and cannot be predicted well.
15. True. They fall during recessions and rise during recoveries.
16. True. With perfectly flexible prices, shifts in demand cannot affect output. They can only affect prices.
17. False. Macroeconomists are no more successful at predicting interest rates than anyone else.
18. True. That is the definition of a recovery.
19. False. They have decreased in magnitude.
20. True. Employment falls during recessions and rises during recoveries.
21. False. With sticky prices, output can diverge from potential GNP.
22. True. In the past 20 years, almost all of the significant declines in the rate of inflation occurred during recession periods.
23. False. The Great Depression was much larger.
24. False. The employment rate is the ratio of employed workers to the working-age population.
25. Economic fluctuations were very large during the 1920s and 1930s, decreased during the 1950s and 1960s, and have increased, although not back to their pre–World War II levels, during the 1970s and 1980s.
26. Macroeconomists are concerned about fluctuations because people can be adversely affected, an example being unemployment and layoffs during recessions.
27. Employment, inflation, interest rates, and exchange rates also undergo fluctuations.
28. Potential output is determined by the productive capacity of the economy, which in turn is determined by the volume of productive factors—capital and labor. It is unrelated to the price level.
29. In the model with flexible prices, output is determined by potential output, and the price level is determined by aggregate demand. In the model with sticky prices, the price level is fixed by assumption, and output is determined by aggregate demand.
30. In the model with flexible prices, since output is determined by potential output, economic fluctuations can only occur when potential output changes. In the model with fixed prices, shifts in aggregate demand can cause fluctuations.
31. During the Great Depression, the decrease in real GNP was too large, 30 percent from 1929 to 1933, to be explained by shifts in potential output.
32. In the long run, an economic model should be able to explain inflation, which the model with sticky prices cannot do.
33. Monetarists believe that steady money growth will best stabilize the growth in aggregate demand. Keynesians believe in a more active use of policy. They feel that changes in taxes and government spending, as well as in the money supply, should be used to offset other sources of instability in the economy.
34. When output is less than potential GNP, there is pressure on prices to adjust downward. When output exceeds potential GNP, there is pressure on prices to adjust upward.

35. Rational expectations means that consumers and firms, when forming their expectations about the future, make the most of the information available to them.
36. New classicals believe that wages and prices adjust very quickly, while new Keynesians believe that they adjust slowly.

Solutions to Review Problems

3. a. The aggregate supply curve is a vertical line where output = potential output = $6500. The aggregate demand curve is downward sloping.
   b. If prices are flexible output equals potential output. Thus $5000 + 3000/P = \$6500$, and $P = 2$.
   c. If prices are sticky and $P = 3$, actual output $Y = 5000 + 3000/3 = \$6000$. Since potential output $Y^* = \$6500$, actual output is below potential, putting downward pressure on the price level.
4. a. The new aggregate supply curve is a vertical line with $Y^* = \$8000$. The aggregate demand curve is unchanged.
   b. If prices are flexible, $5000 + 3000/P = \$8000$, so $P = 1$. The price level is lower than in Problem 3b. This shows that, if prices are flexible, an increase in potential output with unchanged aggregate demand will lower prices.
   c. $Y = 5000 + 3000/3 = \$6000$. Since $Y^* = \$8000$, output is still below potential, and there is still downward pressure on prices.
5. a. The aggregate demand curve has a higher intercept but the same slope as before. The aggregate supply curve is the same as in Problem 4.
   b. If prices are flexible, $6500 + 3000/P = \$8000$, so $P = 2$. The price level is higher than in Problem 4b. This shows that, if prices are flexible, an increase in aggregate demand with unchanged potential output will raise prices.
   c. If prices are sticky and $P = 2$, $Y = 6500 + 3000/P = \$8000$, which is also equal to potential output. There is no pressure on prices to either rise or fall.
6. The rate of inflation was 3.3 percent in 1985 and 2.7 percent in 1986. The expected rate of inflation in 1986 was 3 percent. The real interest rate was 3 percent.

Solutions to MacroSolve Exercises

1. a. On average, there were recessions almost every 5 years. In the period before 1945 there were, by our definition, two recessions, with their troughs in 1933 and 1938.
   b. For the entire period, the average upswing took 2.8 years, and the downswing took 2.1 years.

2. Unemployment is countercyclical; it falls as the GNP gap rises. As more output is produced, there is typically more employment.
3. Interest rates are generally high before recessions, but low in them. They are thus procyclical.
4. There is a tendency for the real interest rate to drop as inflation increases. Nominal interest rates often rise with inflation by less than the inflation increase.
5. Sometimes the two move together, but not always. Whether the real interest rate rises or falls in a recession depends on the monetary and fiscal policies followed. The most recent recessionary period was certainly accompanied by high real interest rates, but the 1974–75 recession was not.

CHAPTER 2   Measuring Economic Performance: Output and Income

Main Objectives

Economic fluctuations are movements in real gross national product around its long-run, potential level, as we saw in Chapter 1. In Chapter 2 we see how gross national product is defined and measured. Three different ways to measure GNP, as spending, production, and income, are discussed and we see how each adds up to the same thing. Beyond mastering the definitions of GNP, you should become familiar with the concepts of saving and investment, and how transactions with the rest of the world relate to domestic GNP.

Key Terms and Concepts

Gross national product (GNP) can be measured in terms of production, income, or spending. **Production GNP** is the dollar value of the goods and services produced during a period of time. **Income GNP** is wages and interest paid by firms, plus profits earned by owners of firms. **Spending GNP** is the amount of goods and services bought by consumers, other firms, and the government, plus **inventories** (goods produced but not yet sold). Through two accounting rules—including inventories in spending and computing profits as sales minus expenses—production GNP, income GNP, and spending GNP are always the same. This is an identity—simply a matter of definition.

It will most often prove useful to define GNP in terms of spending. **Consumption** is spending by households. It includes purchases of durable goods such as automobiles, nondurables goods such as food, and services such as haircuts. **Nonresidential fixed investment** is spending on structures such as office buildings and on equipment for use in business such as computers. **Residential fixed investment** is spending on construction of new houses and apartment buildings. Note that spending on new houses is included in investment, not in consumption. **Inventory investment** is

15

the value of goods that are produced, but not sold, during a given period. If more goods are sold than produced, inventory investment is negative for the period. **Government purchases** is spending on goods and services by state, local, and federal governments.

For a country with a closed economy, one that does not trade with other countries, this would exhaust our categories of spending. Goods produced could either be consumed (except for new houses) if sold to households, invested if sold to firms or added to inventories, or counted as government purchases if sold to the government, so that spending would equal production. We could then say that GNP is equal to consumption plus investment plus government purchases.

Since countries trade with other countries, these categories are incomplete. Some of the goods that we produce are purchased by foreigners. These are our **exports** and are included in our GNP. On the other hand, part of our consumption, investment, and government purchases are of goods produced by foreigners. These are our **imports** and should not be counted as part of our GNP. Exports minus imports is called **net exports**. For an open economy, GNP is equal to consumption plus investment plus government purchases plus net exports. When net exports are positive, there is a **trade surplus**. When net exports are negative, there is a **trade deficit**.

The **capital stock** is the total amount of productive capital— factories, equipment, and houses—in the economy. **Investment** is the flow of new capital that is added during the year to the stock of capital. Since part of the capital stock is always wearing out, or **depreciating**, part of investment goes to maintain the existing level of the capital stock. Net investment is equal to investment minus depreciation. **Net national product (NNP)** includes only net investment. GNP includes gross investment.

GNP can increase either if the physical amount of goods and services produced increases or if prices rise. GNP adjusted for changing prices is called real GNP, and measures the physical amount of production. To clarify the distinction between real GNP and GNP, sometimes the term **nominal GNP** is used for the dollar value of goods and services produced. Nominal GNP is synonymous with GNP.

In order for gross national product to measure the value of production, it is necessary to avoid double counting. Thus only new purchases are counted in spending. Purchases of old houses and used cars are not included because they contributed to GNP when new. Furthermore, only goods purchased at the end of the production line, as final goods, are counted in spending. If General Motors purchases steel to produce an automobile, the steel is an **intermediate good**, and is not counted. When the car is sold, the value of the steel is included as part of the final good.

The concept of **value added** is used to prevent double counting when GNP is computed by production. The value added by a firm is the difference between the revenue a firm earns by selling its products and the amount it pays for intermediate goods produced by other firms. If Goodyear buys rubber and steel to produce steel-belted radial tires, the value added is the difference between what it earns from the tires and what it pays for the rubber and steel. GNP is the sum of the value added by all firms in the economy.

GNP can also be computed as the sum of all incomes in the economy. In the actual statistical accounts, there is no measure of income that is exactly comparable to GNP. The closest is **national income**, which is approximately equal to net national product minus sales and excise taxes. **Personal income** equals national income plus government and business **transfer payments** (social security and other benefits) plus interest on the government debt and from other nonbusiness sources minus social security taxes minus corporate retained earnings. **Disposable personal income**, often just called **disposable income**, is personal income minus income taxes. Disposable income is equal to GNP plus government transfers plus interest on the government debt minus taxes.

Saving is income minus consumption. We can use this definition to analyze saving for various sectors of the economy. **Private saving** is disposable income minus consumption. **Government saving** equals the income received by the government (tax receipts minus government transfers minus interest on the government debt) minus government spending on goods and services. A positive value for government saving is also called a **government budget surplus**. A negative value is a **government budget deficit**. **Rest of world saving** refers to the income that other countries receive from our purchase of their goods and services (our imports) minus their spending on our goods and services (our exports).

Money and bonds are financial liabilities of the government and financial assets of the private sector. The term **government budget identity** means that negative government saving, or the government budget deficit, must be financed either by issuing money or by issuing bonds.

The basic measure of our transactions with the rest of the world is the **merchandise trade balance**, which is our exports of goods minus our imports of goods. The **balance on goods and services** adds net interest payments on foreign investments to the trade balance. The **current account**, which is the most comprehensive measure of our transactions with the rest of the world, adds net international transfers and remittances to the balance on goods and services.

The other side of the rest of the world accounts is the **capital account**, which measures international borrowing and lending. When an

American borrows from a foreigner, either by taking out a loan or by selling a bond, it is a capital inflow or a **capital account surplus**. An American lending to a foreigner falls into the category of a capital outflow or a **capital account deficit**. When the United States imports more than it exports, it runs a current account deficit. In order to finance the deficit, it has to borrow from the rest of the world, creating a capital account surplus. Thus the negative current account is matched by the positive capital account. Put another way, the sum of the current and capital accounts is equal to zero.

The **exchange rate** is the price of dollars in terms of foreign currency, and measures how much foreign currency, say 150 Japanese yen, one can buy with one dollar. When the exchange rate rises, say to 200 yen, foreign goods become cheaper compared to home goods. The **trade-weighted average exchange rate** is an average of the exchange rates between the dollar and several different currencies.

Self-Test

Fill in the Blank

1. Gross national product can be computed by measuring

   _____, _____, or _____.

2. Consumption is spending by _____.

3. The two types of fixed investment are _____ and

   _____.

4. Net investment is gross investment minus _____.

5. _____ investment consists of goods produced but not yet sold.

6. Net exports equal _____ minus _____.

7. To avoid double counting, we include only purchases of _____ when computing GNP.

8. Personal income minus income taxes is _____ personal income.

9. If government saving is negative, there is a government budget

   _____.

10. The measure of our transactions in goods, services, and transfers with the rest of the world is the _____ account.

11. When net exports are positive, there is a trade _____.

12. When net exports are negative, there is a trade _____.

True-False

13. We know that measuring GNP by either production, spending, or income each adds up to the same thing because of long experience with macroeconomic theories.

14. Spending on new houses is the only type of household spending that is not included in consumption.

15. The capital stock increases by the total amount of investment spending.

16. GNP is both the dollar value of all final goods and services produced in this country during a given period of time and the sum of all the value added by firms during the same period.

17. Both nominal and real GNP measure the dollar volume of production.

18. GNP increases if you buy either a new or a used car.

19. If Ford sells more automobiles, GNP will increase whether they are purchased by Americans or foreigners.

20. If you buy 100 shares of IBM stock, it is investment and adds to GNP.

21. If a firm replaces an old typewriter with a new one, it does not add to GNP because the total number of typewriters remains unchanged.

22. If General Motors produces more cars than it sells, this causes a smaller increase in GNP than if it sold all the cars it produced.

23. When the exchange rate rises, foreign goods become cheaper compared to home goods.

24. The exchange rate has been nearly constant during the last ten years.

25. How is GNP computed when measured through spending?

26. What are the components of consumption?

27. What is the relationship between the stock of capital and investment?

28. What happened to real GNP from 1981 to 1986? How does this illustrate an economic cycle?

29. Suppose that the economy is closed and that there is no government. Show that saving must equal investment.

30. Is there any necessity for saving to equal investment in an open economy with a government?

31. Why must a government budget deficit be financed by issuing money or bonds?

32. What is the difference between the merchandise trade balance, the balance on goods and services, and the current account balance?

33. Why does the sum of the current and capital accounts equal zero?

34. How does the current account deficit help finance the government budget deficit?

35. What does the trade-weighted average exchange rate measure?

36. During the past ten years, how have fluctuations in the exchange rate been associated with movements in U.S. output?

Problem Set

Worked Problems

1. Consider a closed economy without a government with expenditure totals given by

$$C = \$1200 \text{ billion} \quad \text{(Consumption)}$$
$$I = \quad 400 \quad\quad\quad \text{(Investment)}$$

   a. What is gross national product?

   b. Show that saving equals investment.

   a. GNP = Consumption + Investment.
   Using Y to denote GNP, Y = C + I = 1200 + 400 = \$1600 billion.

   b. Saving = Income − Consumption = GNP − Consumption.

Using S to denote saving,
S $= Y - C$
$= 1600 - 1200 = \$400$ *billion, which equals investment.*

2. Consider a closed economy with expenditure totals given by

C	=	$1200 billion	(Consumption)
I	=	400	(Investment)
G	=	300	(Government spending)
F	=	200	(Government transfers)
N	=	100	(Interest on the government debt)
T	=	400	(Taxes)

a. What is GNP?

b. What is private saving?

c. What is government saving?

d. What is total saving? Show that it equals investment.

a. GNP = Consumption + Investment + Government spending.
Y $= C + I + G$
$= 1200 + 400 + 300 = \$1900$ *billion.*

b. Private saving = Disposable income – Consumption.

Disposable income = GNP + Government transfers + Interest on the government debt – Taxes.
Using S_p *to denote private saving,*
$S_p = (Y + F + N - T) - C$
$= (1900 + 200 + 100 - 400) - 1200 = \$600$ *billion.*

c. Government saving = Taxes – Government transfers – Interest on the government debt – Government spending.
Using $S_g = T - F - N - G$
$= 400 - 200 - 100 - 300 = -\$200$ *billion.*

d. Total saving = Private saving + Government saving.
S $= S_p + S_g$
$= 600 - 200 = \$400$ *billion, which equals investment.*

3. Consider an open economy with expenditure totals given by

C	=	$1200 billion	(Consumption)
I	=	400	(Investment)
G	=	300	(Government spending)
X	=	–100	(Net exports)
F	=	200	(Government transfers)
N	=	100	(Interest on the government debt)
T	=	400	(Taxes)

a. What is GNP?

b. What is private saving?

c. What is government saving?

d. What is rest of world saving?

e. What is total saving? Show that it equals investment.

a. *GNP = Consumption + Investment + Government spending + Net exports.*
$$Y = C + I + G + X$$
$$= 1200 + 400 + 300 - 100 = \$1800 \text{ billion.}$$

b. *Private saving = Disposable income − Consumption.*
Disposable income = GNP + Government transfers + Interest on the government debt − Taxes.
$$S_p = (Y + F + N - T) - C$$
$$= (1800 + 200 + 100 - 400) - 1200 = \$500 \text{ billion.}$$

c. *Government saving = Taxes − Government transfers − Interest on the government debt − Government spending.*
$$S_g = T - F - N - G$$
$$= 400 - 200 - 100 - 300 = -\$200 \text{ billion.}$$

d. *Rest of world saving = −Net exports.*
Using S_r to denote rest of world saving,
$$S_r = -X$$
$$= \$100 \text{ billion.}$$

e. *Total saving = Private saving + Government saving + Rest of world saving.*
$$S = S_p + S_g + S_r$$
$$= 500 - 200 + 100 = \$400 \text{ billion, which equals investment.}$$

Review Problems

4. Consider an economy with expenditure totals given by

$$C = \$1700 \text{ billion} \quad \text{(Consumption)}$$
$$I = 600 \quad \text{(Investment)}$$

a. What is GNP?

b. What is saving?

c. How much does the capital stock increase during the period?

5. Consider the economy in Problem 4, but with depreciation equal to $200.

a. What is net investment?

b. What is GNP?

c. How much does the capital stock increase during the period?

6. Consider an economy with expenditure totals given by

$$
\begin{array}{lll}
C & = \$1500 \text{ billion} & \text{(Consumption)} \\
I & = 600 & \text{(Investment)} \\
G & = 500 & \text{(Government spending)} \\
F & = 300 & \text{(Government transfers)} \\
N & = 100 & \text{(Interest on the government debt)} \\
T & = 1000 & \text{(Taxes)}
\end{array}
$$

a. What is GNP?

b. What is private saving?

c. What is government saving?

d. What is total saving? Show that it equals investment.

7. Consider an open economy with the same expenditure totals as in Problem 6, except for

$$
X = \$100 \qquad \text{(Net exports)}
$$

a. What is GNP?

b. What is private saving?

c. What is government saving?

d. What is rest of world saving?

e. What is total saving? Show that it equals investment.

8. Consider an economy with expenditure totals given by

$$
\begin{array}{lll}
C & = \$2300 \text{ billion} & \text{(Consumption)} \\
I & = 700 & \text{(Investment)} \\
G & = 800 & \text{(Government spending)} \\
F & = 100 & \text{(Government transfers)} \\
N & = 100 & \text{(Interest on the government debt)} \\
T & = 800 & \text{(Taxes)}
\end{array}
$$

a. What is GNP?

b. What is private saving?

c. What is government saving?

d. What is total saving? Show that it equals investment.

e. What is the government budget deficit?

f. Suppose that money equals $600 and government bonds $800 at the start of the year. If 80 percent of the government deficit is finance by issuing bonds, calculate the new levels of bond and money holdings.

9. Consider an open economy with the same expenditure totals as in Problem 8, except for

$$X = -\$200 \qquad \text{(Net exports)}$$

a. What is GNP?

b. What is private saving?

c. What is government saving?

d. What is rest of world saving?

e. What is total saving? Show that it equals investment.

f. What percentage of the government budget deficit is financed by the current account deficit?

MacroSolve Exercises

1. Tabulate annual data on the ratios to GNP of savings, investment, the government deficit, and net exports.

a. Describe how the ratio of investment to GNP has changed since the 1930s. Why does the share of investment in GNP fall during recessions? Why do you think that the ratio of investment to GNP may have fallen in the 1940s when the GNP gap was high?

b. Confirm that savings equals investment plus the government deficit and net exports. Explain intuitively rather than algebraically why this must always be the case.

c. The U.S. government has run a large deficit since 1980 (compare the ratio of the government deficit to GNP in this period with the previous few years). Does this explain why net exports have been such a large proportion of GNP lately?

d. Why do you think that the government deficit was such a large share of GNP in mid-1975?

2. Plot the trade-weighted exchange rate using quarterly data from 1967 to the present. Between 1981 and 1985, the exchange rate rose sharply.

a. Does this mean that the U.S. dollar became worth more or less in terms of foreign currencies during that period?

b. In this period, would foreign goods becomes relatively more expensive or cheaper for U.S. consumers to buy?

Answers to the Self-Test

1. Spending, production, or income
2. Households
3. Nonresidential and residential
4. Depreciation
5. Inventory
6. Exports minus imports
7. Final
8. Disposable
9. Deficit
10. Current account
11. Surplus
12. Deficit
13. False. We know they are the same simply because of an accounting identity.
14. True. It is included in residential investment.
15. False. It increases by net, not gross, investment.
16. True. The two ways of calculating GNP are equivalent.
17. False. Real GNP measures the physical volume of production.
18. False. It is unchanged if you buy a used car.
19. True. Both domestic consumption and exports add to GNP.
20. False. Investment is spending that adds to or maintains the capital stock. Buying shares of stock is not investment in the sense used by macroeconomists, and does not add to GNP.
21. False. Purchases of new equipment by firms are investment whether they add to or maintain their capital stock.
22. False. The unsold cars constitute inventory investment, which adds to GNP just like consumption.
23. True. When the exchange rate rises, one dollar can buy more foreign currency, making foreign goods cheaper.
24. False. The exchange rate has had large fluctuations during the last ten years.
25. When measured through spending, GNP is equal to consumption plus investment plus government purchases plus net exports.
26. The components of consumption are durable goods, nondurable goods, and services.
27. Investment is the flow of new capital during the year that is added to the existing stock of capital.
28. Real GNP fell from 1981 to 1982, and then rose again in 1983 through 1986 above the 1981 value. This illustrates an economic cycle because it began

with a contraction in real GNP (a recession), reached a trough, and continued with an expansion (a recovery).

29. For a closed economy with no government, GNP is equal to consumption plus investment. From the definition of saving, national income equals consumption plus saving. Since spending on GNP is equal to national income, saving equals investment.

30. In an open economy with a government, total saving, the sum of private, government, and rest of world saving, equals investment.

31. When the government spends more than it collects, it runs a deficit and must borrow to cover the difference. Issuing bonds and money, which are liabilities of the government, is how the government borrows.

32. The merchandise trade balance measures trade in goods. The balance on goods and services adds interest payments on foreign investments, and the current account adds remittances and transfers.

33. When there is a current account deficit, it must be financed by borrowing from the rest of the world, resulting in a matching capital account surplus. The two sum to zero.

34. Both the government budget deficit and the current account deficit are financed by borrowing. When there is a current account deficit, some of the borrowing is from foreigners.

35. The trade-weighted average exchange rate measures the average of the exchange rates between the dollar and several different currencies. The more that a country trades with the U.S., the more weight it receives.

36. The dollar fell during the boom of the late 1970s and rose during the recession of the early 1980s. Other fluctuations in the exchange rate, however, have not been associated with movements in U.S. output.

Solutions to Review Problems

4. a. $Y = C + I = 1700 + 600 = \$2300$.
   b. $S = Y - C = 2300 - 1700 = \$600 = I$.
   c. The capital stock increased by $600, the amount of investment.

5. a. Net investment = Investment (gross) – Depreciation
      $$= 600 - 200 = \$400.$$
   b. GNP is still equal to $2300 because gross, not net, investment is used to calculate it.
   c. The capital stock increases by $400, the amount of net investment.

6. a. $Y = C + I + G$
      $$= 1500 + 600 + 500 = \$2600.$$
   b. $S_p = (Y + F + N + T) - C$
      $$= (2600 + 300 + 100 - 1000) - 1500 = \$500.$$
   c. $S_g = T - F - N - G$
      $$= 1000 - 300 - 100 - 500 = \$100.$$
   d. $S = S_p + S_g$
      $$= 500 + 100 = \$600 = I.$$

7. a. $Y = C + I + G + X$
       $= 1500 + 600 + 500 + 100 = \$2700.$
    b. $S_p = (Y + F + N - T) - C$
       $= (2700 + 300 + 100 - 1000) - 1500 = \$600.$
    c. $S_g = T - F - N - G$
       $= 1000 - 300 - 100 - 500 = \$100.$
    d. $S_r = -X = -\$100.$
    e. $S = S_p + S_g + S_r$
       $= 600 + 100 - 100 = \$600 = I.$
8. a. $Y = C + I + G$
       $= 2300 + 700 + 800 = \$3800.$
    b. $S_p = (Y + F + N - T) - C$
       $= (3800 + 100 + 100 - 800) - 2300 = \$900.$
    c. $S_g = T - F - B - G$
       $= 800 - 100 - 100 - 800 = -\$200.$
    d. $S = S_p + S_g$
       $= 900 - 200 = \$700 = I.$
    e. The government budget deficit is $-S_g$, which equals \$200.
    f. The change in bonds is 80 percent of the 200 government budget deficit, or 160, so the new level of bonds is 960. The change in money is 20 percent of 200, or 40, so the new level of money is \$640.
9. a. $Y = C + I + G + X$
       $= 2300 + 700 + 800 - 200 = \$3600.$
    b. $S_p = (Y + F + N - T) - C$
       $= (3600 + 100 + 100 - 800) - 2300 = \$700.$
    c. $S_g = T - F - N - G$
       $= 800 - 100 - 100 - 800 = -\$200.$
    d. $S_r = -X = \$200.$
    e. $S = S_p + S_g + S_r$
       $= 700 - 200 + 200 = \$700 = I.$
    f. Since the current account deficit, \$200, is the same as the government budget deficit, the entire budget deficit is financed through the current account deficit. This means that foreigners have acquired \$200 in United States bonds or money.

Solutions to MacroSolve Exercises

1. a. Investment has generally been low in recessions, and high in booms. This is made particularly clear by plotting the GNP gap and the investment ratio using quarterly data. The only major exception was during the Second World War, when investment slumped. Investment would not necessarily be expected to behave according to the usual pattern in the middle of a war.
    b. Except for rounding error, the identity holds. Intuitively, investment and government deficit must be financed out of either domestic savings or borrowing from abroad.

c. Plotting net exports and the government deficit confirms that the two have moved in opposite directions since 1980, even though they did not always move in opposite directions previously. The negative net exports are consistent with some national dissaving.

d. There was a temporary tax rebate in mid-1975 that reduced government revenues while expenditures were abnormally high due to the high unemployment rate in 1975.

2. As the exchange rate rose, the dollar became worth more in terms of foreign currencies. U.S. exports therefore became more expensive to foreigners, and U.S. imports became cheaper to domestic consumers.

CHAPTER 3   Monitoring the Economy: Inflation and Employment

Main Objectives

Inflation and unemployment are the two most visible symbols of the economy's performance. Added up, the two have been popularized in presidential campaigns as the "misery index." In the late 1970s, when we had double-digit inflation, rates above 10 percent per year, it was considered imperative that inflation be reduced, even at the cost of provoking a recession. The flip side of the misery index, high unemployment, is the single most important indicator of economic distress. The battle against inflation in the late 1970s drove the unemployment rate above 10 percent in the early 1980s, the largest recession since the Great Depression. In this chapter, you will learn how inflation and unemployment are measured. Also important is the relationship between unemployment and gross national product.

Key Terms and Concepts

The **rate of inflation** is the percentage rate of change in the general price level from one period to the next. There are two ways to measure inflation. The first, **price indexes**, is calculated directly from data on the prices of thousands of goods and services. The best-known price index, the **consumer price index (CPI)**, measures the cost of living for a typical urban family. The weights on the individual prices in the CPI are based on a survey of consumer buying habits. Another widely used index is the **producer price index (PPI)**, which measures the prices charged by producers at various stages in the production process.

The second way to measure inflation is to deflate nominal values by dividing them by the real values they represent. For instance, the ratio of nominal to real GNP is called the **GNP implicit price deflator**, or often just the **GNP deflator**. There are deflators for each component of

GNP. The **consumption deflator**, for example, is the ratio of nominal to real consumption. The CPI and the GNP deflator have differed substantially in the past because the GNP deflator does not include the prices of imported goods and the CPI gave unreasonably heavy weight to the cost of buying a house. In the 1970s, because of rapidly rising oil and house prices, the CPI increased more than the GNP deflator. Recent changes in the way that the CPI weights housing costs are expected to narrow these differences in the future.

People are classified as employed if they are working. **Employment** in the United States is measured by two surveys, one of households and one of establishments where people work. In the long run, employment grows with potential GNP: to create more output firms require more workers. Employment falls with output during recessions, and rises during recoveries. Employment is not a complete measure of the input of labor in production because the average number of hours worked each week also falls during recessions and rises during recoveries. **Total hours of work**, employment multiplied by average hours worked, is a better measure.

If people are not working and are looking for work, they are classified as **unemployed**. The **labor force** is defined as the number of persons sixteen years of age or over who are either working or unemployed. The **unemployment rate** is the percentage of the labor force that is unemployed. There are many people who are not working who are not counted as unemployed including students, those at home taking care of their own children, and people who have become so discouraged about their job prospects that they have stopped looking. People who are not working but who are not looking for work are classified as **out of the labor force**. The **labor force participation rate** is the percentage of the working-age population that is in the labor force.

Unemployment is never equal to zero. There are always people entering the labor force (just turning sixteen, graduating from school, or starting to look for work again), in between jobs, or in professions with high job turnover. Unemployment of such people is called **frictional unemployment**. There are also people with so few skills that they are chronically unemployed. The rate of unemployment that prevails even in normal times, when real GNP equals potential output, is called the **natural rate of unemployment**. It is now usually estimated to be about 6 percent, rising from about 5 percent in the 1960s.

Okun's law is a useful approximation of the cyclical relationship between unemployment and real GNP. It says that for each percentage point by which the unemployment rate is above the natural rate, real GNP is 3 percent below potential GNP. Okun's law is given by

$$\frac{(Y - Y^*)}{Y^*} = -3(U - U^*), \tag{3-1}$$

where U is the unemployment rate, U^* is the natural rate of unemployment, Y is GNP, and Y^* is potential GNP. It is named after the late Arthur Okun of the Brookings Institution. The percentage departure of GNP from potential is called the **GNP gap.**

The **real wage** is the nominal wage divided by the price level. For workers concerned about the real purchasing power of their earnings, the appropriate price level is the CPI or the consumption deflator. Workers who wish to protect themselves against inflation can negotiate **cost-of-living adjustments (COLAs)** to have their payment rise in proportion to the increase in the CPI. The purpose of this is to fix one's real, instead of nominal, wage. Social security payments and many collective-bargaining agreements now incorporate COLAs.

Productivity is the amount of output per unit of input. When economists talk about productivity, they generally mean **labor productivity,** output per hour of labor. Productivity is procyclical, rising during booms and falling in recessions. Productivity growth has been slow since 1973. It has declined in each recession and has not increased enough in each recovery to return to the normal trend.

Self-Test

Fill in the Blank

1. The index that measures the cost of living for a typical urban family is the _____.

2. The _____ measures prices charged by producers at various stages of the production process.

3. The ratio of nominal GNP to real GNP is the _____.

4. The ratio of nominal consumption to real consumption is the

   _____.

5. The _____ is the number of persons sixteen years of age or over who are either working or unemployed.

6. The _____ is the percentage of the labor force that is unemployed.

7. The _____ is the percentage of the working-age population that is in the labor force.

8. The unemployment rate that prevails in normal times is the
_____ of unemployment.

9. Unemployment of people in between jobs is an example of
_____ unemployment.

10. The percentage departure of GNP from potential is called the
_____.

11. The nominal wage divided by the price level is the
_____ wage.

12. Output per hour of labor is called _____.

True-False

13. If the rate of inflation falls, prices decrease.

14. The consumer price index and the consumption deflator are not exactly comparable.

15. The producer price index measures the prices actually paid by consumers.

16. Employment is procyclical.

17. People sixteen years of age or older are classified as either employed or unemployed.

18. If an unemployed person enrolls in school, the unemployment rate decreases.

19. If a student graduates from college and begins to look for a job, the unemployment rate increases.

20. One example of frictional unemployment is when a worker quits one job to search for another.

21. There is no unemployment when real GNP equals potential GNP.

22. The natural rate of unemployment is constant.

23. Real wages decline when oil prices rise.

24. Productivity growth has increased since 1973.

25. What are the two ways that the general price level can be measured?

26. Why might you expect cost-of-living adjustments (COLAs) to have become less popular in the early 1980s than in the late 1970s?

27. Explain why total hours of work is a better measure of labor input to the economy than employment.

28. What is the difference between being unemployed and being out of the labor force?

29. What has happened to the labor force participation rate for women in the last few decades?

30. Why has the natural rate of unemployment increased since the 1960s?

31. What has happened to the labor force since the 1960s that should have contributed to lowering the natural rate of unemployment?

32. What is Okun's law?

33. What is the GNP gap? Is it possible for the GNP gap to be positive as well as negative?

34. How has the real wage fluctuated since 1973?

35. What is the difference between labor productivity and total factor productivity?

36. Describe some of the possible reasons for the slowdown in productivity growth since 1973.

Problem Set

Worked Problems

1. Looking into our crystal ball, we see the following data from the early 1990s:

Year	Unemployment Rate
1991	.05 (5 percent)
1992	.04 (4 percent)
1993	.05 (5 percent)
1994	.06 (6 percent)

a. Assuming that the natural rate of unemployment is 6 percent ($U^* = .06$), calculate the GNP gap for each of the unemployment rates from 1991 to 1994.

b. What is the relationship between GNP and potential GNP for these years?

c. If GNP is $2000 billion in 1993, calculate potential GNP.

a. *According to Okun's law, the GNP gap is $-3 (U - U^*)$ For 1991, with $U = .05$ and $U^* = .06$, $-3(U - U^*) = .03$ (3 percent). The answers for the other years are*

1992	.06 (6 percent)
1993	.03 (3 percent)
1994	.00 (0 percent)

b. *GNP is above or equal to potential GNP for all four years.*

c. *Okun's law states that $(Y - Y^*)/Y^* = $ GNP gap. To calculate potential output, rearrange terms so that $Y^* = Y/(1 + $ GNP gap$)$. For 1993, if $Y = 2000$ and the GNP gap (previously calculated) $= .03$, then $Y^* = 2000/1.03 = \$1941.7$ billion.*

2. We also see the following data on prices from the early 1990s:

Year	CPI
1991	400
1992	440
1993	462
1994	462

a. Calculate the rate of inflation for 1992, 1993, and 1994.

b. Suppose that the increase in the wage rate for a group of workers that sign an employment contract for the 2-year period starting in 1993 is $\Delta W/W = .1$. What happens to the real wage measured in terms of the CPI?

c. Suppose instead that the wage rate is partially indexed to the CPI according to the formula

$$\Delta W/W = .05 + .5 \, \Delta CPI/CPI.$$

What now happens to the real wage?

d. Finally, suppose that the wage rate is completely indexed to the CPI according to

$$\Delta W/W = \Delta CPI/CPI.$$

What happens to the real wage?

e. If, when these contracts were negotiated, workers and employers believed that inflation for 1993 and 1994 would be the same as it was in 1992, was there any reason for either to prefer one formula over the others? Did these preferences change over time once inflation became known?

a. The rate of inflation is

1992	.10 (10 percent)
1993	.05 (5 percent)
1994	.00 (0 percent)

b. Wages increase by 10 percent each year. Prices increase by 5 percent in 1993 and stay the same in 1994, so real wages increase.

c. Wages increase by 7.5 percent in 1993 and 5 percent in 1994. Real wages still increase, although by less than in Part b.

d. The real wage is constant when the nominal wage is completely indexed to the CPI.

e. If inflation had remained at 10 percent in 1993 and 1994 real wages would have been constant with any of the three formulas, so there was no reason for either workers or employers to prefer one over the others. Since the inflation rate declined, workers ended up better off with less indexation (b) while employers would have been better off with more (d).

Review Problems

3. The following unemployment rate (U) data are from the early 1960s:

Year	U
1960	.054 (5.4 percent)
1961	.065 (6.5 percent)
1962	.054 (5.4 percent)
1963	.055 (5.5 percent)

a. Assuming that the natural rate of unemployment was 5 percent ($U^* = .05$), calculate the GNP gap for each of the unemployment rates from 1960 to 1963.

b. Using the theory of price adjustment discussed in Chapter 1, what pressure was there on prices during these years?

c. Real GNP was $832.5 billion in 1963. Calculate potential GNP.

4. These data come from the late 1960s:

Year	U
1966	.037 (3.7 percent)
1967	.037 (3.7 percent)
1968	.035 (3.5 percent)
1969	.034 (3.4 percent)

a. Assuming that the natural rate of unemployment was 5 percent ($U^* = .05$), calculate the GNP gap for each of the unemployment rates from 1966 to 1969.

b. Using the theory of price adjustment discussed in Chapter 1, what pressure was there on prices during these years?

c. Real GNP was $1087.6 billion in 1969. Calculate potential GNP.

5. Now we can examine the late 1970s:

Year	U
1976	.076 (7.6 percent)
1977	.069 (6.9 percent)
1978	.060 (6.0 percent)
1979	.058 (5.8 percent)

a. Assuming that the natural rate of unemployment had risen to 6 percent ($U^* = .06$), calculate the GNP gap for each of the unemployment rates from 1976 to 1979.

b. Using the theory of price adjustment discussed in Chapter 1, what pressure was there on prices during these years?

c. Real GNP was $1479.4 billion in 1979. Calculate potential GNP.

6. We now consider the 1980s:

Year	U
1982	.095 (9.5 percent)
1983	.095 (9.5 percent)
1984	.074 (7.4 percent)
1985	.071 (7.1 percent)

a. Assuming that the natural rate of unemployment is 6 percent ($U^* = .06$), calculate the GNP gap for each of the unemployment rates from 1982 to 1985.

b. Using the theory of price adjustment discussed in Chapter 1, what was the pressure on prices during these years?

c. Real GNP was $1480 billion in 1982. Calculate potential GNP.

7. These data come, once again, from the early 1960s.

Year	CPI
1960	88.7
1961	89.6
1962	90.6
1963	91.7

a. Calculate the rate of inflation for 1961, 1962, and 1963.

b. Suppose that the increase in the wage rate for a group of workers that sign an employment contract for the 2-year period starting in 1962 is $\Delta W/W = .01$. What happens to the real wage measured in terms of the CPI?

c. Suppose instead that the wage rate is partially indexed to the CPI according to the formula

$$\Delta W/W = .005 + .5\ \Delta CPI/CPI.$$

What happens to the real wage?

d. Finally, suppose that the wage rate is completely indexed to the CPI according to

$$\Delta W/W = \Delta CPI/CPI.$$

What happens to the real wage?

e. If, when these contracts were negotiated, workers and employers believed that inflation for 1962 and 1963 would be the same as it was in 1961, was there any reason for either to prefer one formula over the others? Did these preferences change over time once inflation became known?

8. Now use the following data from the late 1960s:

Year	CPI
1966	97.2
1967	100.0
1968	104.2
1969	109.8

a. Calculate the rate of inflation for 1967, 1968, and 1969.

b. Suppose that the increase in the wage rate for a group of workers that sign an employment contract for the 2-year period starting in 1968 is $\Delta W/W = .029$. What happens to the real wage measured in terms of the CPI?

c. Suppose instead that the wage rate is partially indexed to the CPI according to the formula

$$\Delta W/W = .014 + .5 \, \Delta CPI/CPI.$$

What happens to the real wage?

d. Finally, suppose that the wage rate is completely indexed to the CPI according to

$$\Delta W/W = \Delta CPI/CPI.$$

What happens to the real wage?

e. If, when these contracts were negotiated, workers and employers believed that inflation for 1968 and 1969 would be the same as it was in 1967, was there any reason for either to prefer one formula over the others? Did these preferences change over time once inflation became known?

9. The following data are from the late 1970s:

Year	CPI
1976	170.5
1977	181.5
1978	195.4
1979	217.4

a. Calculate the rate of inflation for 1977, 1978, and 1979.

b. Suppose that the increase in the wage rate for a group of workers that sign an employment contract for the 2-year period starting in 1978 is $\Delta W/W = .065$. What happens to the real wage measured in terms of the CPI?

c. Suppose instead that the wage rate is partially indexed to the CPI according to the formula

$$\Delta W/W = .032 + .5 \, \Delta CPI/CPI.$$

What happens to the real wage?

d. Finally, suppose that the wage rate is completely indexed to the CPI according to

$$\Delta W/W = \Delta CPI/CPI.$$

What happens to the real wage?

e. If, when these contracts were negotiated, workers and employers believed that inflation for 1978 and 1979 would be the same as it was in 1977, was there any reason for either to prefer one formula over the others? Did these preferences change over time once inflation became known?

10. We now consider the 1980s:

Year	CPI
1982	289.1
1983	298.4
1984	311.1
1985	322.2

a. Calculate the rate of inflation for 1983, 1984, and 1985.

b. Suppose that the increase in the wage rate for a group of workers that sign an employment contract for the 3-year period starting in 1983 is $\Delta W/W = .10$. What happens to the real wage measured in terms of the CPI?

c. Suppose instead that the wage rate is partially indexed to the CPI according to the formula

$$\Delta W/W = .05 + .5 \, \Delta CPI/CPI.$$

What happens to the real wage?

d. Finally, suppose that the wage rate is completely indexed to the CPI according to

$$\Delta W/W = \Delta CPI/CPI.$$

What happens to the real wage?

e. If, when these contracts were negotiated, workers and employers believed that inflation for 1983 through 1985 would be the same as the average for 1980 through 1982, 10.0 percent, was there any reason for either to prefer one formula over the others? Did these preferences change over time once inflation became known?

MacroSolve Exercises

1. Plot the quarterly growth rates of the CPI and the GNP deflator ("Inflation (CPI)" and "Inflation (GNP)," respectively). Why are the two not always the same. (Hint: what *exactly* do the two indices measure?)

a. What major event helps explain why the growth of the CPI was larger than the growth in the GNP deflator in 1979–80?

b. Why was the CPI inflation rate less than the GNP inflation rate in 1986?

2. Okun's law states that "for each percentage point by which the unemployment rate is *above* the natural rate, real GNP is 3 percent *below* potential GNP. The percentage departure of GNP from potential is called the **GNP gap.**" Using quarterly data, graph the unemployment rate (on the horizontal axis) against the GNP gap (on the vertical axis).

   a. You will see that the curve seems to shift outwards over time. Does this imply that the natural rate of unemployment has risen or fallen over time? (Hint: if the GNP gap is zero for any length of time, then unemployment should be close to the natural rate.)

   b. Compute the slope of the Okun relationship between 1933 and 1944 by tabulating the data for the GNP gap and the unemployment rate. The slope is given by the change in the GNP gap divided by the change in the unemployment rate. Make the same calculation between 1978 and 1983. Has the slope changed? What factors might account for such a change?

   c. How much would the slope coefficient for the 1978–83 period imply that the GNP gap would change if the unemployment rate changed from 7.5 percent to 7.0 percent? This was the actual change in the unemployment rate between 1984 and 1986; explain why the predicted change in the GNP gap might not equal its actual value.

Answers to the Self-Test

1. Consumer price index
2. Producer price index
3. GNP deflator
4. Consumption deflator
5. Labor force
6. Unemployment rate
7. Labor force participation rate
8. Natural rate
9. Frictional
10. GNP gap
11. Real
12. Labor productivity

13. False. The rate of inflation is the percentage of change of the price level. If inflation falls from 10 to 5 percent, prices are still rising.
14. True. They are measured differently, and the CPI gives greater weight to the cost of buying a home.
15. False. The producer price index measures the prices charged by producers at various stages in the production process.
16. True. Employment rises during expansions and falls during recessions.
17. False. They can also be out of the labor force.
18. True. You are counted as out of the labor force if in school full time.
19. True. You are counted as unemployed when you begin to look for a job.
20. True. Others are workers looking for a first job or reentering the labor force.
21. False. The unemployment rate that prevails in normal times is the natural rate of unemployment.
22. False. While it changes only very slowly, it has increased from 5 to 6 percent since the 1960s.
23. True. Oil and labor are both inputs to production. When the price of oil rises, the nominal wage (the price of labor) cannot rise as much as the general price level. Thus the real wage declines.
24. False. The growth of productivity has decreased since 1973.
25. The general price level can be measured either by constructing price indexes or by calculating deflators.
26. COLAs protect workers against inflation. With the slowdown of inflation in the early 1980s, there should be less need for protection.
27. Total hours of work is employment multiplied by the hours of work of the average worker. It is a better measure of labor input than employment because it incorporates how many hours people work.
28. Being unemployed means you are not working and are looking for work. Being out of the labor force means you are neither working nor looking for work.
29. The labor force participation rate for women has increased considerably in the last few decades.
30. The natural rate of unemployment has increased because the baby boom after World War II added to the labor force more young workers, who have higher unemployment rates than older workers.
31. The labor force has become better educated.
32. Okun's law states that for each percentage point by which the unemployment rate is above the natural rate real GNP is 3 percent below potential GNP.
33. The GNP gap is the percentage departure of GNP from potential. It can be positive (GNP can be above potential) if unemployment is below the natural rate.
34. The real wage fell after the oil price increase in 1974, rose during the late 1970s, fell again after the second oil price shock in 1979–80, and rose sharply when oil prices declined in 1986.
35. Labor productivity is output per hour of labor. Total factor productivity is output per generalized unit of input, which includes capital, energy, and materials as well as labor.

36. Increases in oil prices, reduction in expenditures on research and development, and insufficient investment in new machines and factories are some of the possible reasons for the slowdown in productivity since 1973.

Solutions to Review Problems

3. a. The GNP gap is $-3(U - U^*)$. With $U^* = .05$, the gap was

1960	$-.012$ (-1.2 percent)
1961	$-.045$ (-4.5 percent)
1962	$-.012$ (-1.2 percent)
1963	$-.015$ (-1.5 percent)

   b. With the gap between -1.2 and -4.5 percent, GNP was below potential and there was pressure on prices to fall although, for three of the four years, the gap was quite small.

   c. Rearranging Okun's law, $Y^* = Y/(1 + GNP gap)$. For 1963, with $Y = \$832.5$ and the gap $= -.015$, $Y^* = \$845.2$.

4. a. The GNP gap is $-3(U - U^*)$. With $U^* = .05$, the gap was

1966	.039 (3.9 percent)
1967	.039 (3.9 percent)
1968	.045 (4.5 percent)
1969	.048 (4.8 percent)

   b. With the gap between 3.9 and 4.8 percent, GNP was above potential and there was pressure on prices to rise.

   c. Rearranging Okun's law, $Y^* = Y/(1 + GNP gap)$. For 1969, with $Y = \$1087.6$ and the gap $= .048$, $Y^* = \$1037.8$.

5. a. The GNP gap is $-3(U - U^*)$. With $U^* = .06$, the gap was

1976	$-.048$ (-4.8 percent)
1977	$-.027$ (-2.7 percent)
1978	.000 (0 percent)
1979	.006 (0.6 percent)

   b. With the gap between -4.8 and -2.7 percent during 1976 and 1977, GNP was below potential and there was pressure on prices to fall. There was very little pressure on prices during 1978 and 1979.

   c. Rearranging Okun's law, $Y^* = Y/(1 + GNP gap)$. For 1979, with $Y = \$1479.4$ and the gap $= .006$, $Y^* = \$1470.6$.

6. a. The GNP gap is $-3(U - U^*)$. With $U^* = .06$, the gap was

1982	$-.105$ (-10.5 percent)
1983	$-.105$ (-10.5 percent)
1984	$-.042$ (-4.2 percent)
1985	$-.033$ (-3.3 percent)

   b. With the gap between -3.3 and -10.5 percent, GNP was below potential and there was pressure on prices to fall.

c. Rearranging Okun's law, $Y^* = Y/(1 + \text{GNP gap})$. For 1982, with $Y = \$1480$ and the gap $= -.105$, $Y^* = 1480/.895 = \$1654$.

7. a. The rate of inflation was

1961	.010 (1.0 percent)
1962	.011 (1.1 percent)
1963	.012 (1.2 percent)

   b. Wages increase by 1 percent each year. Prices increase by 1.1 percent in 1962 and 1.2 percent in 1963, so real wages fall very slightly.

   c. Wages increase by 1.05 percent in 1962 and 1.1 percent in 1963. Real wages fall very slightly in both 1962 and 1963.

   d. The real wage is constant when the nominal wage is completely indexed to the CPI.

   e. If inflation had remained at 1.0 percent in 1962 and 1962, real wages would have been constant with any of the three formulas, so there was no reason for either workers or employers to prefer one over the others. Since the inflation rate was so close to 1.0 percent, choice of one formula over another would not have made much difference.

8. a. The rate of inflation was

1967	.029 (2.9 percent)
1968	.042 (4.2 percent)
1969	.054 (5.4 percent)

   b. Wages increase by 2.9 percent each year. Prices increase by 4.2 percent in 1968 and 5.4 percent in 1969, so real wages fall.

   c. Wages increase by 3.5 percent in 1968 and 4.1 percent in 1969. Real wages fall, but by less than in Part b.

   d. The real wage is constant when the nominal wage is completely indexed to the CPI.

   e. If inflation had remained at 2.9 percent in 1968 and 1969, real wages would have been constant with any of the three formulas, so there was no reason for either workers or employers to prefer one over the others. Since the inflation rate increased, workers ended up better off with more indexation (d) while employers would have been better off with less (b).

9. a. The rate of inflation was

1977	.065 (6.5 percent)
1978	.077 (7.7 percent)
1979	.113 (11.3 percent)

   b. Wages increase by 6.5 percent each year. Prices increase by 7.7 percent in 1978 and 11.3 percent in 1979, so real wages fall.

   c. Wages increase by 7.1 percent in 1978 and 8.9 percent in 1979. Real wages fall, but by less than in Part b.

   d. The real wage is constant when the nominal wage is completely indexed to the CPI.

   e. If inflation had remained at 6.5 percent in 1978 and 1979, real wages would have been constant with any of the three formulas, so there was no reason for either workers or employers to prefer one over the others. Since the inflation rate increased, workers ended up better off with more indexation (d) while employers would have been better off with less (b).

10. a. The rate of inflation was

1983	.032 (3.2 percent)
1984	.043 (4.3 percent)
1985	.036 (3.6 percent)

 b. Wages increase by 10.0 percent each year. Prices increase by an average of 3.7 percent, so real wages increase.
 c. Real wages increase, but by less than in Part b.
 d. Real wages are constant.
 e. With expected inflation equal to 10 percent, there was no reason for either workers or employers to prefer one over the others. Since inflation was actually below 10 percent, workers ended up better off with less indexation (b) while employers would have been better off with more (d).

Solutions to MacroSolve Exercises

1. The GNP deflator measures the cost of goods and services produced in the economy. The CPI measures the costs of a typical consumer's expenditures. Since the indices measure different things, there is no reason for them to be identical. Over extended periods, they generally move together.
 a. The rise in domestic and international oil prices in 1979–80 increased the cost of consumer goods, without having the same impact on output prices.
 b. The fall in oil prices throughout 1986 led to the opposite result from the 1979–80 period.

2. a. As the curve shifts outwards, the level of unemployment corresponding to a GNP gap of zero increases. This implies that the natural rate of unemployment has increased.
 b. The slope was –2.85 between 1933 and 1944, so that an increase of one percent in the unemployment rate corresponded to a decrease in the GNP gap of 2.85 percent. Between 1978 and 1983, the slope was –2.52. A given change in the unemployment rate now corresponds to a somewhat smaller change in the GNP gap than before the war. In other words, unemployment is somewhat more sensitive to output movements. One possible reason for this (small) change is that unemployment insurance has made unemployment less catastrophic than it was previously.
 c. If the unemployment rate fell by 0.5 percent, the coefficient implies that the GNP gap should increase by 2.52/2 percent, or 1.26 percent. The GNP gap did not change by that much between 1984 and 1986; this is probably because th decline in unemployment resulted from the previous increase in the GNP gap.

CHAPTER 4   Income and Spending

Main Objectives

The first three chapters have given us much to consider: economic fluctuations, gross national product, unemployment rates, inflation rates. These are central concerns of macroeconomists, and they are all related to one another. In Chapter 4, we begin to see how this is so with our first look at the balance between income and spending.

We start with the simplest possible formulation, where GNP and consumption are the only variables to be determined. You should learn the consumption function and the income identity, and know how GNP is determined by combining the two of them through the concept of spending balance. You should also learn how government spending affects GNP through the multiplier, and how the introduction of foreign trade affects the analysis of spending balance.

Key Terms and Concepts

Aggregate demand is the total of the spending demands by the various sectors in the economy. These include **consumption** by households, **investment** by firms, **exports** by foreigners, and **government spending**.

Short-run fluctuations in GNP from its long-run growth path are **demand determined**. Firms normally operate with some excess capacity. When there is an increase in spending demand, they increase production to meet the demand for their goods. If they need additional labor, they can increase the hours per week of their workers, recall laid-off workers, or hire additional workers.

Firms also adjust their prices to changes in demand, but there is a crucial difference between the adjustment of production and the adjustment of prices. Price adjustments are **sticky** compared to production adjustments. The adjustment of prices occurs gradually, while the adjustment of production and employment occurs almost instantaneously.

The **income identity** for a closed economy says that income (Y) equals the sum of consumption (C), investment (I), and government spending (G),

$$Y = C + I + G. \qquad (4\text{-}1)$$

It incorporates two important concepts. First, as shown in Chapter 2, income equals GNP. Second, as discussed above, aggregate demand determines GNP. We use the terms output, income, and GNP interchangeably, always represented by the symbol Y.

The **consumption function** states that consumption depends on disposable income (Y_d), which is equal to income minus taxes,

$$C = a + b Y_d. \qquad (4\text{-}2)$$

There is a subsistence level of consumption, a, about which the individual has no choice. If the individual's income is less than a, he borrows. At income levels above a, he has a choice between consumption and saving. The coefficient b is the **marginal propensity to consume**. It measures how much of an additional dollar of disposable income is spent on consumption. For instance, if we set b equal to .8, we are saying that 80 cents of each additional dollar of disposable income is spent on consumption. The other 20 cents is saved.

If the tax rate is the constant t, total tax payments are the tax rate multiplied by income, tY. Disposable income Y_d = income – taxes = $Y - tY = (1 - t)Y$. By replacing disposable income Y_d with $(1 - t)Y$, the consumption function can be written

$$C = a + b(1 - t)Y. \qquad (4\text{-}3)$$

Spending balance in a closed economy occurs at levels of consumption C and income Y that obey both the consumption function and the income identity. We substitute the consumption function into the income identity, $Y = C + I + G$, and solve for income to obtain

$$Y = a + b(1 - t)Y + I + G$$
$$Y(1 - b(1 - t)) = a + I + G$$
$$Y = \frac{1}{1 - b(1 - t)}(a + I + G). \qquad (4\text{-}4)$$

To solve for consumption, substitute back into the consumption function the value of income when spending balance is attained. Because they can be determined inside the model in this case, income and consumption are called **endogenous variables**. Investment and government spending cannot be determined inside the model—yet—so they are called **exogenous variables**, determined outside the model.

The **multiplier** for a closed economy measures how much a change in investment or government spending changes income. The formula for the multiplier when both investment and government spending are exogenous is $1/(1 - b(1 - t))$. It is greater than one because both b and t are between zero and one, indicating that an increase in either investment or government spending will have a more than proportional effect on income.

The **income identity for an open economy** says that income (Y) equals the sum of consumption (C), investment (I), government spending (G), and net exports (X),

$$Y = C + I + G + X, \tag{4-5}$$

where net exports, equal to exports minus imports, are positive if there is a trade surplus and negative if there is a trade deficit. Since every country trades with the rest of the world, we will simply use the term **income identity** when we mean income identify for an open economy.

The **net export function** relates net exports to income,

$$X = g - mY, \tag{4-6}$$

where g is a constant and m is a coefficient. Net exports depend negatively on income because, as income rises, spending rises. Since part of this rise in spending is on imported goods, imports rise and net exports fall. The coefficient m is called the **marginal propensity to import**, and measures how much of an additional dollar of income is spent on imports.

We now find the value of income at the point of spending balance in an open economy by substituting the net export function, as well as the consumption function, into the income identity, $Y = C + I + G + X$, and solve for income to obtain

$$Y = a + b(1 - t)Y + I + G + g - mY.$$
$$Y(1 - b(1 - t) + m) = a + I + G + g$$
$$Y = \frac{1}{1 - b(1 - t) + m}(a + I + G + g). \tag{4-7}$$

The **open economy multiplier**, which measures the impact of a change in government spending or investment on output in an open economy, is $1/(1 - b(1 - t) + m)$. The open economy multiplier is smaller when the marginal propensity to import m is larger. If m were zero, so that increases in income did not affect imports, the open and closed economy multipliers would be the same. With m greater than zero, the open economy multiplier is smaller than the closed economy multiplier.

We can now analyze the relation between trade deficits and government budget, or fiscal, deficits. Increases in government spending G, if not matched by tax increases, cause fiscal deficits. According to the multiplier, increases in G also cause income Y to rise. When Y increases, imports rise and trade deficits occur.

Self-Test

Fill in the Blank

1. The total of the spending demands in all the sectors of the economy is _____ demand.

2. Variables determined outside a model are called _____ .

3. Variables determined inside a model are called _____.

4. The income identity for a closed economy says that income is the sum of _____, _____, and _____.

5. The income identity for an open economy says that income is the sum of _____, _____, _____, and _____.

6. The _____ is the fraction of an increase in disposable income that is consumed.

7. The _____ is the fraction of an increase in income that is spent on imports.

8. The _____ relates consumption to disposable income.

9. The _____ relates net exports to income.

10. The price level is called _____ because, in the short run, its value is determined by events that have occurred in previous years.

11. The _____ measures how much a change in investment or government spending changes income.

12. The government budget deficit is also called the _____ deficit.

13. Firms normally operate at less than 100 percent capacity utilization.

14. If spending demand increases, firms will increase output before they increase prices.

15. Disposable income is equal to income minus saving.

16. Consumption will equal zero if disposable income equals zero.

17. Spending balance means that the government budget deficit is zero.

18. The income identity says that income is equal to consumption.

19. The multiplier is always greater than the marginal propensity to consume.

20. If the tax rate is zero, the multiplier would equal one.

21. Net exports depend negatively on income.

22. The open economy multiplier measures the impact of a change in government spending on exports.

23. The open economy multiplier is smaller than the closed economy multiplier.

24. Fiscal and trade deficits are unrelated.

Review Questions

25. What are the four components of aggregate demand?

26. What does it mean for short-run fluctuations in GNP to be demand determined?

27. What does it mean for prices to be sticky?

28. What are the two concepts that are incorporated into the income identity?

29. Why does the consumption function depend on disposable, and not total, income?

30. When does spending balance occur?

31. If aggregate demand is less than output produced, how is spending balance achieved?

32. What is the difference between endogenous and exogenous variables?

33. What is the relation between the government spending and investment multipliers?

34. Why is the open economy multiplier smaller than the closed economy multiplier?

35. Why do increases in income cause trade deficits?

36. Why do trade and fiscal deficits occur together?

Problem Set

Worked Problems

1. Consider a closed economy described by the following equations:

$$Y = C + I + G \quad \text{(Income identity)}$$
$$C = 100 + .9\,Y_d \quad \text{(Consumption)}$$

with investment I = \$300 billion, government spending G = \$200 billion, and the tax rate t = .2.

a. What is the level of income when spending balance occurs? What is the multiplier?

b. Suppose government spending increases to \$300 billion. What is the new level of income?

a. *From the income identity,*

$$Y = C + I + G.$$

Using the consumption function, $C = 100 + .9\,Y_d$, and the definition of disposable income, $Y_d = Y - .2Y$,

$$Y = 100 + .9(Y - .2Y) + 300 + 200$$
$$= 600 + .72Y.$$

Subtract .72Y from both sides of the equation,

$$Y - .72Y = 600,$$

factor out Y,

$$Y(1 - .72) = 600,$$
$$.28Y = 600,$$

and multiply both sides by $1/.28 = 3.571$ to obtain the solution,

$$Y = 3.571(600) = \$2143 \text{ billion.}$$

By solving for income, we automatically derive the multiplier. It is the number, 3.571, that multiplies the exogenous components of consumption, investment, and government spending, 600, to get income.

Alternatively, we can use the formula,

$$\frac{1}{1 - b(1 - t)} = \frac{1}{1 - .9(1 - .2)} = \frac{1}{1 - .72} = \frac{1}{.28} = 3.571$$

to find the multiplier. It is important that you learn how to derive the multiplier rather than just memorize the formula, which is correct only if neither investment nor government spending depends on income.

b. *This can be solved in two ways. One is to recalculate Y using the new level of G, 300.*

$$\begin{aligned} Y &= 100 + .9(Y - .2Y) + 300 + 300 \\ &= 700 + .72Y \\ &= 3.571(700) = \$2500 \text{ billion.} \end{aligned}$$

A second is to use the multiplier to calculate the change in Y,

$$\Delta Y = 3.571 \qquad \Delta G = 3.571(100) = 357,$$

and then add the change in Y, 357, to the original value of Y, 2143, to get the new value, \$2500 billion.

2. Consider an open economy described by the following equations:

$$\begin{aligned} Y &= C + I + G + X & \text{(Income identity)} \\ C &= 100 + .9\,Y_d & \text{(Consumption)} \\ X &= 100 - .12Y & \text{(Net exports)} \end{aligned}$$

with investment $I = \$200$ billion, government spending $G = \$200$ billion, and the tax rate $t = .2$.

a. What is the level of income when spending balance occurs? What is the multiplier? Compare the multiplier to the closed economy multiplier in Problem 1.

b. Suppose government spending increases to $300 billion. What is the new level of income?

a. *From the income identity,*

$$Y = C + I + G + X$$

Using the consumption function, $C = 100 + .9\,Y_d$, the net export function, $X = 100 - .12Y$, and the definition of disposable income, $Y_d = Y - .2Y$,

$$Y = 100 + .9(Y - .2Y) + 200 + 200 + 100 - .12Y,$$
$$= 600 + .6Y.$$

Subtract .6Y from both sides of the equation,

$$Y - .6Y = 600,$$

factor out Y,

$$Y(1 - .6) = 600,$$
$$.4Y = 600,$$

and multiply both sides by 2.5 to obtain the solution,

$$Y = 2.5(600) = \$1500 \text{ billion.}$$

By solving for income, we automatically derive the multiplier, 2.5. The open economy multiplier, 2.5, is smaller than the closed economy multiplier, 3.571, for the same marginal propensity to consume and tax rate.
Alternatively, we can use the formula,

$$\frac{1}{1 - b(1 - t) + m} = \frac{1}{1 - .9(1 - .2) + .12} = \frac{1}{.4} = 2.5$$

to find the multiplier.

b. *This can be solved in two ways. One is to recalculate Y using the new level of G, 300.*

$$Y = 100 + .9(Y - .2Y) + 200 + 300 + 100 - .12Y$$
$$= 700 + .6Y$$
$$= 2.5(700) = \$1750 \text{ billion.}$$

A second is to use the multiplier to calculate the change in Y,

$$\Delta Y = 2.5 \qquad \Delta G = 2.5(100) = 250,$$

and then add the change in Y, 250, to the original value of Y, 1500, to get the new value, \$1750 billion.

Review Problems

3. Consider a closed economy described by the following equations:

$$Y = C + I + G \qquad \text{(Income identity)}$$
$$C = 300 + .8 Y_d \qquad \text{(Consumption)}$$

with investment $I = \$300$, government spending $G = \$200$, and the tax rate $t = .2$.

a. What is the level of income when spending balance occurs? What is the multiplier?

b. Consider the same economy, except that investment depends positively on income, so that $I = 300 + .2Y$. What is the level of income and multiplier now?

c. Returning to the investment equation in Part a, suppose that the tax rate is increased to .4. What happens to income and to the multiplier?

4. Consider a closed economy described by the following equations:

$$Y = C + I + G \quad \text{(Income identity)}$$
$$C = 400 + .9\,Y_d \quad \text{(Consumption)}$$

with investment $I = \$400$, government spending $G = \$100$, and the tax rate $t = .5$.

a. What is the level of income when spending balance occurs? What is the multiplier?

b. Suppose government spending increases to $200. What is the new level of income?

5. Consider a closed economy described by the following equations:

$$Y = C + I + G \quad \text{(Income identity)}$$
$$C = 400 + .9\,Y_d \quad \text{(Consumption)}$$

with investment $I = \$300$, government spending $G = \$200$, and the tax rate $t = .3333$.

a. What is the level of income when spending balance occurs? What is the multiplier?

b. Suppose government spending increases to $300. What is the new level of income?

6. Consider an open economy described by the following equations:

$$Y = C + I + G + X \quad \text{(Income identity)}$$
$$C = 300 + .8\,Y_d \quad \text{(Consumption)}$$
$$X = 100 - .04Y \quad \text{(Net exports)}$$

with investment $I = \$200$, government spending $G = \$200$, and the tax rate $t = .2$.

a. What is the level of income when spending balance occurs? What is the multiplier? Compare your answer to the closed economy multiplier in Problem 3.

b. Consider the same economy, except that investment depends positively on income, so that $I = 300 + .2Y$. What is the level of income and multiplier now?

c. Returning to the investment equation in Part a, suppose that the tax rate is increased to .4. What happens to income and to the multiplier?

7. Consider an open economy described by the following equations:

$$\begin{aligned} Y &= C + I + G + X & \text{(Income identity)} \\ C &= 400 + .9Y_d & \text{(Consumption)} \\ X &= 100 - .05Y & \text{(Net exports)} \end{aligned}$$

with investment $I = \$300$, government spending $G = \$100$, and the tax rate $t = .5$.

a. What is the level of income when spending balance occurs? What is the multiplier? Compare your answer to the closed economy multiplier in Problem 4.

b. Suppose government spending increases to $300. What is the new level of income?

8. Consider an open economy described by the following equations:

$$\begin{aligned} Y &= C + I + G + X & \text{(Income identity)} \\ C &= 400 + .9Y_d & \text{(Consumption)} \\ X &= 200 - .1Y & \text{(Net exports)} \end{aligned}$$

with investment $I = \$200$, government spending $G = \$200$, and the tax rate $t = .3333$.

a. What is the level of income when spending balance occurs? What is the multiplier? Compare your answer to the closed economy multiplier in Problem 5

b. Suppose government spending increases to $300. What is the new level of income?

MacroSolve Exercises

1. Using quarterly data, graph consumption on the vertical axis against disposable income.

a. What is the slope of the consumption function (the marginal propensity to consume)?

b. If the tax rate were zero, what would this marginal propensity to consume imply was the value of the multiplier for a closed economy?

c. If the tax rate were 30 percent, what then would be the value of the multiplier?

d. If, in addition, the marginal propensity to import were 0.1, what would be the value of the multiplier?

2. Tabulate the ratio of consumption to disposable income using quarterly data. How can the average propensity to consume be different from the marginal propensity to consume? What does this imply for the value of consumption when income is zero?

3. Tabulate values of the average propensity to consume and the ratio of savings to GNP. Why is the ratio of consumption to income not equal to 1 minus the ratio of savings to GNP?

4. Plot the quarterly growth rates of real GNP and the GNP deflator (Inflation (GNP)). Which would you describe as being more variable? Is this finding compatible with the view that prices are more sticky than output? Is the same true for the entire sample of annual data from 1930 to 1987?

Answers to the Self-Test

1. Aggregate
2. Exogenous
3. Endogenous
4. Consumption, investment, and government spending
5. Consumption, investment, government spending, and net exports
6. Marginal propensity to consume
7. Marginal propensity to import
8. Consumption function
9. Net export function
10. Predetermined
11. Multiplier
12. Fiscal
13. True. Firms normally operate with some excess capacity.
14. True. This is what is means for prices to be "sticky."
15. False. Disposable income is equal to income minus taxes.
16. False. The positive value of the coefficient a in the consumption function, $C = a + bY_d$, means that, rather than starve if disposable income is zero for one year, people will spend some of their savings.
17. False. Spending balance can occur with a positive, negative, or zero government budget deficit.

18. False. The income identity says that income is equal to the sum of consumption, investment, government spending, and net exports.
19. True. The multiplier is greater than one and the marginal propensity to consume is less than one.
20. False. The multiplier would equal $1/(1-b)$ if the tax rate was zero.
21. True. Imports rise when income rises, lowering net exports.
22. False. The open economy multiplier measures the impact of a change in government spending on income.
23. True. If the marginal propensity to import is positive, the open economy multiplier is smaller than the closed economy multiplier.
24. False. Increases in government spending cause both fiscal and trade deficits.
25. The four components of aggregate demand are consumption, investment, government spending, and net exports.
26. Short-run fluctuations in GNP are said to be demand determined because, when there is an increase in spending demand, firms increase production to meet the demand for their goods.
27. Prices are called sticky because they adjust slowly, compared with adjustments in production, to changes in spending demand.
28. The two concepts incorporated into the income identity are that income equals GNP and that aggregate demand determines GNP.
29. The consumption function describes people's choices between consuming and saving. The income available to make such a choice is their after-tax, or disposable, income.
30. Spending balance occurs when the income identity, consumption function, and net export function are satisfied.
31. If a firm produces more output than it can sell, it must either store the additional output, which is costly, or let the output go to waste. The firm is better off by decreasing production, which achieves spending balance.
32. An endogenous variable is determined within the model. An exogenous variable is determined outside the model.
33. The government spending and investment multipliers are equal.
34. The open economy multiplier is smaller than the closed economy multiplier because, in an open economy, part of the induced increase in consumption is spent on imports, which do not add to GNP.
35. When income rises, part of the increase is spent on imports, causing trade deficits.
36. Increases in government spending, which cause fiscal deficits, also raise income, causing trade deficits.

Solutions to Review Problems

3. a. $Y = C + I + G$ for spending balance to hold.
$$= 300 + .8(Y - .2Y) + 300 + 200$$
$$= 800 + .64Y$$
$$= 2.777(800) = \$2222.$$

The government spending multiplier is 2.777. In this case, since neither investment nor government spending depends on income, the formula, $1/(1 - .8(1 - .2))$, will also give the correct answer.

b. $Y = 300 + .8(Y - .2Y) + 300 + .2Y + 200$
$= 800 + .84Y$
$= 6.25(800) = \$5000.$

The multiplier is 6.25. In this case, since investment depends on income, the formula will not give the correct answer.

c. $Y = 300 + .8(Y - .4Y) + 300 + 200$
$= 800 + .48Y$
$= 1.923(800) = \$1538.$

The multiplier, 1.923, decreases because higher taxes lower disposable income. Since the multiplier falls, and the exogenous variables are unchanged, income decreases.

4. a. $Y = 400 + .9(Y - .5Y) + 400 + 100$
$= 900 + .45Y$
$= 1.818(900) = \$1636.$

The multiplier is 1.818.

b. $Y = \$1818$

5. a. $Y = 400 + .9(Y - .3333Y) + 300 + 200$
$= 900 + .6Y$
$= 2.5(900) = \$2250.$

The multiplier is 2.5.

b. $Y = \$2500$

6. a. $Y = C + I + G$ for spending balance to hold.
$= 300 + .8(Y - .2Y) + 200 + 200 + 100 - .04Y$
$= 800 + .6Y$
$= 2.5(800) = \$2000.$

The government spending multiplier is 2.5. It is smaller than the multiplier, 2.777, in Problem 3. In this case, since neither investment nor government spending depends on income, the formula, $1/(1 - .8(1 - .2) + .04)$, will also give the correct answer.

b. $Y = 300 + .8(Y - .2Y) + 200 + .2Y + 200 + 100 - .04Y$
$= 800 + .8Y$
$= 5(800) = \$4000.$

The multiplier is 5. In this case, since investment depends on income, the formula will not give the correct answer.

c. $Y = 300 + .8(Y - .4Y) + 200 + 200 + 100 - .04Y$
$= 800 + .45Y$
$= 1.82(800) = \$1454.5.$

The multiplier, 1.82, decreases because higher taxes lower disposable income. Since the multiplier falls, and the exogenous variables are unchanged, income decreases.

7. a. $Y = 400 + .9(Y - .5Y) + 300 + 100 + 100 - .05Y$
$= 900 + .4Y$
$= 1.67(900) = \$1500.$

The multiplier is 1.67. It is smaller than the multiplier, 1.818, in

Problem 4.
b. $Y = \$1667$
8.   a. $Y = 400 + .9(Y - .3333Y) + 200 + 200 + 200 - .1Y$
$= 1000 + .5Y$
$= 2(1000) = \$2000.$

The multiplier is 2. It is smaller than the multiplier, 2.5, in Problem 5.
b. $Y = \$2200$

Solutions to MacroSolve Exercises

1.   a.   The marginal propensity to consume is about 0.98. In other words, about 98 percent of any increase in disposable income is consumed.
b.   The multiplier would be $1/(1 - 0.98)$, or 50.
c.   If the tax rate were 30 percent, then if income rose by 1 percent, disposable income would rise by only 0.7 percent, and so consumption would increase by 0.98×0.7, or 0.686 percent. So the multiplier would be $1/(1 - 0.686)$, or 3.18.
d.   If the marginal propensity to import were 0.10, the multiplier would be $1/(1 - 0.686 + 0.1)$, or 2.41.
2.   The average propensity to consume is somewhat lower than the marginal propensity to consume. This implies that at zero income, consumption would be negative. Of course, we have never observed (nor are we likely to observe) zero income!
3.   There are two major reasons why the ratio of consumption to disposable income is not equal to 1 minus savings/GNP. First, savings includes not just the savings of consumers but also savings by firms (as undistributed profits) and the government (as budget surpluses). Consequently, even though for an individual the ratio of consumption to income would equal one minus the ratio of savings to income, this does not hold for the economy as a whole. Second, GNP is not equal to disposable income, so the computed fractions are not comparable. If you graph C/Y against S/GNP, however, you will see that they are negatively related, so that a high fraction of GNP saved typically corresponds to a lower ratio of consumption to disposable income.
4.   Real GNP appears to be more variable than is the price level. One measure of variability is the range of variation of the series. The real GNP growth rate varied between −3.4 percent (in the third quarter of 1982) and +7.8 percent (first quarter of 1984). This represents a range of 11.2 percent. By contrast, the inflation rate varied between 2.5 and 9.9 percent, a range of only 7.4 percent. Output is also seen to be more variable than prices in the annual data. Both of these findings are consistent with the hypothesis that prices are more sticky than output.

CHAPTER 5   Financial Markets and Aggregate Demand

Main Objectives

In Chapter 4, we developed the concept of spending balance to show how income is determined in a stylized macroeconomic model. In this chapter, we extend the model by adding financial variables (investment demand, interest rates, money, and prices) to construct a complete, although simplified, picture of how the economy operates in the short run. You should understand how this model can be used to analyze monetary and fiscal policy, and how it is summarized by constructing the aggregate demand curve, one of the basic tools of analysis for the remainder of the book.

Key Terms and Concepts

The **investment function** describes the relation between investment and the interest rate,

$$I = e - dR, \tag{5-1}$$

where I is investment and R is the real interest rate. The constant e measures the part of investment that does not depend on interest rates, while the coefficient d measures how much investment falls when the interest rate increases by 1 percentage point. The relationship is negative because most investment purchases are financed by borrowing. Higher interest rates increase the cost of borrowing, resulting in less investment spending.

The **real interest rate** R is the **nominal interest rate** minus the expected rate of inflation. Investment depends on the real interest rate because investors consider expected inflation when determining the cost of borrowing.

The net export function depends on the interest rate R as well as income Y,

$$X = g - mY - nR. \tag{5-2}$$

Net exports depend negatively on the interest rate because higher U.S. interest rates encourage foreigners to put their funds in dollars, raising the exchange rate. The higher exchange rate lowers exports and raises imports. The coefficient n measures how much net exports fall when the interest rate increases by one percentage point.

Total spending is the sum of consumption, investment, government spending, and net exports. The **total spending function** depends positively on income and negatively on the interest rate:

$$\begin{aligned}
\text{Spending} \quad &= C + I + G + X \\
&= a + b(1 - t)Y + e - dR + g - mY - nR \\
&= a + e + g + [b(1 - t) - m]Y - (d + n)R + G
\end{aligned} \tag{5-3}$$

Money is the sum of currency used by the Federal Reserve System (or Fed), and checking account balances held by the public. Money is the funds individuals want badly enough for transactions that they are willing to forgo the interest they might earn by keeping the funds in another form.[1] The **demand for money** increases with income because, as income rises, people want to make more transactions. It increases with the price level because, as the price level increases, people need more money to make the same real transactions. It decreases with the interest rate because the interest rate is the opportunity cost of holding money. We can summarize this in the algebraic expression

$$M = (kY - hR)P, \tag{5-4}$$

where M is the demand for money, Y is income, R is the interest rate, P is the price level, and k and h are constant coefficients.

The demand for money can also be written in terms of real money, money M divided by the price level P,

$$M/P = kY - hR. \tag{5-5}$$

This says that the demand for real money depends positively on real income and negatively on the interest rate.

The **money supply** is determined by the Fed. We assume that the demand for money always adjusts to equal the supply, which, since it is

---

[1]This simple definition of money has become more complicated since the introduction of interest-bearing checking, but individuals can still choose from alternatives that pay higher interest than checking (such as money market accounts).

set by the Fed, cannot be altered by the actions of asset holders. In practice, the interest rate and, to a lesser extent, income adjust to keep the demand for money equal to its fixed supply. Since the supply of and demand for money are always equal, we also use M to represent the money supply.

The economic model described by the income identity, consumption function, investment function, net export function, and money demand is called the **IS-LM model**. It has two exogenous variables (government spending and the money supply) and five endogenous variables (income, the interest rate, consumption, investment, and net exports). Since prices are sticky and adjust only gradually, they are neither exogenous nor endogenous. We call the price level **predetermined** because, in each period, its value is determined by events that have occurred in previous periods. Another way to think about the price level is as exogenous in the short run and endogenous in the long run.

The **IS curve** shows all the combinations of the interest rate and income that satisfy the income identity, the consumption function, the investment function, and the net export function. It is the set of points for which spending balance occurs. It is downward sloping because lower interest rates cause investment demand to increase, which is consistent with spending balance only if more output is produced. An increase in government spending shifts the IS curve to the right because, for any given level of the interest rate, the increase in G raises Y through the multiplier process. The IS curve is illustrated in Figure 5-1.

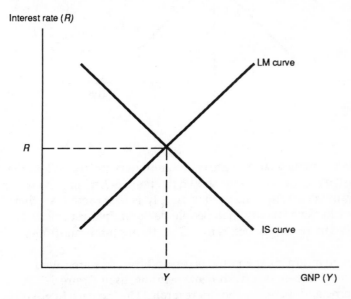

Figure 5-1

61

The **LM curve** shows all combinations of the interest rate and income that satisfy the money demand relationship for a fixed level of the money supply and for a predetermined value of the price level. It slopes upward because, with the nominal money supply fixed by the Fed and the price level predetermined, an increase in income, which increases the demand for money, must be accompanied by an increase in the interest rate, which decreases the demand for money, to keep the demand for money equal to its (fixed) supply. An increase in the money supply shifts the LM curve to the right because, for fixed P, an increase in M is an increase in real money. For any given level of the interest rate, income must rise so that the demand for money equals its new, higher, supply. The LM curve is also illustrated in Figure 5-1.

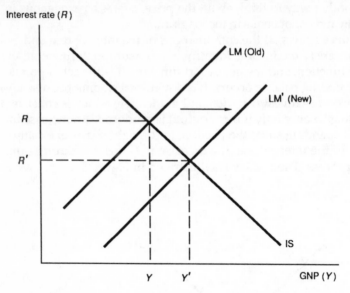

Figure 5-2

Changes in the money supply are called **monetary policy**. When the Fed increases the money supply, as shown in Figure 5-2, income rises and the interest rate falls. When the money supply is first increased, there is more money in the economy than people demand. Interest rates fall and investment increases, which raises GNP through the multiplier process.

Changes in government spending, taxes, and transfers are called **fiscal policy**. An increase in government spending, as in Figure 5-3, increases income and increases the interest rate. The increase in govern-

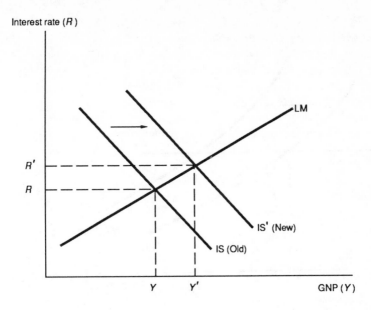

Figure 5-3

ment spending increases income through the multiplier and raises the interest rate because, as GNP increases, the demand for money increases. The interest rate must rise to keep the demand for money equal to its fixed supply. With investment and net exports depending on the interest rate, increases in government spending do not have the full multiplier effect on income. The higher interest rate lowers investment and net exports, offsetting some of the stimulus to GNP caused by government spending. The offsetting negative effect is called **crowding out**.

The coefficients that describe the response of investment (d), net exports (n), and money demand (h) to changes in the interest rate determine the relative effectiveness of monetary and fiscal policy in increasing aggregate demand. If investment and net exports are very sensitive to interest rates ($d + n$ is large), the IS curve is relatively flat. Fiscal policy is weak and monetary policy is strong. If money demand is very sensitive to interest rates (h is large), the LM curve is relatively flat. Fiscal policy is strong and monetary policy is weak. A high spending multiplier also increases the effectiveness of fiscal policy.

The **aggregate demand curve** shows the combinations of price levels and output where the IS and LM curves intersect, or where spending balance occurs and money demand equals money supply. It slopes

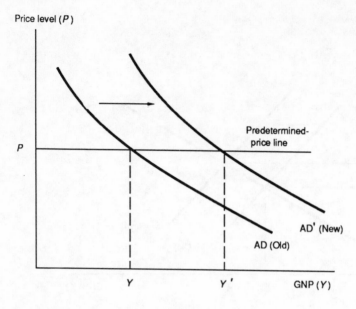

Figure 5-4

downward because a decrease in prices increases real money, shifting the LM curve to the right, lowering interest rates, increasing investment, and increasing output. An increase in either the money supply or government spending, as in Figure 5-4, shifts the aggregate demand curve to the right.

Self-Test

Fill in the blank

1. The _____ describes the relation between investment and interest rates.

2. Net exports depend on _____ and _____.

3. Total spending is the sum of _____, _____, _____, and _____.

4. The total spending function depends _____ on income and _____ on the interest rate.

5. The demand for money _____ with income, _____ with the price level, and _____ with the interest rate.

6. The IS curve is the combination of _____ and _____ for which spending balance occurs.

7. The LM curve illustrates the condition that the demand and supply of _____ are equal.

8. Fiscal policy is made by the _____ .

9. Monetary policy is made by the _____ .

10. Nominal money divided by the price level is _____ money.

11. If investment and net exports are very sensitive to interest rates, fiscal policy is _____ and monetary policy is _____ .

12. If money demand is very sensitive to interest rates, fiscal policy is _____ and monetary policy is _____ .

True-False

13. Investment is negatively related to the interest rate.

14. Net exports are negatively related to the interest rate.

15. In the United States, monetary and fiscal policies are determined by different people.

16. Monetary policy shifts both the IS and LM curves.

17. An increase in government spending will always cause a more than proportional increase in GNP.

18. Increases in the money supply and in government spending have the same effects on income.

19. Increases in the money supply and in government spending have the same effects on interest rates.

20. Increases in the money supply and in government spending have the same effects on the aggregate demand curve.

21. Prices adjust to keep the demand for money equal to the supply of money.

22. The same variable can be exogenous for one model and endogenous for another.

23. If investment and net exports are very sensitive to interest rates, the LM curve is flat.

24. If the price level decreases, the aggregate demand curve shifts to the right.

Review Questions

25. Why does an increase in the interest rate decrease net exports?

26. Why is total spending negatively related to the interest rate?

27. When interest rates rise so that the return on financial assets, such as bonds, is high, does this mean that investment is high?

28. What is the relationship between real and nominal interest rates?

29. What are the implications of crowding out for the effectiveness of government spending?

30. What are the three factors that determine the demand for money, and what are their effects?

31. Why does monetary policy shift the LM, but not the IS, curve?

32. Why does fiscal policy shift the IS, but not the LM, curve?

33. If the money supply and government spending both decrease, what happens to output and the interest rate?

34. What conditions are satisfied along the aggregate demand curve?

35. Can anything besides changes in the money supply or government spending shift the aggregate demand curve?

36. Since decreases in the price level and increases in the money supply both shift the LM curve to the right, why does the former cause a movement along the aggregate demand curve while the latter causes it to shift?

Problem Set

1. Consider an economy described by the following equations:

$$Y = C + I + G + X \qquad \text{(Income identity)}$$
$$C = 100 + .9Y_d \qquad \text{(Consumption)}$$
$$I = 200 - 500R \qquad \text{(Investment)}$$
$$X = 100 - .12Y - 500R \quad \text{(Net exports)}$$
$$M = (.8Y - 2000R)P \quad \text{(Money demand)}$$

with government spending G = \$200 billion, the tax rate t = .2, the nominal money supply M = \$800 billion, and the predetermined price level P = 1.

a. What is the IS curve?

b. What is the LM curve?

c. What are the values of income and the interest rate when spending balance occurs and the demand for money equals the supply of money?

d. What are the values of consumption, investment, and net exports?

a. *We derive the IS curve using the same technique that was used to solve for income in Problem 2 of Chapter 4.*

$$Y = C + I + G + X$$
$$= 100 + .9(Y - .2Y) + 200 - 500R + 200 + 100 - .12Y - 500R$$
$$= 600 + .6Y - 1000R$$
$$= 1500 - 2500R.$$

b. *We derive the LM curve from the equation for money demand, given a fixed level for the money supply and a predetermined value of the price level (1 in this problem):*

$$800 = .8Y - 2000R.$$

Adding 2000R to both sides of the equation,

$$.8Y = 800 + 2000R,$$

and dividing both sides by .8, we obtain

$$Y = 1000 + 2500R,$$

which is the equation for the LM curve.

c. *We compute the values for income and the interest rate by using the IS and LM curves, solving for R, and then solving for Y. Combining the two equations,*

$$1500 - 2500R = 1000 + 2500R,$$

adding 2500R and subtracting 1000 from both sides,

$$500 = 500R,$$
$$R = .10 \ (10 \ percent).$$

substituting the value for R into either the IS or LM curves, Y = $1250 billion.

d. *We determine the values for consumption, investment, and net exports by substituting the computed values of R and Y into the consumption, investment, and net export equations.*

$$
\begin{aligned}
C &= 100 + .9Y_d \\
&= 100 + .9(1 - .2)1250 = \$1000 \ billion. \\
I &= 200 - 500R \\
&= 200 - 50 = \$150 \ billion. \\
X &= 100 - .12Y - 500R \\
&= 100 - 150 - 50 = -\$100 \ billion.
\end{aligned}
$$

2. Derive the aggregate demand curve and show by how much an increase in government spending or real money of $100 billion increases GNP in Problem 1. Compare your answer for government spending to the government spending multiplier in Problem 2 of Chapter 4.

To derive the effects of increases in government spending and real money on income, start with the equation for the LM curve, do not substitute a specific value for real money, and solve for output.

$$M/P = .8Y - 2000R$$
$$Y = 1.25(M/P) + 2500R.$$

Now use the income identity, substitute the consumption, investment, and net export equations, but not a specific value for government spending, and solve for 2500 times the interest rate.

$$
\begin{aligned}
Y &= 100 + .8(Y - .25Y) + 300 - 1000R + G \\
Y &= 400 + .6Y - 1000R + G \\
1000R &= 400 - .4Y + 2.5G \\
2500R &= 1000 - Y + 2.5G.
\end{aligned}
$$

Substitute the spending balance equation into the LM curve, and solve for Y.

$$
\begin{aligned}
Y &= 1.25(M/P) + 1000 - Y + 2.5G \\
2Y &= 1.25(M/P) + 1000 + 2.5G \\
Y &= .625(M/P) + 500 + 1.25G.
\end{aligned}
$$

68

An increase in government spending of 100 raises real GNP by 125. An increase in the money supply of 100, with the price level constant, raises real GNP by 62.5. These are illustrated in Figures 5-2 and 5-3.

In Problem 4.2, with the government spending multiplier equal to 2.5, an increase in government spending of $100 billion raised real GNP by $250 billion. The only difference between the two models is that investment and net exports now depend on the interest rate. This is an example of crowding out. Government spending, in this problem, is only half as effective when the effects of interest rates on investment and net exports are included.

Review Problems

3. Consider an economy described by the following equations:

$$Y = C + I + G + X \quad \text{(Income identity)}$$
$$C = 300 + .8Y_d \quad \text{(Consumption)}$$
$$I = 200 - 1500R \quad \text{(Investment)}$$
$$X = 100 - .04Y - 500R \quad \text{(Net exports)}$$
$$M = (.5Y - 2000R)P \quad \text{(Money demand)}$$

with government spending $G = \$200$, the tax rate $t = .2$, the nominal money supply $M = \$550$, and the predetermined price level $P = 1$.

a. What is the IS curve?

b. What is the LM curve?

c. What are the values of income and the interest rate when spending balance occurs and the demand for money equals the supply of money?

4. Derive the aggregate demand curve and show by how much an increase in government spending or real money increases GNP in Problem 3. Compare your answer for government spending to the government spending multiplier in Problem 6 of Chapter 4.

5. Consider an economy described by the following equations:

$$Y = C + I + G + X \quad \text{(Income identity)}$$
$$C = 400 + .9Y_d \quad \text{(Consumption)}$$
$$I = 300 - 2000R \quad \text{(Investment)}$$
$$X = 100 - .05Y - 1000R \quad \text{(Net exports)}$$
$$M = (.4Y - 1000R)P \quad \text{(Money demand)}$$

with government spending $G = \$100$, the tax rate $t = .5$, the nominal money supply $M = \$180$, and the predetermined price level $P = 1$.

a. What is the IS curve?

b. What is the LM curve?

c. What are the values of income and the interest rate when spending balance occurs and the demand for money equals the supply of money?

6. Derive the aggregate demand curve and show by how much an increase in government spending or real money increases GNP in Problem 5. Compare your answer for government spending to the government spending multiplier in Problem 7 of Chapter 4.

7. Consider an economy described by the following equations:

$$
\begin{aligned}
Y &= C + I + G + X & &\text{(Income identity)} \\
C &= 400 + .9Y_d & &\text{(Consumption)} \\
I &= 200 - 1800R & &\text{(Investment)} \\
X &= 200 - .1Y - 200R & &\text{(Net exports)} \\
M &= (.8Y - 3000R)P & &\text{(Money demand)}
\end{aligned}
$$

with government spending $G = \$200$, the tax rate $t = .3333$, the nominal money supply $M = \$1104$, and the predetermined price level $P = 1$.

a. What is the IS curve?

b. What is the LM curve?

c. What are the values of income and the interest rate when spending balance occurs and the demand for money equals the supply of money?

8. Derive the aggregate demand curve and show by how much an increase in government spending or real money increases GNP in Problem 7. Compare your answer for government spending to the government spending multiplier in Problem 8 of Chapter 4.

MacroSolve Exercises

The MacroSolve program contains a number of the models that are discussed in the text. The following questions make use of the basic model of Chapter 5 of the textbook. The model (called "ISLM, Closed Econ" in the **Select Model** option) is described by the following equations:

$$
\begin{aligned}
Y &= C + I + G \\
C &= 80 + .63Y \\
I &= 750 - 2000R \\
M &= (.1625Y - 1,000R)
\end{aligned}
$$

We assume that the tax rate is 0.1875, so that the marginal propensity to consume out of disposable income is 0.77538.

The equation for the IS and LM curves for this model are also derived in the textbook as:

IS curve: $R = .415 - .000185Y + .0005G$
LM curve: $R = .0001625Y - .001M/P$.

1. Select the above model ("ISLM, Closed Econ"), and tabulate the results with no change in government spending or the money supply. Confirm that the equilibrium interest rate and level of GNP are 5 percent and $4000 billion, respectively.

   a. Increase government spending by $50 billion. Display the shifts of the curves (using the **Display Model** option) to ensure that you understand what is being done. Tabulate the model to find the value of the government spending multiplier. Do you get the same sized multiplier if you increase government spending by $100 billion? Why?

   b. How much is investment "crowded out" by a $50 billion increase in government spending? Explain why investment is crowded out by the increase in government spending. If the money supply is constant, under what conditions on the slopes of the IS and LM curves would there be no crowding out in response to an increase in government spending?

   c. By how much would the Federal Reserve have to increase the money supply to keep investment from being crowded out at all (i.e. keeping investment constant at $650 billion)? If the Federal Reserve Board increases the money supply to avoid any crowding out of investment, what is the value of the government spending multiplier? The size of this multiplier depends on only two parameters in the model. Which are they?

   d. Confirm that the change in savings equals the change in investment plus the change in the government deficit when any exogenous variable is changed. (Hint: Remember that savings equals disposable income less consumption.) What is the economic intuition about why this identity must hold?

2. a. Using the same model, increase the responsiveness of investment to interest rates. Perform the same experiment as in question 1, increasing government spending by $50 billion (with no change in the money supply). Is the multiplier larger or smaller in this case than in question 1? Explain in words why the multiplier changes the way it does.

71

b. Reset the interest elasticity of investment to its default value, but decrease the marginal propensity to consume. Explain in words why the multiplier is larger or smaller than it was in your answer to question 1.

c. Reset the interest elasticity of investment to its default value. Increase the interest elasticity of money demand. Explain in words how and why the multiplier changes.

3. Select the model "ISLM, Closed Econ," and reset all parameters to their default values using the **Change Params** option. By how much does GNP increase when the money supply is increased by $50 billion?

a. If the interest responsiveness of money demand is increased, explain why a given change in the money supply has a smaller effect on GNP than in the default case.

b. Reset the interest responsiveness of money demand to its default value, and decrease the interest elasticity of investment. Explain why this reduces the effect on GNP of a $50 billion increase in the money supply.

c. Is output more responsive to changes in the money supply when the income elasticity of money demand is increased? Explain why.

Answers to the Self-Test

1. Investment function
2. Income and the interest rate
3. Consumption, investment, government spending, and net exports
4. Positively on income and negatively on the interest rate
5. Increases with income, increases with the price level, and decreases with the interest rate
6. Interest rates and income
7. Money
8. The president and Congress
9. Federal Reserve System
10. Real
11. Fiscal policy is weak and monetary policy is strong.
12. Fiscal policy is strong and monetary policy is weak.
13. True. Increases in the interest rate raise the cost of borrowing, lowering investment.
14. True. Increases in the interest rate raise the exchange rate, lowering net exports.
15. True. Monetary policy is determined by the Federal Reserve System. Fiscal policy is determined by Congress and the president.

16. False. Monetary policy shifts the LM curve. Fiscal policy shifts the IS curve.
17. False. This is only correct in the simple multiplier model where investment and net exports do not depend on the interest rate.
18. True. Increases in either the money supply or government spending raise income.
19. False. Increases in the money supply lower interest rates, while increases in government spending raise them.
20. True. They both shift the aggregate demand curve to the right.
21. False. Interest rates and, to a lesser extent, output adjust.
22. True. Investment is exogenous in the simple multiplier model and endogenous in the IS-LM model.
23. False. The sensitivity of investment and net exports to interest rates affects the slope of the IS curve, not the LM curve.
24. False. A decrease in the price level causes a movement along the aggregate demand curve, not a shift of the curve.
25. An increase in the interest rate raises the exchange rate, making U.S. goods more expensive compared to foreign goods. This decreases exports and increases imports, decreasing net exports.
26. Two of the components of total spending are investment and net exports, both of which depend negatively on the interest rate.
27. No. Investment is spending on items such as factories and houses, and has nothing to do with the return on financial assets.
28. The real interest rate equals the nominal interest rate minus the expected rate of inflation.
29. Crowding out decreases the effectiveness of government spending.
30. The demand for money increases with income and the price level, and decreases with the interest rate.
31. Monetary policy changes the supply of money, shifting the LM curve. The IS curve depends on spending balance, which is unaffected by the money supply.
32. Fiscal policy, changes in government spending or taxes, affects spending balance, shifting the IS curve. The LM curve depends on the supply of and demand for money, which are unaffected by spending balance.
33. Since both the IS and LM curves shift to the left, output decreases. You cannot say what happens to the interest rate without knowing the magnitudes of the decreases and the coefficients of the consumption, investment, net export, and money demand equations.
34. Spending balance occurs and the demand for money equals the supply of money.
35. Yes. Changes in the exogenous component of consumption (a), investment (e), or net exports (g) shift the aggregate demand curve by shifting the IS curve.
36. The aggregate demand curve is drawn with P and Y on the axes. A shift of the curve can only be caused by a variable, such as M, that is not on one of the axes. Changes in variables on the axes, P and Y, cause shifts along the curve. For the LM curve, neither P nor M is on the axes, so they can both cause shifts of the curve.

Solutions to Review Problems

3. a. The IS curve is derived from the condition for spending balance.

$$Y = 300 + .8(Y - .2Y) + 200 - 1500R + 200 + 100 - .04Y - 500R$$
$$= 800 + .6Y - 2000R$$
$$= 2000 - 5000R.$$

   b. The LM curve is derived from the condition that the demand for money equal the supply of money with a predetermined price level.

$$550 = .5Y - 2000R$$
$$Y = 1100 + 4000R.$$

   c. Using the IS and LM curves,

$$2000 - 5000R = 1100 + 4000R$$
$$900 = 9000R, R = .10 \text{ (10 percent)}.$$

   Substituting back into either the IS or LM curve, $Y = \$1500$.

4. Starting with the LM curve,

$$M/P = .5Y - 2000R,$$
$$Y = 2(M/P) + 4000R.$$

   Using the condition for spending balance,

$$Y = 300 + .75(Y - .2Y) + 300 - 2000R + G,$$
$$4000R = 1200 - .8Y + 2G.$$

   Substituting the spending balance condition into the LM curve,

$$Y = 2(M/P) + 1200 - .8Y + 2G$$
$$= 1.11(M/P) + 666.7 + 1.11G.$$

   An increase in government spending has less effect on output than in the earlier problem because of crowding out.

5. The technique for this problem is the same as for Problem 3.

   a. $Y = 400 + .9(Y - .5Y) + 300 - 2000R + 100 + 100 - .05Y - 1000R$
$$= 900 + .4Y - 3000R$$
$$= 1500 - 5000R.$$

   b. $180 = .4Y - 1000R$
$$Y = 450 + 2500R.$$

   c. $R = .14 \text{ (14 percent)}, Y = \$800$.

6. The technique for this problem is the same as for Problem 4. From the LM curve,

$$Y = 2.5(M/P) + 2500R.$$

   From the condition for spending balance,

$$2500R = 666.67 - .5Y + .83G.$$

Substituting the spending balance condition into the LM curve,

$$Y = 1.67(M/P) + 444.5 + .55G.$$

This illustrates that crowding out can cause an increase in government spending to have a less than proportionate effect on income, a result that is not possible if investment and net exports do not depend on the interest rate.

7. The technique for this problem is the same as for Problem 3.

a. $Y = 400 + .9(Y - .3333Y) + 200 - 1800R + 200 + 200 - .1Y - 200R$
$= 1000 + .5Y - 4000R$
$= 2000 - 4000R.$

b. $1104 = .8Y - 3000R$
$Y = 1380 + 3750R.$

c. $R = .08$ (8 percent), $Y = \$1680.$

8. The technique for this problem is the same as for Problem 4.
From the LM curve,

$$Y = 1.25(M/P) + 3750R.$$

From the condition for spending balance,

$$3750R = 1500 - .94Y + 1.875G.$$

Substituting the spending balance condition into the LM curve,

$$Y = .64(M/P) + 773.2 + .97G.$$

Government spending is less effective because of crowding out.

Solutions to MacroSolve Exercises

1. a. GNP rises by $72 billion, so the multiplier is 72/50 or 1.44. Because the model is linear, this multiplier is the same size for any change in government spending.
   b. When government spending increases by $50 billion, investment drops by $23 billion because of the increase in the interest rate. If either the LM or IS curves were horizontal there would be no crowding out. In the former case, the interest rate would not change, so investment would be constant.
   c. If the Federal Reserve increases the money supply by $20 billion, the interest rate is approximately constant. If there is no crowding out, the multiplier is $1/(1 - c(1 - t))$, where c is the marginal propensity to consume and t is the tax rate. In this case, the multiplier would be $1/(1 - .63)$, or 2.7.
   d. If G is increased by $50 billion (and the money supply is held fixed), the deficit increases by 37, and investment falls by 23, the difference

(14) equals the change in savings. The increase in savings is equal to the increase in disposable income (58.5) less the increase in consumption (45); hence savings increases by $13.5. Aside from rounding error, the increase in the deficit and investment equals the increase in savings.

2. a. The multiplier falls, as the increase in the interest rate caused by the rise in government spending crowds out more investment.
   b. The multiplier falls because the drop in the MPC causes more savings and less consumption to follow each round of income increase.
   c. The multiplier increases as the LM curve becomes flatter because the increase in interest rates following a fiscal expansion is smaller, so there is less crowding out.

3. GNP increases $144 billion.
   a. As the LM curve is flatter, the GNP increase is smaller as the change in interest rates caused by a change in the money supply is smaller.
   b. If the interest elasticity of investment drops, monetary policy becomes less able to affect investment by changing interest rates, so the GNP increase is smaller.
   c. As the income elasticity of money demand increases, the effect of money on output decreases. This is because the increase in income caused by the money supply increase leads to a greater increase in the demand for money than in the default case.

CHAPTER 6   Aggregate Supply and Price Adjustment

Main Objectives

Focusing solely on aggregate demand, we have seen how to determine GNP and the interest rate in the short run. Chapter 6 turns to aggregate supply, which determines output in the long run, and price adjustment, which describes the transition between the short and the long run. In learning these two essential concepts, you should become familiar with both the determinants of aggregate supply—the labor force, the capital stock, and technology—and the role expectations of inflation play in the price-adjustment process.

Key Terms and Concepts

Aggregate supply, or **potential GNP**, describes the amount of output that the basic resources of the economy—labor and capital—are capable of producing. The three factors that determine aggregate supply are potential employment, the capital stock, and the production function.

Potential employment (N^*) is the volume of employment that would occur if everyone was working who wanted to at the prevailing real wage. At potential employment, the unemployment rate is not equal to zero. It equals the natural rate—about 6 percent.

The **capital stock** (K) is the amount of equipment, structures, and land in the economy. Although the capital stock changes with net investment, increments to capital are so small compared with the existing stock that we take the capital stock to be exogenous.

The **production function** tells us how much output can be produced from a given amount of capital and labor. Potential GNP is the amount of output that can be produced, given the existing capital stock, when employment equals potential employment. **Potential GNP** does not depend on the price level because neither of its determinants, potential employment and the capital stock, depends on the price level.

In the short run, as we saw in Chapter 5, the price level is predetermined and the level of output is determined by aggregate demand. Output can be above or below its potential level. When output is above potential GNP, unemployment, as we saw in Chapter 3 when we discussed Okun's law, is below the natural rate. When output is below potential GNP, unemployment is above the natural rate. In the long run, as shown in Figure 6-1, output is determined by aggregate supply and the price level is determined by aggregate demand. Output is equal to potential GNP and unemployment is equal to the natural rate.

The process of **price adjustment** describes the transition from the short to the long run. Prices rise when output is above potential GNP and fall when it is below potential GNP. When prices are rising, the **rate of inflation**, which is the rate of change of the price level, is positive. When prices are falling, the inflation rate is negative. An algebraic formulation of price adjustment, called the Phillips curve, is

$$\pi = f(Y_{-1} - Y^*)/Y^*, \tag{6-1}$$

where π is the rate of inflation, $(P - P_{-1})/P_{-1}$, and Y^* is potential GNP. Prices are predetermined because the current price level is determined by last period's output, Y_{-1}.

The process of price adjustment needs to be modified because workers and firms form expectations of future inflation. The Phillips curve with an expectations term is

$$\pi = \pi^e + f(Y_{-1} - Y^*)/Y^*, \tag{6-2}$$

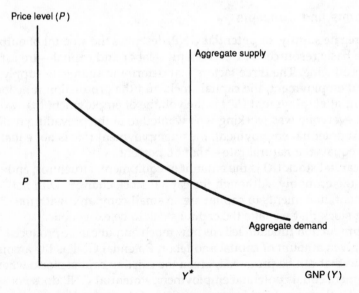

Figure 6-1

78

where π^e is the **expected rate of inflation**. It says that inflation equals expected inflation plus a term that is positive if output is greater than potential and negative if output is less than potential. Incorporating expectations of inflation into the Phillips curve makes it possible for inflation to be positive even if output is below potential GNP.

If inflation were fairly constant from year to year, the best forecast of current inflation π would be last period's inflation π_{-1}. The price-adjustment equation would become

$$\pi = \pi_{-1} + f(Y_{-1} - Y^*)/Y^*. \tag{6-3}$$

When inflation is variable, other factors such as previous years' inflation rates and expectations of future money supply growth would also influence expected inflation.

The price-adjustment equation with expected inflation equal to last period's inflation, Equation 6-3, has three important properties. First, the only way to reduce inflation is to have a recession. Output must be below potential GNP for inflation to be less than last period's inflation. Second, the larger the gap between actual and potential GNP, the greater the increase in the inflation rate (or decrease in the inflation rate if the gap is negative). Third, if output is permanently above potential GNP inflation will rise without bound; this is called the **accelerationist** or **natural rate property**.

Aggregate demand, aggregate supply, and price adjustment can be combined to analyze the short- and long-run effects of monetary and fiscal policy. For the moment, assume that expected inflation is always zero so that price adjustment is described by Equation 6-1. Suppose that, beginning with output equal to potential GNP, the Fed increases the money supply. In the short run, with predetermined prices, the stimulus to aggregate demand lowers interest rates and raises output above potential as described in Chapter 5. This causes inflation, as can be seen from the price-adjustment equation, 6-1. The inflation causes prices to rise over time, decreasing real money and output. As output falls toward potential, the rate of inflation decreases. In the long run, output returns to potential GNP with zero inflation at the original interest rate and a higher price level. Monetary policy is neutral in the long run. All real variables—GNP, consumption, investment, net exports, and interest rates—return to their original levels.

Fiscal policy, such as an increase in government spending, looks very similar to monetary policy. Output rises above potential in the short run. This causes inflation, which increases prices and drives output back to potential in the long run. There are, however, important differences between monetary and fiscal policy. Fiscal policy raises interest rates in the short run. As prices rise, real money falls and interest rates keep rising. In the long run, potential output is attained with both higher prices and higher interest rates. *The sum of investment and net exports*

is decreased by the same amount that government spending is increased.
This is called **complete crowding out**. Even though fiscal policy does not
change real output in the long run, it is not neutral because it changes
investment, net exports, and interest rates.

Expansionary monetary and fiscal policies are illustrated in Figure
6-2. Both expansionary policies shift the aggregate demand curve to
the right. In the short run, output rises along the predetermined price
line. Over time, prices rise and output falls along the aggregate demand
curve until, in the long run, output returns to potential.

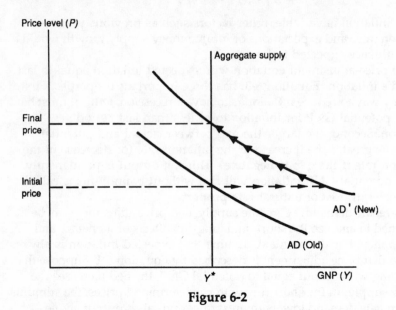

Figure 6-2

The above description of monetary and fiscal policy is incomplete
because it ignores the impact of expected inflation. Incorporating
expected inflation into the Phillips curve does not affect either the
short-run or the long-run results. What is does change is the **dynamics**:
the transition between the short and the long run. With expected
inflation always equal to zero, as in Equation 6-1, past inflation
influences current inflation only because, by raising current prices, it
affects the difference between actual and potential output. With
expected inflation equal to last period's inflation, as in Equation 6-3,
past inflation also influences current inflation directly. The major
difference for monetary and fiscal policy is that the transition from the
short to the long run is no longer smooth. Inflation increases as output
falls toward potential, driving prices above their long-run level.
Output falls below potential, causing a recession that finally brings
inflation down. Prices fall and output rises as the economy cycles back

to the long run. Prices and output are said to **overshoot** their long-run levels. The cyclical movement of prices and output along the aggregate demand curve in response to expansionary policy is shown in Figure 6-3.

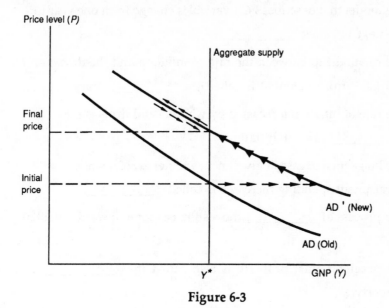

Figure 6-3

Self-Test

Fill in the Blank

1. Aggregate _____ describes the amount of output that the basic resources of the economy are capable of producing.

2. The volume of employment that the entire population would choose given existing incentives is called _____ employment.

3. The production function shows how much output can be made from given amounts of _____ and _____ .

4. The amount of output that would be produced if employment were at its potential level and all existing capital were in use is called

_____.

81

5. Another name for potential GNP is the _____ level of output.

6. The model that describes how variables change from one year to the next is called _____ .

7. The relationship between the rate of inflation and the deviation of real GNP from potential is called the _____ curve.

8. The rate of inflation forecasted by workers and firms is the _____ rate of inflation.

9. The long-run decrease in investment and net exports when government spending increases is called _____ .

10. The process of _____ moves the economy toward potential GNP.

11. The accelerationist property is also called the _____ property.

12. Prices and output _____ their long-run levels when the process of price adjustment is cyclical.

True-False

13. Although potential employment is exogenous, it is not constant.

14. Aggregate supply does not depend on the price level.

15. In the short run, output can be below or above its potential level.

16. In the short run, unemployment can be above or below the natural rate.

17. The unemployment rate is zero when employment is equal to potential employment.

18. The current price level does not depend on the current level of output.

19. Expected inflation is always equal to last year's inflation.

20. If expected inflation is equal to last year's inflation, it is necessary to have a recession to reduce the rate of inflation.

21. If expected inflation is equal to last year's inflation, output can only be permanently raised above potential by having inflation increase without bound.

22. In the long run fiscal policy completely crowds out investment and net exports.

23. Monetary policy is neutral in both the short and long run.

24. Fiscal policy is neutral in both the short and long run.

Review Questions

25. What are the three determinants of aggregate supply?

26. Why do we assume that the capital stock is exogenous?

27. How is output determined in the short run?

28. How is output determined in the long run?

29. What is the relation between output and unemployment?

30. What is the accelerationist property?

31. Describe the process of price adjustment when firms do not expect prices to rise in the future.

32. How does expected inflation change the process of price adjustment?

33. If there is no expected inflation, describe what happens to GNP and prices when the Fed increases the money supply.

34. How does expected inflation change you answer to Question 33?

35. What happens to GNP and prices when government spending is increased if there is no expected inflation?

36. How does your answer to Question 35 change if there is expected inflation?

Problem Set

Worked Problems

1. Suppose the economy has the aggregate demand curve

$$Y = 500 + 1.25G + .625(M / P)$$

and the price-adjustment schedule

$$\pi = (Y_{-1} - 1250)/1250 + \pi^e.$$

Government spending is $200 billion and the money supply is $800 billion.

a. Assume that expected inflation, π^e, is always zero. Starting from $P_0 = .8$, describe the path of the economy until GNP is within 1 percent of its long-run value.

b. Assume that $\pi^e = \pi_{-1}$. Describe the path of the economy, again starting from $P_0 = .8$ with zero inflation. How does your answer differ from that of Part a?

a. *The initial level of output, Y_0, is found from the aggregate demand curve by setting $P_0 = .8$ and using the given values for government spending and the money supply.*

$$Y_0 = 500 + 1.25 (200) + .625 (800)/.8$$
$$= \$1375 \text{ billion.}$$

The inflation rate, π_1, is found from the price-adjustment curve,

$$\pi_1 = (1375 - 1250)/1250 = .1 \ (10 \text{ percent}),$$

and determines the next year's price level:

$$P_1 = .8 + .8(.1) = .88.$$

Y_1 can now be determined by substituting P_1 into the aggregate demand curve, and so on. The complete answer is present below.

Year	π	P	Y
0	.000	.80	1375
1	.100	.88	1318
2	.055	.93	1289
3	.031	.96	1271
4	.017	.98	1262

Output is initially above potential GNP. Prices rise and output falls smoothly until potential GNP is attained with $P = 1$.

b. *The technique for this part is the same as for Part a except that, when computing inflation, last year's inflation needs to be incorporated. This does not affect π_1, since $\pi_0 = 0$, but $\pi_2 = .055 + \pi_1 = .155$, and so on. This affects the rest of the answer.*

Year	π	P	Y
0	.000	.80	$1375
1	.100	.88	1318
2	.155	1.02	1242
3	.149	1.17	1177
4	.088	1.27	1143
5	.002	1.27	1143
6	-.084	1.16	1180
7	-.140	1.00	1250

Output is initially above potential GNP. As above, prices begin to rise and output falls, but now output falls below potential. This causes prices first to stop rising, and then to fall. Output recovers to potential. The numerical answer gives only the first part of the cycle because inflation does not equal zero when output equals potential GNP.

2. Using the same model as in Problem 1, increase government spending by $50 billion starting from potential GNP with the price level $P = 1$.

   a. Calculate the paths of inflation, the price level, and GNP for the first 5 years, in the case where expected inflation is always zero.

   b. Perform the same calculations, this time for 10 years, in the case where expected inflation equals last period's inflation.

a. Initially, in Year 0, GNP equals potential with $\pi = 0$ and $P = 1$. The increase in government spending first affects output, which can be calculated from the aggregate demand curve with G = $250 billion.

$$Y_1 = 500 + 1.25(250) + .625(800)/1$$
$$= \$1313 \text{ billion.}$$

The inflation rate, π_2, is found from the price-adjustment curve,

$$\pi_2 = (1313 - 1250)/1250 = .05 \text{ (5 percent),}$$

and determines the next year's price level:

$$P_2 = 1 + 1(.05) = 1.05.$$

Y_2 can now be determined by substituting P_2 into the aggregate demand curve, and so on. The complete answer is presented below.

Year	π	P	Y
0	.000	1.00	$1250
1	.000	1.00	1313
2	.050	1.05	1289
3	.031	1.08	1275
4	.020	1.10	1266
5	.013	1.11	1261

The increase in government spending shifts the aggregate demand curve to the right. In the short run, output increases above potential with unchanged prices. Over time, prices rise and output falls smoothly until potential GNP is restored.

b. The technique for this part is the same as for Part a except that, when computing inflation, last year's inflation needs to be incorporated. This does not affect π_2, since $\pi_1 = 0$, but $\pi_3 = .031 + \pi_2 = .081$, and so on. This affects the rest of the answer.

Year	π	P	Y
0	.000	1.00	$1250
1	.100	1.00	1313
2	.050	1.05	1289
3	.081	1.14	1253
4	.083	1.23	1217
5	.057	1.30	1197
6	.015	1.32	1191
7	-.032	1.28	1204
8	-.069	1.19	1232
9	-.083	1.09	1271
10	-.066	1.02	1303

Output is initially above potential GNP. As above, prices begin to rise and output falls, but now output falls below potential. This causes prices first to stop rising, and then to fall. Output recovers to potential. The numerical answer gives only part of the cycle because inflation does not equal zero when output equals potential GNP.

Review Problems

3. Suppose the economy has the aggregate demand curve

$$Y = 667 + 1.11G + 1.11(M/P),$$

and the price-adjustment schedule,

$$\pi = (Y_{-1} - 1500)/1500 + \pi^e.$$

Government spending is $200 and the money supply is $550.

a. Assume that expected inflation, π^e, is always zero. Starting from $P_0 = 1.4$, describe the path of the economy until GNP is within 1 percent of its long-run value.

b. Assume that $\pi^e = \pi_{-1}$. Describe the path of the economy, again starting from $P_0 = 1.4$, with zero inflation. How does your answer differ from that of Part a?

4. Using the same model as in Problem 3, increase the money supply by $100 starting from potential GNP with the price level $P=1$.

a. Calculate the paths of inflation, the price level, and GNP for the first 5 years, in the case where expected inflation is always zero.

b. Perform the same calculations, this time for 7 years, in the case where $\pi^e = \pi_{-1}$.

5. Suppose the economy has the aggregate demand curve

$$Y = 445 + .55G + 1.67(M/P),$$

and the price-adjustment schedule,

$$\pi = .8(Y_{-1} - 800)/800 + \pi^e.$$

Government spending is $100 and the money supply is $180.

a. Assume that expected inflation, π^e, is always zero. Starting from $P_0 = .8$, describe the path of the economy until GNP is within 1 percent of its long-run value.

b. Assume that $\pi^e = .4\pi_{-1}$. Describe the path of the economy, again starting from $P_0 = .8$ with zero inflation. How does your answer differ from that of Part a?

6. Using the same model as in Problem 5 above, decrease government spending by $20 and the money supply by $20 starting from potential GNP with the price level $P = 1$.

a. Calculate the paths of inflation, the price level, and GNP for the first 5 years, in the case where expected inflation is always zero.

b. Perform the same calculation, this time for 7 years, in the case where $\pi^e = .4\pi_{-1}$.

7. Suppose the economy has the aggregate demand curve

$$Y = 734 + 1.21G + .64(M/P)$$

and the price-adjustment schedule

$$\pi = (Y_{-1} - 1680)/1680 + \pi^e.$$

Government spending is \$200 and the money supply is \$1100.

a. Assume that expected inflation, π^e, is always zero. Starting from $P_0 = .8$, describe the path of the economy until GNP is within 1 percent of its long-run value.

b. Assume that $\pi^e = \pi_{-1}$. Describe the path of the economy, again starting from $P_0 = .8$ with zero inflation. How does your answer differ from that of Part a?

8. Using the same model as in Problem 7, increase the money supply by 10 percent starting from potential GNP with the price level $P = 1$.

a. Calculate the paths of inflation, the price level, and GNP for the first five years, in the case where expected inflation is always zero.

b. Perform the same calculation, this time for seven years, in the case where expected inflation equals last period's inflation.

MacroSolve Exercises

In this chapter, we continue to use the basic model of aggregate demand developed in Chapter 5. To it, we add consideration of potential output, and price adjustment when output differs from potential output. The price adjustment schedule that we add has the form:

$$\pi = 0.8(Y_{-1} - Y^*)/Y^* + \pi^e$$

1. Suppose, first, that $\pi^e = 0$ (i.e., that agents in the economy do not expect any inflation). This model is available in the **Select Model** option as "AD/PA zero exp π." Change government spending by \$100 billion and make a table of the multipliers (the change in GNP per dollar change in government spending) for each time period. Explain in words why the steady-state (or long-run) multiplier differs from its value in the previous chapter.

2. Now select the default model ("AD/PA, Closed Econ") in which inflation expectations are determined in the following manner:

$$\pi^e = .4\pi_{-1} + .2\pi_{-2}.$$

Repeat the analysis of question 1 with this new model. Explain why the time taken for the multiplier to settle down to its long-run value differs from the previous case.

3. Is adjustment of the price level to a change in the money supply faster or slower when inflation expectations respond to past inflation (as in question 2) than when they do not (question 1)? Explain why.

4. Increase the responsiveness of prices to output (using the **Change Params** option).

   a. How does this increase alter the time pattern of output following a reduction in government spending?

   b. How does it affect the degree to which investment is crowded out following an increase in government expenditure? Explain the mechanism that accounts for this change.

5. The first four years of the Reagan administration (1981 to 1985) were marked by tight monetary policy and expansionary fiscal policy.

   a. Use the default dynamic model ("AD/PA, Closed Econ") to show what would be predicted to happen to interest rates, output, savings (which you can calculate as the difference between disposable income and consumption), and investment.

   b. Check the actual data for the U.S. economy during this period by plotting, tabulating, or graphing them to see if the theoretical predictions for these variables actually occurred. Were there any significant deviations from the model's predicted results? If so, can you give reasons for them?

Answers to the Self-Test

1. Supply
2. Potential
3. Labor and capital
4. Potential GNP
5. Full-employment
6. Dynamic
7. Phillips
8. Expected
9. Complete crowding out
10. Price adjustment

11. Natural rate
12. Overshoot
13. True. It grows steadily as the population grows.
14. True. Aggregate supply is the same as potential GNP. It depends on potential employment and the capital stock, neither of which depends on the price level.
15. True. In the short run, aggregate demand determines output at a predetermined price. It is only over time that price adjustment moves output toward potential GNP.
16. True. In the short run, with sticky prices, unemployment can be above or below its long run, natural, rate.
17. False. It is equal to the natural rate of unemployment, which is now about 6 percent.
18. True. Current prices are affected by past, but not current, output. This is what is meant by prices being predetermined.
19. False. Other factors, such as people's expectations of future monetary policy, also influence expected inflation.
20. True. Real GNP must fall below potential GNP, setting the economy into a recession, for current inflation to be reduced below last year's inflation.
21. True. The rate of inflation would have to increase each year to keep inflation above expected inflation and output above potential output.
22. True. In the long run the decrease in investment and net exports exactly equals the increase in government spending, and output is unchanged.
23. False. While monetary policy is neutral in the long run, it is not neutral in the short run.
24. False. Fiscal policy is not neutral in either the short or the long run.
25. The determinants of aggregate supply are the number and productivity of people available for work, the amount of equipment, structures, land, and other types of capital, and the technology.
26. Although the capital stock changes over time by the amount of net investment, each year's change is very small compared to the existing stock. As an approximation, we take the capital stock to be exogenous.
27. In the short run, output is determined by the intersection of the aggregate demand curve and the predetermined price level.
28. In the long run, output is determined by the vertical aggregate supply curve.
29. When output is above (below) potential GNP, unemployment is below (above) the natural rate. Unemployment equals the natural rate when output equals potential GNP.
30. The accelerationist property is that, if real GNP is kept above potential permanently, inflation will increase without bound.
31. With no expected inflation, prices will rise (inflation will be positive) if output is greater than potential GNP, and will fall (inflation will be negative) if output is less than potential GNP.
32. With expected inflation, if output is greater than potential GNP, inflation will be higher than expected inflation. If output is less than potential GNP, inflation will be lower than expected inflation.

33. An increase in the money supply shifts the aggregate demand curve to the right. In the short run, output increases and the price level is unchanged. Over time, prices rise and output falls. In the long run, output returns to potential at a higher price level. Money is neutral in the long run—consumption, investment, net exports, and interest rates return to their original levels.

34. Since prices are predetermined, expectations of inflation do not change the short-run results. Once prices begin to rise, people expect more inflation, which in turn increases actual inflation. Price adjustment is no longer smooth. Prices and output cycle before the long run is attained. The results for the long run are also unaffected by expectations of inflation.

35. An increase in government spending also shifts the aggregate demand curve to the right. Output increases with an unchanged price level in the short run. Over time, prices rise and output falls. In the long run, output returns to potential at a higher price level. There is complete crowding out in the long run. The higher interest rate causes investment and net exports to decrease by the same amount that government spending increased.

36. The answer to this question is the same as the answer to Question 34. Expectations of inflation affect the transition from the short to the long run, but they do not change either the short- or the long-run results.

Solutions to Review Problems

3. a.

Year	π	P	Y
0	.000	1.40	$1325
1	-.117	1.24	1382
2	-.079	1.14	1423
3	-.051	1.08	1453
4	-.031	1.05	1472

b.

Year	π	P	Y
0	.000	1.40	$1325
1	-.117	1.24	1382
2	-.196	1.00	1500
3	-.196	.80	1652
4	-.095	.72	1732
5	.060	.76	1692
6	.188	.90	1565
7	.231	1.11	1387

		Year	π	P	Y
4.	a.	0	.000	1.00	$1500
		1	.000	1.00	1611
		2	.074	1.07	1561
		3	.041	1.11	1537
		4	.024	1.14	1524
		5	.016	1.16	1512
	b.	Year	π	P	Y
		0	.000	1.00	$1500
		1	.000	1.00	1611
		2	.074	1.07	1561
		3	.115	1.19	1494
		4	.111	1.32	1435
		5	.067	1.41	1401
		6	.001	1.41	1400
		7	-.067	1.32	1437
5.	a.	Year	π	P	Y
		0	.000	.80	$876
		1	.076	.86	849
		2	.049	.90	833
		3	.033	.93	823
		4	.023	.95	816
	b.	Year	π	P	Y
		0	.000	.80	$876
		1	.076	.86	849
		2	.079	.93	824
		3	.056	.98	806
		4	.030	1.01	798
		5	.009	1.02	795
6.	a.	Year	π	P	Y
		0	.000	1.00	$800
		1	.000	1.00	756
		2	-.044	.96	768
		3	-.032	.93	777
		4	-.023	.91	783
		5	-.017	.89	788

		Year	π	P	Y
b.		0	.000	1.00	$800
		1	.000	1.00	756
		2	-.044	.96	768
		3	-.050	.91	782
		4	-.038	.88	794
		5	-.021	.86	799
		6	-.010	.85	803
		7	-.001	.85	804
7.	a.	Year	π	P	Y
		0	.000	.80	1856
		1	.105	.88	1773
		2	.055	.93	1734
		3	.032	.96	1709
		4	.017	.98	1697
	b.	Year	π	P	Y
		0	.000	.80	1856
		1	.105	.88	1773
		2	.160	1.02	1666
		3	.151	1.17	1575
		4	.089	1.27	1529
		5	-.001	1.27	1529
		6	-.091	1.15	1586
		7	-.056	1.09	1625
8.	a.	Year	π	P	Y
		0	.000	1.00	1680
		1	.000	1.00	1750
		2	.042	1.04	1719
		3	.023	1.06	1704
		4	.014	1.07	1696
		5	.009	1.08	1693
	b.	Year	π	P	Y
		0	.000	1.00	1680
		1	.000	1.00	1750
		2	.042	1.04	1719
		3	.065	1.11	1675
		4	.062	1.18	1633
		5	.034	1.22	1611
		6	-.007	1.21	1615
		7	-.045	1.15	1646

Solutions to MacroSolve Exercises

1. The multipliers for the first six periods are 1.44, 0.96, 0.43, 0.29, and 0.20. By the tenth period, the multiplier has become zero. The reason for the decline in the multiplier is that as prices rise, the real money supply contracts, shifting the LM curve to the left and reducing investment by increasing interest rates. As time progresses, GNP returns to its equilibrium value and the decrease in investment is exactly equal to the increase in government spending. Consumption returns to its starting value. (If you increase the number of simulation periods to 16, you will see this exactly.)

2. By the fourth period, the multiplier is already close to zero. The adjustment to its long-run value is faster because the price level increases faster than in the previous case.

3. Adjustment is faster, but the price level overshoots its long-run level with adaptive expectations.

4. a. Output returns to equilibrium faster when the responsiveness of prices to output increases.

   b. Investment is crowded out faster by an increase in government spending, since the faster increase in prices causes interest rates to rise more rapidly.

5. a. Interest rates will definitely rise. Output and savings will fall or rise depending on whether the decrease in the money supply was more or less severe than the fiscal expansion. Since interest rates rise, investment will necessarily fall. You should check for yourself how savings and output respond to different values of M and G.

   b. Plotting I/GNP and interest rates shows that their movements are consistent with the model's predictions. The GNP gap reveals that GNP fell considerably until 1983 and recovered thereafter, suggesting that the monetary tightness was more significant than the initial fiscal expansion. Plotting the growth rates of money and prices confirms that the real money supply (but not the nominal money supply) decreased at the start of the period.

CHAPTER 7　Macroeconomic Policy: A First Look

Main Objectives

When we considered monetary and fiscal policy in Chapter 6, we saw that neither could be used to increase output permanently above potential GNP. A more realistic goal of macroeconomic policy is to guide the economy as it returns to potential GNP following a disturbance. Another is to reduce inflation if it has become too high, as in the late 1970s. Macroeconomic policy-making often presents difficult choices between policies that eliminate recessions quickly and those that keep inflation low. Chapter 7 introduces the economic policy decisions made by the Fed and by the administration, and how macro-economists analyze these decisions. Its examination of recent Fed policies to reduce inflation gives you some practice with the macroeconomic analysis developed in Chapters 4–6.

Key Terms and Concepts

Economic shocks or **disturbances** are events other than policy changes that move the economy away from potential GNP. An **aggregate demand disturbance** is one that shifts the aggregate demand curve. Examples of aggregate demand disturbances are changes in investment, net export, and money demand. A **price disturbance** is an event that shifts the price-adjustment curve. Examples of price disturbances are increases in the price of imported oil and widespread anticipation of inflation by firms that leads them to increase prices.

In the short run, aggregate demand disturbances change output without affecting prices. In the absence of a policy response, the analysis of aggregate demand disturbances is exactly the same as the analysis of monetary and fiscal policy in Chapter 6. For instance, an increase in investment demand shifts the aggregate demand curve to the right, raising output above potential in the short run. Over time, prices rise and output falls until potential GNP is again attained.

Another example is an increase in money demand, which has exactly the same effects as a decrease in the money supply.

Price disturbances affect both output and prices in the short run. Consider a positive price shock, such as an oil price shock, that shifts up the price-adjustment curve. In the short run, the price level rises, dropping output below potential GNP. If there is no policy response, the process of price adjustment will cause prices to fall slowly and output to rise until potential output is eventually restored at the original price level. The economy is in a recession until potential GNP is attained. The path taken by the economy following a price disturbance is illustrated in Figure 7-1.

Activist or **countercyclical stabilization policy** is monetary or fiscal policy that attempts to counter the effects of *aggregate demand disturbances*. These are considered undesirable because they cause fluctuations in real GNP and in inflation. Suppose that an increase in money demand shifts the aggregate demand curve to the left. With no policy response, there will be a recession until falling prices raise real money sufficiently to restore potential GNP. Instead of allowing the economy to suffer through the recession, the Fed can increase the money supply to meet the additional demand for money. This immediately shifts the aggregate demand curve to the right, restoring potential output. Shifts to investment demand can be similarly counteracted.

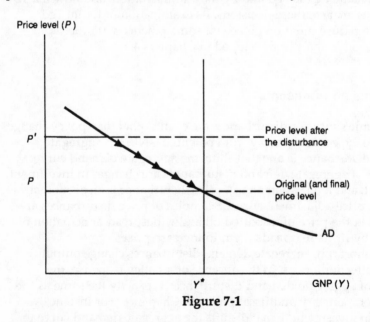

Figure 7-1

Accommodative monetary policy is an increase in the money supply in response to a *price disturbance*. A policy that holds the money supply constant is called **nonaccommodative**. A price disturbance increases the price level and decreases output below potential in the short run. This presents The Fed with several difficult choices. While accommodative policy, as shown in Figure 7-2, returns output quickly to potential, it has the cost of further increasing the price level. Nonaccommodative policy, however, causes a sustained recession until prices fall. A more extreme alternative, decreasing the money supply to fight inflation, deepens the recession.

If policy reacts in a systematic manner to economic disturbances, then it is no longer exogenous. A **policy rule** is a description of endogenous economic policy. Many economists favor adopting policy rules because their use may have favorable effects through expectations and because a binding rule may prevent attempts to increase output above potential GNP.

Policy rules are also important because of **time inconsistency**, the temptation of policy-makers, in order to stimulate the economy, to announce one plan and then enact another. In such situations, policy rules can be advantageous if they commit policy-makers to follow their announced plans. One policy rule is the monetarist proposition to fix the rate of growth of the money supply. Another is accommodative monetary policy, increasing the money supply in response to a price disturbance.

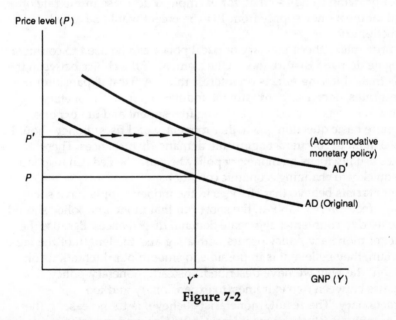

Figure 7-2

Disinflation is a reduction in the *rate* of inflation. **Deflation** (a negative rate of inflation) is a reduction in the price level itself. The problem of disinflation is closely related to the problem of how to respond to price shocks. In order to lower inflation, the Fed must decrease the rate of growth of the money supply. From the Phillips curve with expectations of inflation equal to last period's inflation,

$$\pi = \pi_{-1} + f(Y_{-1} - Y^*)/Y^*, \tag{7-1}$$

we know that it is necessary to have a recession to lower inflation. The Fed has two choices. It can lower the money supply slowly, causing a small recession, but only gradually decreasing inflation and restoring potential output. Alternatively, it can decrease the money supply quickly, creating a large recession, but quickly bringing down inflation and returning the economy to potential output. With a choice between a long-lasting small recession and a shorter large recession, there are no easy answers. Starting in 1979, with inflation over 10 percent, the Fed decreased money supply growth very quickly. This caused the largest recession since the Great Depression but also brought the inflation rate to under 4 percent in 1984.

Expansionary (or **looser**) monetary policy is an increase in the money supply, while expansionary fiscal policy is an increase in government purchases, an increase in transfers, or a decrease in taxes. **Contractionary** (or **tighter**) policy is the reverse. The words expansionary and contractionary are sometimes used to measure changes against growing trends so that, for example, a decrease in the rate of growth of the money supply from 10 to 5 percent would be called contractionary.

In principle, either monetary or fiscal policy can be used to counteract aggregate demand disturbances. One element of the choice between the two is their differing effects on interest rates. A fiscal expansion raises interest rates, decreasing investment and net exports. A monetary expansion lowers interest rates, raising investment and net exports.

A more basic question is whether monetary and fiscal policy should be used at all to counteract aggregate demand disturbances. These debates usually focus on monetary policy because the Fed can respond more quickly to changing economic conditions.

Monetarists believe that changes in the money supply have such strong effects on real GNP in the short run that monetary policy should not be used to counteract aggregate demand disturbances. Because the impact of monetary policy occurs with a lag and the length of the lag is uncertain, they believe it is impossible to smooth out fluctuations on real GNP the way we have described. Instead, monetary policy alternates between two extremes: to expansionary and too contractionary. The result, monetarists believe, is to increase, rather than to mitigate, fluctuations in real GNP. A second monetarist argument against activist stabilization policy is that, for short-run political reasons, governments are tempted to overstimulate the economy past potential GNP, causing higher and higher rates of inflation.

New classical macroeconomists take issue with our assumption of price stickiness. They believe prices can adjust instantaneously. If so, any systematic attempt to use monetary policy to affect real GNP will offset by changes in the price level. New classical macroeconomists also believe that disinflation can be accomplished much more quickly and at much lower cost than we have argued. We will discuss new classical economics in Chapter 14. Both monetarists and new classical macroeconomists advocate a constant rate of growth of the money supply, but for completely different reasons. Monetarists believe that monetary policy has such powerful effects on real GNP in the short run that it should not be used for stabilization. New classical macroeconomists believe that, since systematic monetary policy has no effect on real GNP, even in the short run, its growth should be kept constant in order to stabilize prices.

Self-Test

Fill in the Blank

1. A shock to investment, net export, or money demand is an

   _____.

2. A price disturbance shifts the _____.

3. Policy that attempts to counter aggregate demand disturbances is called _____ or _____ stabilization policy.

4. Policies that increase the money supply in response to price shocks are called _____ policies.

5. Holding the money supply constant in response to price shock is called a _____ policy.

6. Disinflation is the problem of _____ the rate of inflation.

7. Deflation is a reduction in the _____.

8. The temptation of policy-makers to announce one plan and then enact another is called _____.

9. An increase in the money supply is _____ monetary policy.

99

10. An increase in government purchases is _____ fiscal policy.

11. An increase in taxes is _____ fiscal policy.

12. A decrease in the rate of growth of the money supply is called

_____.

13. Aggregate demand disturbances do not affect the price level in the short run.

14. Price shocks do not affect output in the short run.

15. Monetarists believe that monetary policy should be used to counter aggregate demand disturbances.

16. New classical macroeconomists believe that monetary policy should be used to counter aggregate demand disturbances.

17. Aggregate demand disturbances do not affect output in the long run.

18. Price shocks do not affect the price level in the long run.

19. An oil price increase is an example of an aggregate demand disturbance.

20. Using appropriate monetary policy, it is possible to reduce inflation without causing a recession.

21. Monetary and fiscal policy can both be used to counteract aggregate demand disturbances.

22. Monetary and fiscal expansions both raise net exports.

23. Lowering the rate of inflation is called deflation.

24. New classical macroeconomists believe that it is very costly to reduce the rate of inflation.

Review Questions

25. What is the difference between an aggregate demand disturbance and a price disturbance?

26. Describe several examples of aggregate demand and price disturbances.

27. Describe the effects of a contractionary aggregate demand disturbance, such as a decrease in investment demand, with no change in policy.

28. How can countercyclical stabilization policy be used to counter the effects of a contractionary aggregate demand disturbance?

29. Describe the effects of a positive price shock with no change in policy?

30. How can accommodative monetary policy be used in response to a price shock?

31. Contrast the views of monetarists and new classical macroeconomists regarding the use of monetary policy.

32. What is a policy rule? What are two examples of such a rule?

33. Why are policy rules advantageous, compared to exogenous policy, in situations involving time inconsistency?

34. What are the choices faced by the Fed if it wishes to reduce the rate of inflation?

35. What happened to inflation and GNP, starting in 1979, after the Fed lowered the rate of growth of the money supply?

36. Why do monetary and fiscal expansions have different effects on investment and net exports?

Problem Set

Worked Problems

1. Suppose the economy has the aggregate demand curve

$$Y = 500 + 1.25G + .625(M/P) + Z_d$$

and the price-adjustment schedule

$$\pi = (Y_{-1} - Y^*)/Y^*,$$

where Z_d is an aggregate demand shock. Potential GNP $Y^* = \$1250$ billion, government spending $G = \$200$ billion, and the money supply $M = \$800$ billion.

a. Starting at potential output with the price level $P = 1$ and inflation $\pi = 0$, an aggregate demand disturbance $Z_d = -\$100$

billion occurs in the first year. No further shocks occur ($Z_d =$ -\$100 billion in all future years). Describe the path of the economy until GNP is within 1 percent of its long-run value.

b. How can the Fed offset the aggregate demand disturbance and keep output equal to potential GNP?

a. *In the first year output decreases by 100 (the amount of the aggregate demand disturbance) to \$1150 billion. The inflation rate π_2 is found from the price-adjustment curve,*

$$\pi_2 = (1150 - 1250)/1250 = -.08(-8 \text{ percent}),$$

and determines the price level:

$$P_2 = 1 + 1(-.08) = .92.$$

Output is found from the aggregate demand curve using the given values for government spending, the money supply, and the aggregate demand disturbance:

$$Y_2 = 500 + 1.25(200) + .625(800)/.92 - 100$$
$$= \$1193 \text{ billion}$$

The inflation rate π_3 can be computed by substituting Y_2 into the price-adjustment curve, and so on. It takes 5 years to return to within 1 percent of potential GNP:

Year	π	P	Y
0	.000	1.00	\$1250
1	.000	1.00	1150
2	-.080	.92	1193
3	-.045	.88	1219
4	-.025	.86	1233
5	-.014	.85	1240

The aggregate demand disturbance lowers output below potential at an unchanged price level. Over time, prices fall and output rises until potential GNP is restored.

b. *In order to offset the shock, the money supply should be increased so that $.625 (\Delta M/P) = -Z_d$. The money supply is therefore raised by 160 to \$960 billion.*

2. Suppose the economy had the aggregate demand curve

$$Y = 500 + 1.25G + .625(M/P)$$

and the price-adjustment schedule

$$\pi = (Y_{-1} - Y^*)/Y^* + Z_p,$$

where Z_p is a price shock. Potential GNP $Y^* = \$1250$ billion, government spending $G = \$200$ billion, and the money supply $M = \$800$ billion.

a. Starting at potential output with the price level $P = 1$ and inflation $\pi = 0$, a price disturbance of 10 percent occurs in the first year ($Z_p = .1$). No further shocks occur ($Z_p = 0$ in all future years). Describe the path of the economy until GNP is within 1 percent of its long-run value.

b. Suppose that, starting in the first year, the Fed increases the money supply by 5 percent. Compare the new path of prices and output to the original path.

a. *The first year's price level is raised from 1 to 1.1 by the 10 percent price disturbance. Output is found from the aggregate demand curve,*

$$Y_1 = 500 + 1.25(200) + .625(800)/1.1$$
$$= \$1250 \text{ billion,}$$

which determines the inflation rate π_2, and so on.

Year	π	P	Y
0	.000	1.00	$1250
1	.100	1.10	1205
2	-.036	1.06	1222
3	-.023	1.04	1233
4	-.014	1.03	1238

The price disturbance raises prices and lowers output below potential. Over time, prices fall and output rises until potential GNP is restored.

b. *The technique for this part is the same as for Part a except that, starting in Year 1, the new money supply is substituted in the aggregate demand curve. The accommodative policy restores output to within 1 percent of potential in 3 years at the cost of a higher price level.*

Year	π	P	Y
0	.000	1.00	$1250
1	.100	1.10	1227
2	-.018	1.08	1236
3	-.011	1.07	1242

3. Suppose the economy has the aggregate demand curve

$$Y = 667 + 1.11G + 1.11(M/P) + Z_d$$

and the price-adjustment schedule

$$\pi = (Y_{-1} - Y^*)/Y^*,$$

where Z_d is an aggregate demand shock. Potential GNP $Y^* = \$1500$, government spending $G = \$200$, and the money supply $M = \$550$.

a. Starting at potential output with the price level $P = 1$ and inflation $\pi = 0$, an aggregate demand disturbance $Z_d = -\$150$ occurs in the first year. No further shocks occur ($Z_d = -\$150$ in all future years). Describe the path of the economy until GNP is within 1 percent of its long-run value.

b. How can the Fed offset the aggregate demand disturbance and keep output equal to potential GNP?

4. Suppose the economy has the aggregate demand curve

$$Y = 667 + 1.11G + 1.11(M/P)$$

and the price-adjustment schedule

$$\pi = (Y_{-1} - Y^*)/Y^* + Z_p,$$

where Z_p is a price shock. Potential GNP $Y^* = \$1500$, government spending $G = \$200$, and the money supply $M = \$550$.

a. Starting a potential output with the price level $P = 1$ and inflation $\pi = 0$, a price disturbance of 15 percent occurs in the first year ($Z_p = .15$). No further shocks occur ($Z_p = 0$ in all future years). Describe the path of the economy until GNP is within 1 percent of its long-run value.

b. Suppose that, starting in the first year, the Fed increases the money supply by 4 percent. Compare the new path of prices and output to the original path.

5. Suppose the economy has the aggregate demand curve

$$Y = 445 + .55G + 1.67(M/P) + Z_d$$

and the price-adjustment schedule

$$\pi = (Y_{-1} - Y^*)/Y^*,$$

where Z_d is an aggregate demand shock. Potential GNP $Y^* = \$800$, government spending $G = \$100$, and the money supply $M = \$180$.

a. Starting at potential output with the price level $P = 1$ and inflation $\pi = 0$, an aggregate demand disturbance $Z_d = $-\$50$ occurs in the first year. No further shocks occur ($Z_d = $-\$50$ in all future years). Describe the path of the economy until GNP is within 1 percent of its long-run value.

b. How can the Fed offset the aggregate demand disturbance and keep output equal to potential GNP?

6. Suppose the economy has the aggregate demand curve

$$Y = 445 + .55G + 1.67(M/P)$$

and the price-adjustment schedule

$$\pi = (Y_{-1} - Y^*)/Y^* + Z_p,$$

where Z_p is a price shock. Potential GNP $Y^* = \$800$, government spending $G = \$100$, and the money supply $M = \$180$.

a. Starting at potential output with the price level $P = 1$ and inflation $\pi = 0$, a price disturbance of 10 percent occurs in the first year ($Z_p = .1$). No further shocks occur ($Z_p = 0$ in all future years). Describe the path of the economy until GNP is within 1 percent of its long-run value.

b. Suppose that, starting in the first year, the Fed increases the money supply by 5 percent. Compare the new path of prices and output to the original path.

7. Suppose the economy has the aggregate demand curve

$$Y = 734 + 1.21G + .64(M/P) + Z_d$$

and the price-adjustment schedule

$$\pi = (Y_{-1} - Y^*)/Y^*,$$

where Z_d is an aggregate demand disturbance. Government spending $G = \$200$, the money supply $M = \$1100$, and potential output $Y^* = 1680$.

a. Starting at potential output with the price level $P = 1$ and inflation $\pi = 0$, an aggregate demand disturbance $Z_d = $-\$100$ occurs in the first year. No further shocks occur ($Z_d = $-\$100$ in all future years). Describe the path of the economy until GNP is within 1 percent of its long-run value.

b. How can the Fed offset the aggregate demand disturbance and keep output equal to potential GNP?

8. Suppose the economy has the aggregate demand curve

$$Y = 734 + 1.21G + .64(M/P)$$

and the price-adjustment schedule

$$\pi = (Y_{-1} - Y^*)/Y^* + Z_p,$$

where Z_p is a price disturbance. Government spending $G = \$200$, the money supply $M = \$1100$, and potential output $Y^* = 1680$.

a. Starting at potential output with the price level $P = 1$ and inflation $\pi = 0$, a price disturbance of 20 percent occurs in the first year ($Z_p = .20$). No further shocks occur ($Z_p = 0$ in all future years). Describe the path of the economy until GNP is within 1 percent of its long-run value.

b. Suppose that, starting in the first year, the Fed increases the money supply by 10 percent. Compare the new path of prices and output to the original path.

MacroSolve Exercises

In this chapter we continue to assume that the aggregate demand side of the economy is given by the model in Chapter 4, and add to our price adjustment equation the influence of supply shocks. Our price adjustment equation becomes:

$$\pi = \pi^e + 0.8(Y_{-1} - Y^*)Y^* + Z$$

where Z represents a price shock. This model is called "AD/PA, Closed Econ."

For your answers to questions 1 to 4, you may find it useful to alter the display of the model results (using **Select Display** in the screen option menu) to plot the time paths of the price level and real GNP on the right-hand side of the screen. You will then be able to trace out movements similar to those in Figure 7-7 of the textbook.

1. Select a price shock of 10 percent. Assume that government spending and the money supply are kept constant.

a. How much output is "lost" in the following five periods, where lost output is measured as the sum of the deviation of output from potential output over those years?

b. Increase the responsiveness of investment to interest rates. Is the output loss greater or smaller than it was with less responsive investment? Explain in words why this is the case, emphasizing the role of changes in the interest rate in transmitting price shocks to the real side of the economy.

c. Reset the interest responsiveness of investment to its default, and make prices less responsive to aggregate demand. Explain why the price shock has a more prolonged depressing effect on GNP when prices are more "sticky."

2. Continue to assume that the 10 percent price shock hits the economy, and reset all parameters to their default values. Compare the output loss following the price shock in the last case to the case where the Federal Reserve allows the money supply to increase sufficiently to keep output constant in the first period.

a. Explain why increasing the money supply to exactly $660 billion is the right amount to keep output constant in the first period.

b. Compare the output loss over the first six years with that in the previous question.Why would a government ever choose not to accommodate a price shock in this manner?

3. Suppose that instead of changing the money supply, the government increases its own expenditure to keep output constant in the period of the price shock.

a. Explain how the solution differs from the previous case where the money supply was increased.

b. What variables are significantly different in the last period of the two (monetary and fiscal policy response) simulations? What explains their differences? Why might a policy maker prefer one over the other?

4. Compare the effects on the economy of the accommodating policy response to a supply shock (as in question 2) with those resulting from an extinguishing policy (for example, one that reduced the money supply by $60 billion)? Are there reasons why the government might prefer the extinguishing policy (a) in the short run, or (b) in the long run?

5. A somewhat naive characterization of the 1960s debates between Keynesians and monetarists is to assert that Keynesians believed that the interest elasticity of money demand was very high and the interest elasticity of investment demand was very low. Monetarists were portrayed as believing the opposite—that the interest elasticity of money demand is low, while the interest

elasticity of investment demand is high. To answer the following questions, select the ISLM model ("ISLM, Closed Econ").

a. Show how the shapes of the IS and LM curves differ in the "Keynesian" and "monetarist" cases (by altering the elasticities in the **Change Params** option of the RUN THE MODEL menu).

b. Repeat the last question using the flexible price model ("AD/PA, Closed Econ"). Does this model still have "Keynesian" and "monetarist" conclusions under the assumptions made above (a) in the short run, and (b) in the long run? Explain why your answers to (a) and (b) are different.

Answers to the Self-Test

1. Aggregate demand disturbance
2. Price-adjustment curve
3. Activist or countercyclical
4. Accommodative
5. Nonaccommodative
6. Reducing
7. Price level
8. Time inconsistency
9. Expansionary
10. Expansionary
11. Contractionary
12. Contractionary
13. True. Aggregate demand disturbances only affect output in the short run.
14. False. Price shocks affect both output and the price level in the short run.
15. False. Monetarists believe that monetary policy should not be used to counter such disturbances.
16. False. New classical macroeconomists believe that monetary policy is incapable of countering such disturbances.
17. True. In the long run, output is equal to potential GNP, which is unaffected by aggregate demand disturbances.
18. True. Unless there is a policy response, prices return to their original level in the long run.
19. False. An oil price increase is a price shock.
20. False. Any attempt to reduce inflation must lower output below potential GNP, causing a recession.
21. True. Both monetary and fiscal policy shift the aggregate demand curve.
22. False. While monetary expansions raise net exports, fiscal expansions lower them.
23. False. Disinflation is a reduction in the rate of inflation. Deflation is negative inflation.

24. False. New classical macroeconomists believe that inflation can be reduced with low cost.
25. Aggregate demand disturbances shift the aggregate demand curve while price disturbances shift the price-adjustment curve.
26. Changes in investment, net exports, and money demand are examples of aggregate demand disturbances while oil price shocks and expectations of inflation are examples of price disturbances.
27. In the short run, output declines at an unchanged price level. Over time, prices fall and output increases until potential GNP is restored.
28. Expansionary fiscal or monetary policy can be used to shift the aggregate demand curve to the right, restoring potential GNP without a prolonged recession.
29. In the short run, prices rise and output falls. Over time, prices fall and output increases until potential GNP is restored.
30. Accommodative monetary policy, increasing the money supply in response to a price shock, shortens the recession at the cost of increasing the price level.
31. Monetarists believe that monetary policy should not be used to counter aggregate demand disturbances because it is too powerful and will be misused. New classical macroeconomists believe that it should not be used because it is powerless to affect real GNP.
32. A policy rule is a description of endogenous economic policy. Two examples of policy rules are the monetarist proposition to fix the rate of growth of the money supply and an accommodative monetary policy that increases the money supply in response to a price shock.
33. The advantage of policy rules is that they can commit policy-makers to follow their announced plans.
34. The Fed can decrease the money supply sharply, causing a quick reduction in inflation but a large recession, or it can decrease the money supply more gradually, causing a slower reduction in inflation but also a smaller recession.
35. Inflation remained high through 1981. It dropped sharply in 1982, and fell to under 4 percent by 1984. There was a large recession, with GNP 11 percent below potential in 1982, followed by a recovery.
36. Monetary and fiscal expansions have different effects on investment and net exports because they have different effects on interest rates.

Solutions to Review Problems

3. a.

Year	π	P	Y
0	.000	1.00	$1500
1	.000	1.00	1350
2	-.100	.90	1417
3	-.055	.85	1457
4	-.029	.83	1479
5	-.014	.82	1485

b. The money supply should be increased by $135 to $685.

4. a.

Year	π	P	Y
0	.000	1.00	$1500
1	.015	1.15	1420
2	-.053	1.09	1450
3	-.034	1.05	1469
4	-.021	1.03	1483

b.

Year	π	P	Y
0	.000	1.00	$1500
1	.015	1.15	1441
2	-.039	1.11	1464
3	-.024	1.08	1475
4	-.017	1.06	1487

The accommodative policy mitigates the recession at the cost of a higher price level.

5. a.

Year	π	P	Y
0	.000	1.00	$800
1	.000	1.00	750
2	-.062	.94	771
3	-.037	.91	782
4	-.022	.89	788
5	-.015	.88	793

b. The money supply should be increased by $30 to $210.

6. a.

Year	π	P	Y
0	.000	1.00	$800
1	.010	1.10	773
2	-.033	1.06	783
3	-.022	1.04	790
4	-.013	1.03	793

b.

Year	π	P	Y
0	.000	1.00	$800
1	.010	1.10	787
2	-.016	1.08	792

The accommodative policy mitigates the recession at the cost of a higher price level.

7. a.

Year	π	P	Y
0	.000	1.00	$1680
1	.000	1.00	1580
2	-.060	.94	1625
3	-.033	.91	1650
4	-.018	.89	1663

b. The money supply should be increased by $156 to $1256.

8. a.

Year	π	P	Y
0	.000	1.00	$1680
1	.200	1.20	1563
2	-.070	1.12	1607
3	-.044	1.07	1633
4	-.028	1.04	1653
5	-0.16	1.02	1664

b.

Year	π	P	Y
0	.000	1.00	$1680
1	.200	1.20	1621
2	-.035	1.16	1644
3	-.021	1.14	1658
4	-.013	1.12	1664

The accommodative policy mitigates the recession at the cost of a higher price level.

Solutions to MacroSolve Exercises

1. a. $621 billion.
   b. $631 billion. Initially, more output is lost since the increase in the interest rate caused by the price shock (through the reduction in the real money supply) reduces investment more. Offsetting this somewhat is the fact that the deeper initial recession causes the price level to fall back to equilibrium more quickly, thus bringing down interest rates in the later periods of the simulation.
   c. Stickier prices cause the real money supply to remain low for longer, keeping up interest rates and hence depressing investment and output for longer.
2. a. The required increase in the money supply is $60 billion, or 10 percent. This increase is exactly sufficient to keep the real money supply fixed in the face of a 10 percent price shock.
   b. The output lost is $336 billion. The output loss is far lower when there is monetary accommodation, but the price level will be 10 percent higher in the long run. This may be undesirable. A superior policy might be to allow the money supply to increase only temporarily.
3. Increasing G by $110 billion keeps GNP almost constant in the first period.
   a. The output loss is $320 billion. Compared to the monetary accommodation policy, the interest rate and the government deficit are higher and investment is lower.
   b. In the fiscal accommodation case, the final price level is lower (it returns to 1.0), but the interest rate is permanently higher, and

111

investment is permanently lower. If long-run economic growth is affected by the amount of investment (see Chapter 13 of the textbook), this might be an undesirable side effect of the fiscal policy. At any rate, it must be weighted against the costs imposed by a higher price level in the monetary accommodation scenario.

4. The output loss is $741 billion in the extinguishing simulation, concentrated in the first few periods. In the short run this is unattractive from the perspective of a policy maker, but the recovery from the price shock is more rapid in the extinguishing case, and the price level reverts eventually to its original value. In the long run, therefore, a policy maker will find some good aspects of an extinguishing policy.

5. a. In the Keynesian case, the IS curve is steeper (as investment is less sensitive to interest rates) and the LM curve is flatter than in the monetarist case.

   b. In the monetarist case, fiscal policy is weak as the steep LM curve makes interest rates rise greatly when government spending rises, and the high interest elasticity of investment thus depresses investment a good deal. Monetary policy is strong because investment, and hence output, is strongly increased by a reduction in interest rates.

6. In the short run, the Keynesian and monetarist conclusions still hold. However, in the long run, fiscal policy simply affects interest rates, and monetary policy only affects the price level. GNP is unaffected by either.

PART II

The Micro Foundations
of Aggregate Demand

CHAPTER 8   Consumption Demand

Main Objectives

A basic principle of microeconomics is that people set their consumption plans in order to maximize their satisfaction, or utility. The simple consumption function discussed in Chapter 4, which says that people consume a constant fraction of their current disposable income, is an incomplete description of consumer behavior. Chapter 8 develops a more complete description by examining the empirical evidence regarding consumption and by relating consumption not only to current income, but to expectations of future income and to interest rates as well. You should learn the more sophisticated consumption model. Also, you should understand the implications of this model for the IS-LM analysis developed in Chapter 5 and for the analysis of price adjustment developed in Chapter 6. Indeed, a habit you should begin in this chapter is always to consider the impact of any new details on the model developed in Chapters 4, 5, and 6.

Key Terms and Concepts

Consumption is spending by households. Macroeconomists break consumption into three broad categories: durable goods, or those that are consumed over a number of years, like automobiles; non-durable goods, or those that are consumed during the year that they are purchased, like laundry detergent; and services, or professional attention, such as a visit to the barber or the doctor.

The central relationship between consumption and GNP is that, over the long run, **consumption expenditures** and GNP grow at about the same rate, but, over short-run business cycles, consumption expenditures fluctuate less than GNP. These fluctuations would be even smaller if we measured true consumption rather than consumption expenditures, so that consumer durables would be counted as providing consumption over the years that they are used rather than being considered as fully consumed during the period in which they are purchased.

One reason that consumption fluctuates less than GNP in the short run is because consumption depends on personal disposable income, which itself fluctuates less than GNP. Depreciation, taxes, and retained earnings by corporations are all part of GNP but not part of disposable income, while transfers from the government such as unemployment insurance and social security are part of disposable income but not part of GNP. Disposable income does not fall as much as GNP during recessions because tax collections decline while transfers increase. Tax collections and transfers are called **automatic stabilizers** because of their built-in stabilizing effect on disposable income.

The **Keynesian consumption function** discussed in Chapter 4 relates consumption to current disposable income,

$$C = a + bY_d \qquad (8\text{-}1)$$

where b, the marginal propensity to consume, has been measured at about .91 for the Unites States.

While this equation fits the data fairly well, there are aspects of consumption that it cannot explain, One of these is that, on average, fluctuations in consumption are not only smaller than fluctuations in GNP, they are smaller than fluctuations in disposable income: while the long-run marginal propensity to consume is equal to .91, the short-run marginal propensity to consume is equal to .78. If consumption actually followed the simple Keynesian consumption function, the short- and long-run marginal propensities to consume would be equal.

Two theories of consumption were developed during the 1950s in response to the defects in the simple Keynesian consumption function. The **permanent income theory**, developed by Milton Friedman, postulates that consumption depends not on current income, but on a measure of a family's average long-run, or permanent, income.

$$C = b_p Y_p, \qquad (8\text{-}2)$$

where Y_p is permanent income and b_p is a coefficient. Empirical tests by Friedman, using a weighted average of current and past incomes as a proxy for permanent income, demonstrated that his formulation fit the data better than the simple Keynesian consumption function.

The **life-cycle theory**, developed by Franco Modigliani, is based on a family planning consumption over its entire lifetime and incorporates assets into the Keynesian consumption function:

$$C = b_1 Y_d + b_2 A, \qquad (8\text{-}3)$$

where A is assets held by the family and b_1 and b_2 are coefficients. Empirical work by Albert Ando of the University of Pennsylvania and

116

Franco Modigliani found that, as predicted by the life-cycle theory, holdings of assets influence consumption.

The text highlights the similar feature of the permanent-income and life-cycle theories; each is a **forward-looking theory of consumption**. The most important aspect of forward-looking theories is that expected future, as well as current, income influences consumption. Families face an **intertemporal budget constraint**: they cannot have significantly negative assets. This constraint limits their consumption, but within it they can choose a wide range of consumption plans.

Without further assumptions, the forward-looking theory allows for such a wide range of consumption plans that it cannot be tested. Therefore, economists qualify it by assuming that most people prefer to keep their consumption fairly steady from year to year, rather than have their consumption fluctuate with their yearly income. Other factors come into play in determining which smooth consumption path a family will choose. For instance, the **bequest motive**, which describes parents' preferences for assets at the end of their lifetimes, must also be known in order to determine whether the family will choose a high or a low smooth consumption path.

The most important proposition of the forward-looking theory of consumption is the difference between the **marginal propensity to consume out of a temporary change in income** and the **marginal propensity to consume out of a permanent change in income**. Consider a tax cut that raises disposable income. If the tax cut is permanent, the increase in disposable income is also permanent and consumption will increase by the marginal propensity to consume times the change in income. If the tax cut is temporary, disposable income will return to its original level once the tax cut ends. A family's lifetime disposable income will increase much less than if the tax cut were permanent, which will cause consumption to increase much less than under a permanent cut.

Another feature of the forward-looking theory of consumption involves **anticipated changes in income**. Suppose a permanent tax cut was announced on year in advance. With the announcement, people would know that their lifetime disposable income had increased and would immediately raise their consumption. The increase in consumption would occur before the tax cut actually took place.

The forward-looking theory of consumption has been extensively tested over the last thirty years. The most compelling evidence in favor of the forward-looking theory as opposed to the simple Keynesian theory is that the short-run marginal propensity to consume is smaller than the long-run marginal propensity to consume. Additional evidence comes from examining two temporary changes in policy: the tax surcharge of 1968 and the tax rebate and social security bonus of 1975. In both cases, the response of consumption to the change in disposable income was small.

Recent empirical work on the forward-looking theory, using rational expectations to measure future income prospects, raises some interesting questions. This research indicates that consumption is more responsive to temporary changes in income than the forward-looking theory predicts, although clearly not as responsive as in the simple Keynesian theory. Other research involving individual family histories, using panel or longitudinal surveys, produces the same result. One explanation for these results is that some consumers are **liquidity constrained**—they cannot borrow as easily as the forward-looking model suggests.

Real interest rates also influence consumption. If the real interest rate is positive, as it generally is, people have an incentive to defer spending. On the other hand, consumption today is preferred to consumption in the future, and this is measured by the **rate of time preference**. If the real interest rate is greater than the rate of time preference, people will shift some of their consumption toward the future. These effects, like all relative price changes, are theoretically ambiguous. Higher real interest rates also raise income, which would tend to increase consumption. Indeed, the effects of real interest rates on consumption have not been strongly confirmed empirically.

The issues raised in this chapter have conflicting effects on the slope of the IS curve. Forward-looking consumers have a smaller marginal propensity to consume out of disposable income than is predicted by the Keynesian consumption function, making the multiplier smaller and the IS curve steeper than it seemed in Chapter 5. On the other hand, higher real interest rates decrease consumption, making GNP more sensitive to the interest rate and the IS curve flatter than in Chapter 5. Which effect dominates is an empirical question.

The forward-looking theory of consumption also has implications for shifts in the IS curve due to tax changes. If a tax cut is permanent, the IĨ curve will shift much more than if it is temporary. Expectations of future tax cuts will also shift the IS curve.

Self-Test

Fill in the Blank

1. Over short-run business cycles, consumption expenditures fluctuate

   _____ than GNP.

2. Changes in taxes and transfers that cause disposable income to fluctuate less than GNP are called _____.

3. The short-run marginal propensity to consume is _____ than the long-run marginal propensity to consume.

4. The forward-looking theory of consumption combines the _____ and _____ theories.

5. The _____ limits the amount of consumption by a family over a period of years.

6. The forward-looking theory of consumption assumes that most people prefer to keep a _____ consumption path.

7. The forward-looking theory of consumption predicts that the effects of tax changes will differ depending on whether they are _____ or _____ .

8. Consumers are _____ if they cannot borrow as easily as the forward-looking model suggests.

9. The _____ is the relative price between present and future consumption.

10. The _____ measures the preference for consumption today over consumption in the future.

11. Forward-looking theories have a _____ marginal propensity to consume than is predicted by the Keynesian consumption function.

12. According to the forward-looking theory, anticipated tax changes shift the _____ .

13. Consumption fluctuates less than consumption expenditures.

14. The relation between consumption expenditures and GNP is the same over short-run business cycles as it is over the long run.

15. Automatic stabilizers decrease fluctuations in disposable income.

16. According to the simple Keynesian consumption function, the short-run marginal propensity to consume is equal to the long-run marginal propensity to consume.

17. The intertemporal budget constraint means that, in any single year, a family cannot consume more than its disposable income.

18. People choose a smooth consumption path because of the bequest motive.

19. The simple Keynesian consumption function predicts that consumption will respond equally to temporary and permanent tax cuts.

20. The forward-looking theory of consumption predicts that consumption will respond equally to temporary and permanent tax cuts.

21. According to the forward-looking theory the announcement of a tax cut one year in the future will increase consumption immediately.

22. If consumers ar liquidity constrained, consumption would respond more to temporary changes in income than the forward-looking theory predicts.

23. If consumption is negatively related to the real interest rate, the IS curve is flatter.

24. According to the forward-looking theory, the IS curve is steeper than it seemed in Chapter 5.

Review Questions

25. What is the difference between consumption and consumption expenditures?

26. What is the most important reason that consumption fluctuates less than GNP?

27. What is the major piece of evidence against the simple Keynesian consumption function?

28. What is the basic difference between the forward-looking theory of consumption and the simple Keynesian consumption function?

29. What does the forward-looking theory assume about people's preferences for steady versus erratic consumption?

30. Describe the early empirical evidence on the permanent-income and the life-cycle theories.

31. Why did the 1968 tax surcharge and the 1975 tax rebate provide support for the forward-looking theory?

32. What is the recent empirical evidence that points out defects in the forward-looking theory?

33. Why does consumption depend on the real interest rate?

34. Why does the forward-looking theory of consumption affect the slope of the IS curve?

35. Why do temporary tax changes cause smaller shifts of the IS curve than permanent tax changes?

36. Why do expectations of future tax cuts shift the IS curve?

Problem Set

Worked Problems

1. Suppose that consumption is of the form

$$C = 500 + .8Y_p,$$

where Y_p is permanent disposable income. Suppose also that consumers estimate their permanent disposable income by a simple average of disposable income in the current and past year:

$$Y_p = .5(Y_d + Y_{d-1}),$$

where Y_d is current disposable income.

a. Suppose that disposable income Y_d is equal to $5000 billion in Years 1 and 2. What is consumption in Year 2?

b. What are the short- and long-run marginal propensities to consume?

c. Suppose that disposable income increases to $6000 billion in Year 3 and then remains at $6000 billion in all future years. What is consumption in Years 3 and 4 and all remaining years?

Explain why consumption responds the way it does to an increase in income.

a. *Permanent income in Year 2 = .5(5000 + 5000) = $5000 billion. Consumption in Year 2 = 500 + .8(5000) = $4500 billion.*

b. *The short-run marginal propensity to consume = (.8)(.5) = .4. The long-run marginal propensity to consume = .8.*

c. *Permanent income in Year 3 = .5(6000 + 5000) = $5500 billion. Consumption in Year 3 = 500 + .8(5500) = $4900 billion. Permanent income in Year 4 and all remaining years = .5(6000 + 6000) = $6000 billion. Consumption in Year 4 and all remaining years = 500 + .8(6000) = $5300 billion. Consumption responds less in Year 3 than in Year 4 and thereafter because the short-run marginal propensity to consume is smaller than the long-run marginal propensity to consume.*

2. Suppose that consumption is given by

$$C = 100 + .9Y_d - 1000R$$

rather than by the consumption function in Problem 1 of Chapter 5. Add this consumption function to the other three equations of the IS-LM model:

$$Y = C + I + G + X \qquad \text{(Income identity)}$$
$$I = 200 - 500R \qquad \text{(Investment)}$$
$$X = 100 - .12Y - 500R \qquad \text{(Net exports)}$$
$$M = (.8Y - 2000R)P \qquad \text{(Money demand)}$$

with government spending G = $200 billion, the the tax rate t = .2, the nominal money supply M = $800 billion, and the predetermined-price level P = 1.

a. What is the IS curve? Compare it with the IS curve in Problem 1 of Chapter 5.

b. Derive the aggregate demand curve and calculate the effect of increases in government spending or real money on GNP. Compare your answer with Problem 2 of Chapter 5.

a. *As in Chapter 5, the IS curve is derived by substituting consumption, investment, net exports, and government spending into the income identity:*

$$Y = 1500 - 5000R.$$

It is flatter than the IS curve in Chapter 5, $Y = 1500 - 2500R$, because consumption depends negatively on the interest rate.

b. *The aggregate demand curve is calculated as in Chapter 5. From the LM curve,*

$$Y = 1.25(M/P) + 2500R.$$

From the condition for spending balance,

$$2500R = 500 - .5Y + 1.25G.$$

Substituting the spending balance condition into the LM curve, we derive the aggregate demand curve:

$$Y = .83(M/P) + 333 + .83G.$$

Because the IS curve is flatter, increases in government spending have less effect on GNP than in Chapter 5, while increases in real money have more effect.

Review Problems

3. Suppose that consumption is of the form

$$C = 200 + .9Y_p,$$

where Y_p is permanent disposable income. Suppose also that consumers estimate their permanent disposable income by a weighted average of disposable income in the current and past years:

$$Y_p = .7Y_d + .3Y_{d-1},$$

where Y_d is current disposable income.

a. Suppose that disposable income Y_d is equal to $6000 in Years 1 and 2. What is consumption in Year 2?

b. Suppose that disposable income increases to $7000 in Year 3 and then remains at $7000 in all future years. What is consumption in Years 3 and 4 and all remaining years?

c. What are the short- and long-run marginal propensities to consume? How do they explain your answer to Part b?

4. Suppose that consumption is of the form

$$C = 300 + .9Y_p,$$

where Y_p is permanent disposable income. Suppose also that consumers estimate their permanent disposable income by a weighted average of disposable income in the current and past two years:

$$Y_p = .6Y_d + .3Y_{d-1} + .1Y_{d-2},$$

123

where Y_d is current disposable income.

a. Suppose that disposable income Y_d is equal to \$8000 in Years 1, 2, and 3. What is consumption in Year 3?

b. Suppose that disposable income increases to \$9000 in Year 4 and then remains at \$9000 in all future years. What is consumption in Years 4, 5, and 6 and all remaining years?

c. What are the short- and long-run marginal propensities to consume?

5. Suppose that consumption is given by

$$C = 300 + .8Y_d - 1000R$$

rather than by the consumption function in Problem 3 of Chapter 5. Completing the IS-LM model,

$$\begin{aligned} Y &= C + I + G + X &&\text{(Income identity)}\\ I &= 200 - 1500R &&\text{(Investment)}\\ X &= 100 - .04Y - 500R &&\text{(Net exports)}\\ M &= (.5Y - 2000R)P &&\text{(Money demand)} \end{aligned}$$

with government spending $G = \$200$, the tax rate $t = .2$, the nominal money supply $M = \$550$, and the predetermined-price level $P = 1$.

a. What is the IS curve? Compare it with the IS curve from Problem 3 of Chapter 5.

b. Derive the aggregate demand curve and calculate the effect of increases in government spending or real money on GNP. Compare your answer with Problem 4 of Chapter 5.

6. Suppose that consumption is given by

$$C = 400 + .9Y_d - 1500R$$

rather than by the consumption function in Problem 5 of Chapter 5. Completing the IS-LM model,

$$\begin{aligned} Y &= C + I + G + X &&\text{(Income identity)}\\ I &= 300 - 2000R &&\text{(Investment)}\\ X &= 100 - .05Y - 1000R &&\text{(Net exports)}\\ M &= (.4Y - 1000R)P &&\text{(Money demand)} \end{aligned}$$

with government spending $G = \$100$, the tax rate $t = .5$, the nominal money supply $M = \$180$, and the predetermined-price level $P = 1$.

a. What is the IS curve? Compare it with the IS curve in Problem 5 of Chapter 5.

124

b. Derive the aggregate demand curve and calculate the effect of increases in government spending or real money on GNP. Compare your answer with Problem 6 of Chapter 5.

7. Suppose that consumption is given by

$$C = 400 + .9Y_d - 1750R$$

rather than by the consumption function in Problem 7 of Chapter 5. Completing the IS-LM model,

$$\begin{aligned}
Y &= C + I + G + X && \text{(Income identity)} \\
I &= 200 - 1800R && \text{(Investment)} \\
X &= 200 - .1Y - 200R && \text{(Net exports)} \\
M &= (.8Y - 3000R)P && \text{(Money demand)}
\end{aligned}$$

with government spending G = \$200 billion, the tax rate t = .3333, the nominal money supply M = \$1104 billion, and the predetermined-price level $P = 1$.

a. What is the IS curve? Compare it with the IS curve in Problem 7 of Chapter 5.

b. Derive the aggregate demand curve and calculate the effect of increases in government spending or real money on GNP. Compare your answer with Problem 8 of Chapter 5.

MacroSolve Exercises

1. Plot on the screen the behavior of the annual value of the average propensity to consume (APC—the ratio of consumption to disposable income). What might explain the atypical behavior of the APC in the Great Depression and in the Second World War? Is your explanation consistent with the permanent income hypothesis? (Hint: It might also be helpful to graph disposable income on the horizontal axis against consumption on the vertical axis.)

2. Provide an explanation that is consistent with the permanent income hypothesis of the unusual behavior of the ratio of consumption to income in 1968 and 1975. To see this behavior, either plot or tabulate the quarterly time series of the APC or graph consumption expenditures against disposable income. (The textbook discusses these periods in Chapter 8.)

3. Using the basic fixed price model in MacroSolve ("ISLM, Closed Econ"), investigate the implications of changing the marginal propensity to consume.

a. Explain how and why the slope of the IS curve changes when the marginal propensity to consume increases.

b. Is the government spending multiplier lager or smaller when the marginal propensity to consume is larger? Why?

c. Is the effect of a change in the money supply on GNP larger or smaller when the marginal propensity to consume is larger? Why?

4. In the basic AD/PA model, does an increased responsiveness of consumption to current income lead to faster or slower adjustment to equilibrium GNP following a cut in the money supply? Explain in words why this is.

Answers to the Self-Test

1. Less
2. Automatic stabilizers
3. Less
4. Permanent-income and life-cycle
5. Intertemporal budget constraint
6. Steady
7. Temporary or permanent
8. Liquidity constrained
9. Real interest rate
10. Rate of time preference
11. Smaller
12. IS curve
13. True. Consumption expenditures count consumer durables, such as automobiles, when they are purchased rather than over the time they are used.
14. False. Over the long run, consumption expenditures and GNP grow at about the same rate, but, over short-run business cycles, consumption expenditures fluctuate less than GNP.
15. True. Automatic stabilizers such as taxes, which fall during recessions, and transfers, which rise, are the reason that disposable income fluctuates less than GNP.
16. True. The simple Keynesian consumption function is that consumption depends on current disposable income, which equates the short- and long-run marginal propensities to consume.
17. False. The intertemporal budget constraint limits consumption over a period of many years, not for any single year.
18. False. People choose a smooth consumption path because they prefer steady to erratic consumption. The bequest motive determines which smooth path they choose.
19. True. They both raise current disposable income by the same amount.

20. False. A temporary tax cut causes only a small increase in lifetime disposable income, and so causes only a small increase in consumption.
21. True. The announcement of a future tax cut increases lifetime disposable income and, to maintain a smooth consumption path, consumption increases immediately.
22. True. Liquidity-constrained consumers are not able to borrow sufficiently to smooth consumption as much as the forward-looking
23. True. A negative relation between consumption and the real interest rate makes GNP more sensitive to the interest rate and the IS curve flatter.

24. False. The forward-looking theory incorporates two conflicting factors, making the total effect ambiguous.
25. The distinction applies only to consumer durables. Consumption expenditure occurs when the good, such as a car, is purchased. Consumption occurs at the car is used up.
26. The most important reason that consumption fluctuates less than GNP is that consumption depends on disposable income, which itself fluctuates less than GNP.
27. The short-run marginal propensity to consume is less than the long-run marginal propensity to consume.
28. The simple Keynesian consumption function depends only on current disposable income, while the forward-looking theory depends on both current and expected disposable income.
29. It assumes that people prefer steady rather than erratic consumption.
30. Milton Friedman found that the permanent-income formulation of the consumption function fit the data better than the simple Keynesian formulation. Albert Ando and Franco Modigliani found that, as predicted by the life-cycle theory, assets as well as disposable income influence consumption.
31. Both the 1968 tax surcharge and the 1975 tax rebate were temporary. As predicted by the forward-looking theory, neither had much effect on consumption.
32. Recent empirical evidence assuming rational expectations finds that consumption is more sensitive to temporary changes in income than would be predicted by the forward-looking theory. Studies using individual family histories find the same result.
33. The real interest rate, as the relative price between present and future consumption, influences the choice of whether to consume more today or more tomorrow.
34. According to the forward-looking theory, the multiplier is smaller than in Chapter 5, making the IS curve steeper, but consumption depends on real interest rates, making the IS curve flatter.
35. Temporary tax changes have less effect on consumption than permanent tax changes, causing smaller shifts of the IS curve.
36. Expectations of future tax cuts increase consumption, shifting the IS curve.

Solutions to Review Problems

3. a. Permanent income in Year 2 = .7(6000) + .3(6000) = $6000. Consumption in Year 2 = 200 + .9(6000) = $5600.

   b. Permanent income in Year 3 = .7(7000) + .3(6000) = $6700. Consumption in Year 3 = 200 + .9(6700) = $6230. Permanent income in Year 4 and all remaining years = $7000. Consumption in Year 4 and all remaining years = 200 + .9(7000) = $6500.

   c. The short-run marginal propensity to consume = (.9)(.7) = .63. The long-run marginal propensity to consume = .9. In Part b, consumption in Year 3 increases by $630, the short-run marginal propensity to consume, .63, times the change in disposable income, $1000. Consumption in Year 4 and thereafter increases by $900, the long-run marginal propensity to consume, .9, times the change in income.

4. a. Consumption in Year 3 = $7500.

   b. Consumption in Year 4 = $8040, in Year 5 = $8310, and in Year 6 and in all subsequent years = $8400.

   c. The short-run marginal propensity to consume = .54. The long-run marginal propensity to consume = .9.

5. a. The IS curve is $Y = 2000 - 7500R$. It is flatter than the IS curve in Chapter 5.

   b. The aggregate demand curve is $Y = 1.3(M/P) + 523 + .87G$. Because the IS curve is flatter, increases in government spending have less effect on GNP than in Chapter 5, while increases in real money have more effect.

6. a. The IS curve is $Y = 1500 - 7500R$. It is flatter than the IS curve in Chapter 5.

   b. The aggregate demand curve is $Y = 1.88(M/P) + 334 + .42G$. Because the IS curve is flatter, increases in government spending have less effect on GNP than in Chapter 5, while increases in real money have more effect.

7. a. The IS curve is $Y = 2000 - 7500R$. It is flatter than the IS curve in Chapter 5.

   b. The aggregate demand curve is $Y = .83(M/P) + 533 + .67G$. Because the IS curve is flatter, increases in government spending have less effect on GNP than in Chapter 5, while increases in real money have more effect.

Solutions to MacroSolve Exercises

1. The increase in the APC in the depression could be a rational response to the expected increase in future income when the "temporary" recession was over. When income is temporarily low, the permanent income hypothesis predicts a decrease in savings. The decline in the APC in the Second World War could be due to "patriotic" saving, to rationing, or

could be a response to uncertainty about future income levels (many expected a recession to follow the war).

2. There was a temporary tax surcharge in 1968 and a temporary tax rebate in 1975. Since neither change affected permanent income, consumption would not be expected to change much. Hence the ratio of consumption to current income should rise in the first case and fall in the second — which it did.

3. a. The IS curve becomes flatter as a lower proportion of income is saved.
   b. The multiplier is increased because a given increment to income results in more consumer spending the larger is the MPC.
   c. The increase in GNP from an increase in the money supply is greater for the same reason as above.

4. Adjustment is slower with a higher MPC because the initial recession is deeper due to the larger multiplier and is followed by greater overshooting.

CHAPTER 9   Investment Demand

Main Objectives

Investment is the most volatile component of aggregate demand. Chapter 9 expands the simple investment demand function of Chapter 5 by examining the microeconomic underpinnings of investment behavior. You should learn how investment, influenced by the forward-looking behavior of firms, depends in a systematic way on output as well as on interest rates. You should also be able to explain the effects of investment models in the IS-LM framework.

Key Terms and Concepts

Investment is the flow of newly produced capital goods. It consists of three subcategories: **nonresidential fixed investment**, or business purchases of new plants and equipment; **residential fixed investment**, or construction of new houses and apartments; and **inventory investment**, or increases in stocks of goods produced but not yet sold.

The **desired capital stock** is the amount of factories, equipment, and supplies that firms desire. It is determined by equating the marginal cost and the marginal benefit of employing more capital. Firms need to be forward looking in order to determine the marginal benefit.

The **rental price of capital** is the cost of using capital for one year. It depends on the real price of new equipment, the real interest rate, and the rate of depreciation:

$$R^K = (R + d)P^K, \tag{9-1}$$

where R^K is the rental price of capital, R is the interest rate, d is the rate of depreciation, and P^K is the price of new equipment.

Since the rental price of capital is the cost of using capital, the desired capital stock declines if the rental price of capital rises. The desired capital stock increases if planned output rises because it is generally advantageous to use more of both capital and labor to produce additional output. It also increases if the wage rises because a higher wage lowers the cost of capital relative to labor. Algebraically,

$$K^* = k(W/R^K)Y, \qquad (9\text{-}2)$$

where K^* is the desired capital stock, W is the wage, R^K is the rental price of capital, Y is output, and k is a coefficient.

The **investment function** shows the amount of investment a firm will undertake during the year. If there is no depreciation, investment equals the change in the actual capital stock, $K - K_{-1}$. If there are no lags in the investment process so that firms can attain their desired capital stock within one year, investment can be written as the difference between the desired capital stock and last year's capital stock,

$$I = K^* - K_{-1} = K(W/R^K)Y - K_{-1}, \qquad (9\text{-}3)$$

where I is investment; The investment function shows that investment depends positively on the wage rate and output, and negatively on the rental price of capital. Since the rental price of capital rises with the real interest rate, investment depends negatively on the interest rate.

The **accelerator** describes the relation between investment and output. If the desired capital stock is attained within one year, this year's capital stock, K, depends on this year's output, Y, and so last year's capital stock, K_{-1}, depends on last year's output, Y_{-1}. Then the level of investment, I, which is the change in the capital stock, ΔK, depends on the change in output, ΔY. When output accelerates—when its change gets bigger—investment increases.

A large part of investment serves to replace, rather than add to, the capital stock. The **rate of depreciation** is the fraction of the capital stock that wears out each year. If a constant fraction d of the existing capital stock wears out each year, the net investment function, Equation 9-3, can be changed into a gross investment function by adding d times K_{-1} to the right-hand side of the equation.

Lags in the investment function prevent the capital stock from being adjusted to its desired level immediately. For many investment projects, such as building a new factory, there is a lag of several years between the decision to invest and the completion of the project. These lags can be modeled by modifying the investment function,

$$I = s(K^* - K_{-1}), \qquad (9\text{-}4)$$

where s is the fraction of the difference between the desired and actual capital stock that can be changed within one year. Studies indicate that the value of s is between one-tenth and one-third.

The **Tax Reform Act of 1986** had substantial effects on investment. While the reduction in the corporate tax rate lowered the rental price of capital, the elimination of the investment tax credit and reduction of the accelerated depreciation of capital for tax purposes raised it. The total effect was to raise the rental price of capital by about 10 percent, thereby reducing investment. More positively, by eliminating tax-based incentives, the Tax Reform Act should cause investment to be allocated more efficiently.

As with consumption, the effect of tax changes on investment depends on whether the changes are temporary or permanent. **Anticipated tax changes** can have perverse effects: for instance, expectations of an increase in the investment tax credit one year from now will decrease current investment as firms wait for the tax credit to come into effect before starting investment projects. Expectations of the elimination of the investment tax credit can explain why investment rose at the end of 1985, just before the credit was eliminated, and then fell in early 1986.

Residential investment can be analyzed in much the same way as business investment. One difference is that the annual rate of depreciation for business equipment is about 10 percent while the rate of depreciation for houses is about 2 percent. Consequently, the real interest rate is a much larger fraction of the rental price of housing than it is of the rental price of business capital, and residential investment is much more sensitive to fluctuations in interest rates than is business investment. Monetary policy, through its effect on interest rates, has a very large effect on residential construction.

Inventory investment can also be analyzed like business investment. The **pipeline function** describes inventories that are an intrinsic part of the production process, such as automobile parts held by a car manufacturer. The **buffer stock function** describes finished goods that are ready for sale, such as automobiles held by a car dealer. About two-thirds of inventories are held for the pipeline function, with the other third for the buffer stock function.

Investment depends positively on real GNP and negatively on the real interest rate. In terms of the IS-LM framework, the dependence of investment on GNP increases the multiplier, raising the intercept of the IS curve and making it flatter. Because of lags in the investment process, the response of investment to changes in interest rates is small in the very short run and increases over time. This makes the IS curve close to vertical in the very short run, but flatter over longer periods.

Self-Test

Fill in the Blank

1. The three categories of investment spending are _____, _____, and _____.

2. Fluctuations in investment are _____ than fluctuations in real GNP.

3. The cost of capital to a firm is measured by the _____ of capital.

4. Firms invest if their actual capital stock differs from their _____ capital stock.

5. The desired capital stock depends on the _____, _____, and _____.

6. If there is no depreciation, investment is the change in the _____.

7. Investment depends _____ on the wage rate, _____ on the rental price of capital, and _____ on output.

8. The _____ shows the amount of investment a firm will undertake during the year.

9. The _____ is the fraction of the capital stock that wears out each year.

10. _____ in the investment function prevent the capital stock from being adjusted to its desired level immediately.

11. The accelerator describes the effect of the _____ of output on the _____ of investment.

12. The two functions of inventories are the _____ and _____ functions.

True-False

13. Investment is the least volatile component of aggregate demand.

14. The rental price of capital increases if the rate of depreciation rises.

15. The desired capital stock increases when output rises.

16. Investment is high when wages are high.

17. When the price of new equipment rises investment is high.

18. The actual capital stock is always equal to the desired capital stock.

19. Gross investment is equal to the change in the capital stock.

20. The accelerator describes the effect of the level of output on the change of investment.

21. The Tax Reform Act of 1986 has caused investment to be allocated less efficiently.

22. Anticipated and unanticipated tax credits have the same effects on investment.

23. Monetary policy has more effect on residential investment than on business fixed investment.

24. Inventory investment tends to be closely related to changes in production.

Review Questions

25. Why do firms need to be forward looking when they determine their desired capital stock?

26. How is the rental price of capital determined?

27. What are the determinants of the desired capital stock?

28. Why does investment depend negatively on the real interest rate?

29. Why does the level of investment depend on the change of output?

30. Why are there lags in the investment process?

31. Describe how the tax system influences investment.

32. Why is residential investment very sensitive to fluctuations in the interest rate?

33. What is the relation between the interest sensitivity of investment and the slope of the IS curve?

34. Why do lags in the investment process make the IS curve steeper in the very short run?

35. How did the Tax Reform Act of 1986 affect investment?

36. How can the increase in investment during the fourth quarter of 1985 be explained by the Tax Reform Act of 1986?

Problem Set

1. Suppose that the demand for investment is given by

$$I = .5(K^* - K_{-1}),$$

where K^* is the desired stock of capital given by

$$K^* = .025(Y/R),$$

where Y is output and R is the interest rate. Assume that there is no depreciation.

a. Calculate the desired capital stock in Year 1 if output is $1000 billion and the interest rate is .1 (10 percent).

b. What is the level of investment in Year 1 if the capital stock in Year 0 was $150 billion?

c. Assuming that output and the interest rate are constant, what is investment in Years 2 and 3 and all subsequent years?

a. *The desired capital stock* $K^* = .025(1000)/.1 = \$250$ *billion.*

b. *Investment* $I_1 = .5(250 - 150) = \$50$ *billion.*

c. *The capital stock* K_1 *increases by* I_1 *to* $\$200$ *billion. Since the desired capital stock* K^* *is unchanged,*

$$I_2 = .5(250 - 200) = \$25 \text{ billion.}$$

Similarly,

$$I_3 = .5(250 - 225) = \$12.5 \text{ billion.}$$

Investment will decrease by one-half each year and will eventually approach zero.

2. Suppose that investment is given by

$$I = 200 - 500R + .2Y$$

rather than by the investment function in Problem 1 of Chapter 5. Add this investment function to the other three equations of the IS-LM model:

$$
\begin{aligned}
Y &= C + I + G + X & &\text{(Income identity)} \\
C &= 100 + .9Y_d & &\text{(Consumption)} \\
X &= 100 - .12Y - 500R & &\text{(Net exports)} \\
M &= (.8Y - 2000R)P & &\text{(Money demand)}
\end{aligned}
$$

with government spending $G = \$200$ billion, the tax rate $t = .2$, the nominal money supply $M = \$800$ billion, and the predetermined-price level $P = 1$.

a. What is the IS curve? Compare it with the IS curve in Problem 1 of Chapter 5.

b. Derive the aggregate demand curve and calculate the effect of increases in government spending or real money on GNP. Compare your answer with Problem 2 of Chapter 5.

a. *As in Chapter 5, the IS curve is derived by substituting consumption, investment, net exports, and government spending into the income identity:*

$$Y = 3000 - 5000R.$$

Because investment depends positively on income, the multiplier is greater than in the sample problem of Chapter 5. This makes the IS curve flatter with a larger intercept.

b. *The aggregate demand curve is calculated as in Chapter 5. From the LM curve,*

$$Y = 1.25(M/P) + 2500R.$$

From the condition for spending balance,

$$2500R = 1000 - .5Y + 2.5G.$$

Substituting the condition for spending balance into the LM curve, we derive the aggregate demand curve,

$$Y = .83(M/P) + 667 + 1.67G.$$

Because of the larger multiplier, increases in both government spending and in real money have more effect on GNP than in the model used in Chapter 5.

Review Problems

3. Suppose that the demand for investment is given by

$$I = .2(K^* - K_{-1}),$$

where K^* is the desired stock of capital given by

$$K^* = .01(Y/R),$$

where Y is output and R is the interest rate. Assume that there is no depreciation.

a. Calculate the desired capital stock in Year 1 if output is $2000 and the interest rate is .05 (5 percent).

b. What is the level of investment in Year 1 if the capital stock in Year 0 was $200?

c. Assuming that output and the interest rate are constant, what is investment in Years 2 and 3 and all subsequent years?

4. Answer Problem 3 if the interest rate is .10 (10 percent).

5. Suppose that investment is given by

$$I = 200 - 1500R + .2Y$$

rather than by the investment function in Problem 3 of Chapter 5. Complete the IS-LM model:

$$
\begin{aligned}
Y &= C + I + G + X & &\text{(Income identity)} \\
C &= 300 + .8Y_d & &\text{(Consumption)} \\
X &= 100 - .04Y - 500R & &\text{(Net exports)} \\
M &= (.5Y - 2000R)P & &\text{(Money demand)}
\end{aligned}
$$

with government spending $G = \$200$, the tax rate $t = .2$, the nominal money supply $M = \$550$, and the predetermined-price level $P = 1$.

a. What is the IS curve? Compare it with the IS curve in Problem 3 of Chapter 5.

b. Derive the aggregate demand curve and calculate the effect of increases in government spending or real money on GNP. Compare your answer with Problem 4 of Chapter 5.

6. Suppose that investment is given by

$$I = 300 - 2000R + .1Y$$

rather than by the investment function in Problem 5 of Chapter 5. Completing the IS-LM model:

$$
\begin{aligned}
Y &= C + I + G + X & &\text{(Income identity)} \\
C &= 400 + .9Y_d & &\text{(Consumption)} \\
X &= 100 - .05Y - 1000R & &\text{(Net exports)} \\
M &= (.4Y - 1000R)P & &\text{(Money demand)}
\end{aligned}
$$

with government spending $G = \$100$, the tax rate $t = .5$, the nominal money supply $M = \$180$, and the predetermined-price level $P = 1$.

a. What is the IS curve? Compare it with the IS curve in Problem 5 of Chapter 5.

b. Derive the aggregate demand curve and calculate the effect of increases in government spending or real money on GNP. Compare your answer with Problem 6 of Chapter 5.

7. Suppose that investment is given by

$$I = 200 - 1800R + .1Y$$

rather than by the investment function in Problem 7 of Chapter 5. Completing the IS-LM model:

$$
\begin{aligned}
Y &= C + I + G + X & \text{(Income identity)} \\
C &= 400 + .9Y_d & \text{(Consumption)} \\
X &= 200 - .1Y - 200R & \text{(Net exports)} \\
M &= (.8Y - 3000R)P & \text{(Money demand)}
\end{aligned}
$$

with government spending $G = \$200$, the tax rate $t = .3333$, the nominal money supply $M = \$1104$, and the predetermined-price level $P = 1$.

a. What is the IS curve? Compare it with the IS curve in Problem 7 of Chapter 5.

b. Derive the aggregate demand curve and calculate the effect of increases in government spending or real money on GNP. Compare your answer with Problem 8 of Chapter 5.

MacroSolve Exercises

1. Graph the ratio of investment to GNP against the real interest rate for both annual and quarterly data.

   a. Describe the relationship that you see. Is it compatible with the theoretical model in Chapter 9?

   b. Why might the relationship between investment and the real interest rate be obscured in the graph?

   c. How might you be able to distinguish whether the movements in the real interest rate are causing the changes in investment, or whether fluctuations in investment are shifting the IS curve and causing interest rates to change?

2. Compare the behavior of the ratio of investment to GNP and the growth rate of GNP for both annual and quarterly data. (Hint: try graphing one series against the other, and plotting both the time series on the same screen.) Is this relationship consistent with the theoretical model in Chapter 9? Would you expect to see a closer

relation between investment and the GNP gap or between investment and the growth in GNP?

3. How does the interest elasticity of investment affect the size of the government spending multiplier in the fixed-price ISLM model? Use the model ("ISLM, Closed Econ") to illustrate your answer.

4. a. How does the interest elasticity of investment affect the size and time pattern of the government spending multiplier in the dynamic AD/PA model? Explain why.

   b. Why does the interest elasticity of investment have no effect on the long-run government spending multiplier?

   c. Is the output cost of reducing the price level by cutting the money supply higher or lower the more responsive is investment to interest rates? Explain why.

Answers to the Self-Test

1. Nonresidential fixed investment, residential fixed investment, and inventory investment.
2. Greater
3. Rental price
4. Desired
5. Wage rate, level of output, and rental price of capital
6. Actual capital stock
7. Positively, negatively, and positively
8. Investment function
9. Rate of depreciation
10. Lags
11. Change of output on the level of investment
12. Pipeline and buffer stock
13. False. Investment is the most volatile component of aggregate demand.
14. True. Higher depreciation raises the rental cost of capital, which increases the rental price.
15. True. With higher output, firms want to use more capital in production.
16. True. High wages cause firms to substitute toward capital, which raises the desired capital stock and investment.
17. False. An increase in the price of new equipment raises the rental price of capital, which lowers the desired capital stock and investment.
18. False. Lags in the investment process can cause the actual and desired capital stock to differ.
19. False. Net investment is equal to the change in the capital stock. Gross investment also includes investment to replace depreciated capital.
20. False. The accelerator describes the effect of the change of output on the level of investment.

21. False. By eliminating tax-based incentives, the Tax Reform Act of 1986 should cause investment to be allocated more efficiently.

22. False. An unanticipated tax credit raises investment immediately. An anticipated tax credit first decreases investment while firms wait for the credit to occur.

23. True. Residential investment is more sensitive to interest rates than business fixed investment.

24. True. Most inventory investment is for the pipeline function, which closely follows changes in production.

25. Firms determine their desired capital stock by equating the marginal benefits of capital to the rental cost of capital. They need to be forward looking in order to determine the marginal benefits.

26. The rental price of capital is the price of new equipment multiplied by the sum of the real interest rate plus the rate of depreciation.

27. The determinants of the desired capital stock are the wage rate, the level of output, and the rental price of capital.

28. A higher real interest rate raises the rental price of capital, lowering the desired capital stock and investment.

29. In a world without depreciation, the level of investment is the change in the capital stock. Since the level of the capital stock depends on the level of output, the change in the capital stock depends on the change in output.

30. Much investment spending, such as building new factories, takes time and cannot be completed within one year.

31. Taxation of capital decreases investment. Tax incentives for investment, such as the investment tax credit, stimulate investment.

32. Because the rate of depreciation of houses is low, the interest rate is a large fraction of the rental price of housing and residential investment is very sensitive to fluctuations in the interest rate.

33. The greater the interest sensitivity of investment, the flatter the IS curve.

34. Lags in the investment process make investment very insensitive to interest rates in the very short run, making the IS curve steeper in the very short run than it is otherwise.

35. The Tax Reform Act of 1986 raised the rental price of capital, lowering investment.

36. Expectations that, as part of the Tax Reform Act, the investment tax credit would be eliminated beginning in 1986 raised investment in the fourth quarter of 1985.

Solutions to Review Problems

3. a. The desired capital stock $K^* = .01(2000)/.05 = \$400$.
   b. Investment $I_1 = .2(400 - 200) = \$40$.
   c. The capital stock K_1 increases by 40 to 240. Since the desired capital stock K^* is unchanged,

$$I_2 = .2(400 - 240) = \$32.$$
$$I_3 = .2(400 - 272) = \$25.6$$

Investment will decrease by one-fifth each year and will eventually approach zero.

4. a. The desired capital stock $K^* = .01(2000)/.1 = \$200$.
   b. Investment $I_1 = .2(400 - 400) = 0$ since the actual capital stock equals the desired capital stock.
   c. Investment equals zero in all subsequent years.

5. a. The IS curve is $Y = 4000 - 10,000R$. It is flatter with a larger intercept than the IS curve in Chapter 5.
   b. The aggregate demand curve is $Y = 1.43(M/P) + 857 + 1.43G$. Because the multiplier is larger, increases in both government spending and real money have more effect on GNP than in Chapter 5.

6. a. The IS curve is $Y = 1800 - 6000R$. It is flatter with a larger intercept than the IS curve in Chapter 5.
   b. The aggregate demand curve is $Y = 1.76(M/P) = 470 + .58G$. Because the multiplier is larger, increases in both government spending and real money have more effect on GNP than in Chapter 5.

7. a. The IS curve is $Y = 2500 - 5000R$. It is flatter with a larger intercept than the IS curve in Chapter 5.
   b. The aggregate demand curve is $Y = .71(M/P) + 857 + 1.07G$. Because the multiplier is larger, increases in both government spending and real money have more effect on GNP than in Chapter 5.

Solutions to MacroSolve Exercises

1. a. There is little evidence from the graph that investment responds either positively or negatively to either real or nominal interest rates.
   b. Possible reasons for the lack of evidence:
      1. Investment should be related to the rental cost of capital; the real interest rate is just one component of this cost.
      2. Investment is also greatly affected by output movements; just graphing investment against the interest rate is insufficient to show the full relationship.
      3. Interest rates and investment may both be high at the same moment because investment is high for a different reason such as a tax cut. Thus, even though high interest rates should decrease investment, a graph of one against the other may show that interest rates and investment are sometimes positively related.
   c. If interest rates are affecting investment, we would expect the two variables to be negatively related. If IS fluctuations are causing movements in both variables, we would expect to see a positive relationship.

2. There is a clear positive relationship between the growth of GNP and the investment ratio, consistent with the model of Chapter 9. The accelerator

hypothesis suggests that investment should be more closely related to the change in output than to the output gap.

3. If the interest elasticity of investment is increased, the multiplier will be smaller as there is more crowding out, as interest rates rise.

4. a. If the interest elasticity of investment rises, the multiplier will be smaller, and the adjustment to equilibrium more rapid.

   b. The long-run multiplier is zero, as output returns to potential output eventually. This finding is unaffected by the interest elasticity of investment.

   c. Since investment and, hence, output respond more to a change in interest rates, the recession will be deeper. But it will also be shorter, as prices will adjust more rapidly.

CHAPTER 10

Foreign Trade and the Exchange Rate

Main Objectives

During the 1980s, issues involving foreign trade and the exchange rate have played a central role in the performance of the U.S. economy. The unprecedented trade deficit and roller coaster ride of the dollar have led to proposals for protectionism and exchange-rate stabilization. Chapter 10 discusses the causes of trade imbalances and exchange-rate fluctuations, considers the effects of these foreign influences on the U.S. economy, and analyzes whether proposals for protectionism and exchange-rate stabilization will do more harm than good.

Key Terms and Concepts

Exports are sales of goods and services to the rest of the world. **Imports** are purchases of goods and services from the rest of the world. **Net exports** are exports minus imports. There is a **trade surplus** when exports are greater than imports and a **trade deficit** when imports are greater than exports. A trade deficit must be financed by borrowing from abroad. This borrowing is called a **capital inflow**.

The **exchange rate** is the price of one currency in terms of another. For the United States, it is the amount of foreign currency that can be bought with one dollar, for example 3 West German marks. If more foreign currency can be bought with one dollar, say 4 marks, then we say that the dollar rises or **appreciates** with respect to that currency. If less foreign currency can be bought with one dollar, then the dollar falls or **depreciates**.

Currencies are traded in the foreign exchange market, which is a worldwide network of banks rather than a single organized market. For a variety of reasons, the major industrialized countries fixed exchange rates prior to 1971. Today's international monetary system is called a **floating or flexible exchange rate system** because there is a free market in foreign exchange. The **trade-weighted exchange rate** is an average of several different exchange rates, each weighted by the amount of trade with the United States. It measures the exchange rate between the United States and the rest of the world.

The **real exchange rate** is a measure of the relative price of goods produced in the United States compared to the price of goods produced in the rest of the world (ROW),

$$\text{Real exchange rate} = EP/P_W, \tag{10-1}$$

where E is the trade-weighted exchange rate, P is the U.S. price level, and P_W is the ROW price level. The exchange rate E is sometimes called the **nominal exchange rate**. In the short run, both the U.S. and ROW price levels are predetermined and the real exchange rate, EP/P_W, varies with the exchange rate (E). In the long run, prices are flexible and the real exchange rate is constant. **Purchasing power parity** is a theory proposing that the real exchange rate is constant. It does not hold for the short run, but does for the long run.

The **net export function** relates net exports to real income and the real exchange rate,

$$X = g - mY - n(EP/P_W), \tag{10-2}$$

where g is a constant and m and n are coefficients. Net exports depend negatively on real income because, as domestic income rises, our imports increase. The coefficient m is called the **marginal propensity to import**. Net exports depend negatively on the real exchange rate because a higher real exchange rate makes our goods more expensive relative to foreign goods. This increases our imports and decreases our exports.

When the U.S. interest rate rises in comparison to other interest rates, U.S. assets become more attractive and the dollar appreciates. The positive relation between the real exchange rate and the U.S. interest rate can be expressed as

$$EP/P_W = q + vR, \tag{10-3}$$

where q is a constant and v is a coefficient. Combining the equation for the real exchange rate with the net export function enables us to derive the open economy IS curve, which was discussed in Chapter 5.

The **open economy IS curve** differs from the closed economy IS curve in two ways. First, net exports depend negatively on income, which makes the open economy multiplier, $1/[1 - b(1 - t) + m]$, smaller than the closed economy multiplier and the IS curve steeper. This reduction in the size of the multiplier is called **leakage**. Second, as can be seen by combining Equations 10-2 and 10-3, net exports depend negatively on the interest rate. This makes the IS curve flatter. The LM curve is the same as for a closed economy.

Expansionary monetary policy lowers inters rates, causes the exchange rate to depreciate, and increases output above potential in the short run. Over time, prices rise and output falls towards potential. In the long run, the real exchange rate returns to parity and the nominal exchange rate depreciates by the increase in the price level. As in the closed economy, monetary policy is neutral in the long run.

Expansionary fiscal policy increases interest rates, causes the exchange rate to appreciate, increase the trade deficit (or reduces the trade surplus), and raises output above potential in the short run. The government budget deficit is partially financed by the capital inflow from abroad. Over time, prices rise and output falls towards potential. In the long run, the interest rate and real exchange rate are permanently higher.

Changes in the exchange rate have an immediate impact on the price level for a small country by changing the price of imports. The situation is quite different for the United States. Importers tend to keep the dollar price of their goods stable through swings in the exchange rate. For the large U.S. economy, movements in the exchange rate do not create price shocks.

Protectionist measures include **tariffs** on imports, **quotas** on the quantity of imports, and outright **bans** on some imports. They help domestic producers by lessening foreign competition but hurt consumers by raising prices on imported goods. Th effects on prices are sticky for tariffs, but immediate for quotas. Protection stimulates net exports and shifts the IS curve outward, raising interest rates and the exchange rate.

The Fed can **stabilize** the exchange rate by using monetary policy to keep the interest rate constant, which would make the LM curve perfectly flat. In that case, monetary policy could not be used for other goals, such as preventing fluctuations in unemployment or prices. With a flat LM curve, fiscal policy becomes more powerful but spending disturbances, such as investment shocks, that shift the IS curve cause large movements in GNP.

The theory of **interest rate parity** proposes that the interest rate differential between dollar bonds and bonds denominated in foreign currency $(R - R_W)$ is equal to the expected rate of depreciation of he dollar. **Covered interest rate parity** predicts that the interest rate differential is equal to the percentage difference between the forward or future and current exchange rate. Covered interest rate parity holds almost exactly, while interest rate parity holds only approximately.

Self-Test

Fill in the Blank

1. Net exports are _____ minus _____ .
2. Exchange rates are _____ when they are determined by market forces.
3. When the United States runs a trade deficit, the amount we borrow from abroad is the _____ .
4. The nominal exchange rate adjusted for changes in purchasing power between the United States an the ROW is the _____.
5. The theory that the real exchange rate is constant is called _____ .
6. The net export function says that net exports depend negatively on _____ and _____ .
7. The coefficient that describes how much imports rise when income rises is the _____ .
8. The difference between United States and ROW interest rates is called the _____ .
9. Interest rate parity suggests that the interest rate differential is equal to the _____ .
10. The reduction in the size of the multiplier because net exports depend negatively on income is called _____ .
11. Protectionist measures include _____ , _____ , and _____ on imports.
12. The Fed can limit exchange-rate fluctuations by using monetary policy to _____ the exchange rate.

13. Appreciation of the dollar occurs when the exchange rate rises.

14. Since the exchange rate is flexible, the United States is powerless to affect it.

15. The theory of purchasing power parity says that the nominal exchange rate is constant.

16. Movements in nominal and real exchange rates are unrelated.

17. When domestic income rises, net exports fall.

18. When the real exchange rate appreciates, net exports fall.

19. The exchange rate and interest rate are negatively correlated.

20. The open-economy LM curve is steeper than the closed-economy LM curve.

21. For an open economy, monetary policy is not neutral in the long run because increases in the money supply depreciate the exchange rate.

22. Changes in the exchange rate have an immediate impact on the U.S. price level.

23. Protectionist measures appreciate the exchange rate.

24. The Fed can stabilize the exchange rate and allow interest rates to fluctuate.

Review Questions

25. Why is the open-economy multiplier smaller than the closed-economy multiplier?

26. Compare the slope of the open- and closed-economy IS curves.

27. What are the short- and long-run effects of a decrease in government spending?

28. What are the short- and long-run effects of a decrease in the money supply?

29. What is the relation between the government budget deficit and capital inflow from abroad?

30. Why does the exchange rate appreciate when the interest rate rises?

31. Briefly describe today's international monetary system.

32. Why do changes in the exchange rate have different impacts on the price level of the U.S. than they do for a small country?

33. Why do protectionist measures help domestic producers but hurt consumers?

34. Why does exchange-rate stabilization increase fluctuations of GNP in response to spending disturbances?

35. Why can't monetary policy be used both to stabilize the exchange rate and to stabilize prices?

36. Explain the difference between interest rate parity and covered interest rate parity.

Problem Set

Worked Problems

1. Consider the following macroeconomic model:

$Y = C + I + G + X$	(Income identity)
$C = 100 + .8YD$	(Consumption)
$I = 300 - 1000R$	(Investment)
$X = 195 - .1Y - 100(EP/P_W)$	(Net exports)
$EP/P_W = .75 + 5R$	(Real exchange rate)
$M = (.8Y - 2000R)P$	(Money demand)

   with government spending G = $200 billion, the tax rate $t = .25$, and the money supply M = $800 billion. The U.S. price level P is predetermined at 1 and ROW price level P_W is always equal to 1.

   a. What are the IS curve, the LM curve, and values of Y, R, and E predicted by this model?

   b. Derive the aggregate demand curve. Calculate the effect of an increase in government spending of $50 billion on Y, R, and E.

   a. *The IS curve is derived by substituting the values for C, I, G, and X into the income identity:*

   $$Y = 1440 - 3000R.$$

   The LM curve is derived by equating money supply and demand:

   $$Y = 1000 + 2500R.$$

   Values for Y and R are found from the IS and LM curves:

   $$Y = \$1200 \text{ billion}, R = .08 \text{ (8 percent).}$$

148

With P = P$_W$ = 1, E = EP/P$_W$ = .75 + 5(.08) = 1.15.

b. *The aggregate demand curve is calculated as in Chapter 5. From the LM curve,*

$$Y = 1.25(M/P) + 2500R.$$

From the condition for spending balance,

$$2500R = 867 - .83Y + 1.67G.$$

Substituting the spending balance condition into the LM curve, we derive the aggregate demand curve:

$$Y = .68(M/P) + 474 + .91G.$$

If G increases by $50 billion to $250 billion,

$$Y = 474 + .68(800) + .91(250) = \$1246 \text{ billion.}$$

The interest rate can be calculated from the LM curve:

$$R = [Y - 1.25(M/P)]/2500$$
$$= [1246 - 1.25(800)/1]/2500 = .098 \ (9.8 \text{ percent}).$$

With P = P$_W$ = 1, E = 1.24.

2. Assume that prices in Problem 1 adjust according to the price-adjustment equation

$$\pi = .5(Y_{-1} - Y^*)Y^*,$$

where π is the rate of inflation and potential output Y^* is equal to $1200 billion. As in Problem 1, increase government spending by $50 billion starting from potential GNP. Calculate the paths of inflation, the price level, output, the interest rate, and the real and nominal exchange rates for 4 years. Describe the economy after prices have fully adjusted.

The technique for calculating π, P, and Y is described in Problem 2 of Chapter 6. Once Y is determined, R can be found from either the IS or LM curve. Knowing R, the real exchange rate can be calculated. The nominal exchange rate E (with P$_W$ = 1) is equal to the real exchange rate divided by P.

Year	π	P	Y	R	EP/P$_W$	E
0	.000	1.00	$1200	.080	1.15	1.15
1	.000	1.00	1246	.098	1.24	1.24
2	.019	1.02	1235	.102	1.26	1.24
3	.015	1.04	1224	.103	1.27	1.23
4	.012	1.04	1224	.105	1.28	1.23

Once prices adjust fully, output will return to its original level. The real interest rate and the real exchange rate will both be higher. The nominal exchange rate will also appreciate, but not as much as the real exchange rate.

3. Consider the following macroeconomic model:

$$Y = C + I + G + X \qquad \text{(Income identity)}$$
$$C = 300 + .75YD \qquad \text{(Consumption)}$$
$$I = 300 - 2000R \qquad \text{(Investment)}$$
$$X = 500 - .2Y - 200(EP/P_W) \qquad \text{(Net exports)}$$
$$EP/P_W = .5 + 5R \qquad \text{(Real exchange rate)}$$
$$M = (.5Y - 2000R)P \qquad \text{(Money demand)}$$

with government spending G = \$200, the tax rate t = .2, and the money supply M = \$550. The U.S. price level P is predetermined at 1 and ROW price level P_W is always equal to 1.

a. What are the IS curve, the LM curve, and values of Y, R, and E predicted by this model?

b. Derive the aggregate demand curve. Calculate the effect of an increase in the money supply of \$100 on Y, R, and E.

4. Assume that prices in Problem 3 adjust according to the price-adjustment equation

$$\pi = (Y_{-1} - Y^*)Y^*,$$

where π is the rate of inflation and potential output Y^* is equal to \$1500. As in Problem 3, increase the money supply by \$100 starting from potential GNP. Calculate the paths of inflation, the price level, output, the interest rate, and the real and nominal exchange rates for 4 years. Describe the economy after prices have fully adjusted.

5. Consider the following macroeconomic model:

$$Y = C + I + G + X \qquad \text{(Income identity)}$$
$$C = 400 + .8YD \qquad \text{(Consumption)}$$
$$I = 400 - 3000R \qquad \text{(Investment)}$$
$$X = 114 - .2Y - 40(EP/P_W) \qquad \text{(Net exports)}$$
$$EP/P_W = .75 + 5R \qquad \text{(Real exchange rate)}$$
$$M = (.4Y - 1000R)P \qquad \text{(Money demand)}$$

with government spending G = \$100, the tax rate t = .5, and the money supply M = \$180. The U.S. price level P is predetermined at 1 and ROW price level P_W is always equal to 1.

a. What are the IS curve, the LM curve, and values of Y, R, and E predicted by this model?

b. Derive the aggregate demand curve and calculate the effect of increases in government spending and the money supply of $20 on Y, R, and E.

6. Assume that prices in Problem 5 adjust according to the price-adjustment equation

$$\pi = (Y_{-1} - Y^*)Y^*,$$

where π is the rate of inflation and potential output Y^* is equal to $750. As in Problem 5, increase the money supply and government spending by $20 starting from potential GNP. Calculate the paths of inflation, the price level, output, the interest rate, and the real and nominal exchange rates for 4 years. Describe the economy after prices have fully adjusted.

MacroSolve Exercises

In this chapter, we continue to use the basic fixed price and sticky price models of the previous chapters, but we add to them the implications of an open economy with a flexible exchange rate. The model is called "AD/PA, Open, Flex E" in MacroSolve. The motivation for the following equations is sketched here, and is explained fully in Chapter 10 of the textbook. First, we add an equation for net exports (Equation 10-2 in the text):

$$X = 500 - .1Y - 100 \, EP/P_w.$$

We assume that the world price level (P_w) is a constant, 1.0, and that the exchange rate satisfied Equation 10-4 in the textbook:

$$EP/P_w = 0.75 + 5R.$$

Together these yield an equation for net exports:

$$X = 425 - .1Y - 500R.$$

1. Graph the ratio of net exports to GNP against the exchange rate using quarterly data. Why would it not be valid to conclude from recent experience that a high exchange rate necessarily leads to low net exports?

2. Compare the size of the government expenditure multiplier in the closed economy ISLM model ("ISLM, Closed Econ") with that in the open economy flexible exchange rate ISLM model ("ISLM, Open,

151

Flex E″). Explain why the open economy multiplier is smaller than the closed economy multiplier.

3. Compare the size of the response of GNP to a monetary expansion in the open and closed economy ISLM models.

   a. Why is the strength of monetary policy hardly affected by the open economy assumption? Discuss exactly what happens to the interest rate and the exchange rate that lead to this result.

   b. Since the change in the money supply leads to a change in the exchange rate, and a change in the exchange rate leads net exports to change, which in turn causes total expenditure to change, why does the IS curve not shift when there is a monetary expansion?

4. Increase the marginal propensity to import. How is the government spending multiplier changed? What is the effect of a money supply increase on GNP and the interest rate? Explain why the changes in the model's behavior occur.

5. The first four years of the Reagan administration (1981 to 1985) were marked by tight monetary policy and expansionary fiscal policy. In addition, the exchange rate was allowed to float. Using the flexible rate ISLM model, analyze the effect of these policies.

   a. Describe what happens to the exchange rate, net exports, and output. How do the output and interest rate changes compare with the same policy experiment in the closed economy case? Explain why the openness of the economy affects the output and interest rate responses.

   b. Repeat the analysis for the comparable dynamic models. (Hint: you may find it helpful to use the **Change Display** option to show the time paths of these variables on the screen.) Why does output regain its equilibrium value slower in the open economy case?

6. a. Select the closed economy dynamic model and increase government spending by $50 billion. Calculate for the first two years of the policy the increase in the budget deficit, the change in investment, and the change in savings. Is the budget deficit primarily financed by a reduction in investment or an increase in savings? Do the same for the final simulation period—is the financing of the deficit generally the same as in the previous periods?

   b. Repeat for the open economy dynamic model with a flexible exchange rate. Calculate the changes in the government deficit, investment, savings, and net exports in the first two periods and the last. Explain why the pattern of financing changes in this model. What variables account for this change?

Answers to the Self-Test

1. Exports minus imports
2. Floating or flexible
3. Capital inflow
4. Real exchange rate
5. Purchasing power parity
6. Real income and the real exchange rate
7. Marginal propensity to import
8. Interest rate differential
9. Expected rate of depreciation
10. Leakage
11. Tariffs, quotas, and bans
12. Stabilize
13. True. When the exchange rate rises, one dollar can buy more foreign currency.
14. False. U.S. monetary and fiscal policies have powerful effects on the exchange rate.
15. False. Purchasing power parity says that the real exchange rate is constant, not that the nominal exchange rate is constant.
16. False. Nominal and real exchange rates move closely together in the short run.
17. True. Higher domestic income increases imports, causing net exports to fall.
18. True. Real exchange rate appreciation increases the relative price of domestic goods, causing net exports to fall.
19. False. They move together, or are positively correlated.
20. False. The closed- and open-economy LM curves are identical.
21. False. It is the real, not the nominal , exchange rate that matters for the neutrality of money. Increases in the money supply do not change the long-run real exchange rate.
22. False. Importers tend to keep the dollar price of their goods stable in the short run.
23. True. Protection shifts the IS curve outward, raising interest rates and appreciating the exchange rate.
24. False. In order to stabilize the exchange rate, the Fed holds interest rates constant.
25. The open-economy multiplier is smaller than the closed-economy multiplier because imports are negatively related to income.
26. We do not know which IS curve is steeper. The open-economy IS curve is steeper because the multiplier is smaller, but it is flatter because net exports depend negatively on the interest rate.

27. In the short run, a decrease in government spending lowers interest rates, depreciates the exchange rate, causes a trade surplus, and lowers output. In the long run, prices fall, output returns to potential , and the real exchange rate and interest rate are lower.

28. In the short run, a decrease in the money supply raises interest rates, appreciates the exchange rate, and lowers output. In the long run, prices fall, output returns to potential, the nominal interest rate appreciates by the amount that prices fall, and the real exchange rate is unchanged.

29. The government budget deficit is partially financed by borrowing abroad, causing a capital inflow.

30. When the interest rate rises, domestic assets become more attractive and the exchange rate appreciates.

31. Today's international monetary system is a floating or flexible exchange-rate system.

32. Exchange-rate changes immediately affect the price level for a small country by changing the price of imports. The U.S. is insulated from these price changes in the short run because importers keep the dollar price of their goods stable.

33. Protectionist measures help domestic producers by reducing foreign competition but hurt consumers by raising prices of imports.

34. The Fed stabilizes the exchange rate by keeping the interest rate constant. This makes the LM curve flat, increasing fluctuations of GNP when spending disturbances shift the IS curve.

35. Both price and exchange rate stabilization require the Fed to set the money supply, and it can only be set at one level at a time.

36. Interest rate parity means that the interest rate differential equals the expected rate of depreciation. Covered interest rate parity means that the interest rate differential equals the difference between the forward and current exchange rate.

Solutions to Review Problems

3. a. The IS curve is $Y = 2000 - 5000R$. The LM curve is $Y = 1100 + 4000R$. $Y = 1500$, $R = .10$, and $E = 1.0$.

   b. The aggregate demand curve is $Y = 1.11(M/P) + 741 + .74G$. If M increases by \$100 to \$650, $Y = \$1611$, $R = .078$, and $E = .89$.

4.

Year	π	P	Y	R	EP/P_W	E
0	.000	1.00	\$1500	.100	1.00	1.00
1	.000	1.00	1611	.078	.89	.89
2	.074	1.07	1563	.087	.94	.88
3	.042	1.11	1536	.091	.97	.86
4	.024	1.14	1524	.096	.98	.86

Once prices fully adjust, output will return to its original level. The nominal exchange rate will depreciate by the same percentage that prices increase. The real interest rate and the real exchange rate will both be unchanged.

5. a. The IS curve is $Y = 1230 - 4000R$. The LM curve is $Y = 450 + 2500R$. $Y = 750$, $R = .12$, and $E = 1.35$.
    b. The aggregate demand curve is $Y = 1.54(M/P) + 425 + .48G$. If M and G increase by 20, $Y = \$791$, $R = .116$, and $E = 1.33$.

6.

Year	π	P	Y	R	EP/P_W	E
0	.000	1.00	$750	.120	1.35	1.35
1	.000	1.00	791	.116	1.33	1.33
2	.054	1.05	775	.120	1.35	1.29
3	.034	1.09	767	.123	1.37	1.26
4	.022	1.11	759	.123	1.37	1.23

Once prices fully adjust, output will return to its original level. The real interest rate and the real exchange rate will both be slightly higher because of the increase in government spending. The nominal exchange rate will depreciate because it is more affected by the increase in the money supply than by the increase in government spending.

Solutions to MacroSolve Exercises

1. There is a predominantly negative relationship. However, it is not possible to say which causes which, since both the exchange rate and net exports respond to changes in exogenous variables.
2. The multiplier is smaller, because the increase in the interest rate causes the exchange rate to appreciate, which reduces net exports and hence attenuates the increase in GNP.
3. a. An increase in the money supply reduces interest rates increasing investment and GNP and reducing net exports, but it also leads to an exchange rate depreciation when the exchange rate is flexible, which attenuates the net export decline. The net effect is that net exports are little changed by the increase in the money supply, so the effect is much the same in both the closed and open economy models.
    b. The slope of the IS curve is changed by the train of events described, but not its position.
4. The government spending multiplier would decrease as more of the increased income would be spent on imported goods which do not increase domestic production, and hence GNP.
5. a. There will be an appreciation of the exchange rate, net exports will likely fall, and output may increase or decrease depending on the relative strengths of monetary and fiscal policy.

The interest rate and output will generally be lower in the open economy case because of the appreciation of the exchange rate and the decline in net exports.

b. The open economy case suffers a larger recession and greater oscillations of GNP about its equilibrium value.

6. a. 62 percent ($23 billion of the $37 billion) of the government deficit is financed by a reduction in investment in the first period. In the long run, 100 percent of the financing comes from a decline in investment.

b. 46 percent of the government deficit is financed by a reduction in investment in the first period, and 80 percent is so financed in the long run. The appreciation of the exchange rate leads to a capital inflow of $10 billion to finance the remainder.

CHAPTER 11 The Government's Budget Deficit and Aggregate Demand

Main Objectives

The record-setting U.S. government budget deficit of the 1980s has focused attention on the government's influence on the economy. We have already glimpsed the government's influence on aggregate demand: it purchases goods and services, it makes transfer payments such as social security and unemployment compensation, and it taxes personal and business income. Until now, we have treated the government as exogenous—not explained by our model. Chapter 11 looks closely at each of these influences, and ties them into the model. You should learn how the government reacts to economic fluctuations and how these reactions influence economic policy. You should also understand the relation between deficits, consumption, and interest rates.

Key Terms and Concepts

The **government budget** is a summary of the government's yearly spending plans. It consists of both **outlays**, purchases of goods and services and transfer payments, and **receipts**, taxes and other revenue. The government budget includes both the federal budget and state and local government budgets.

Automatic stabilizers are government transfer programs that respond to the state of the economy. These include social security, unemployment insurance, food stamps, welfare, and Medicaid. In a recession, with low income and high unemployment, transfer payments from these program automatically increase.

Tax receipts also rise and fall with economic fluctuations. The **elasticity of real tax receipts** with respect to real GNP is 1.86—for every 1 percent change in real GNP tax receipts change by 1.86 percent.

The most important reason the elasticity is greater than 1 is that the income tax system is progressive—tax rates rise and fall with income. **Discretionary** changes in tax rates during recessions, such as the tax cuts of the early 1960s and early 1980s, also contribute to the high elasticity of real tax receipts.

Inflation combined with progressive income taxes automatically causes tax receipts to rise because, as people's nominal incomes increase, they move into higher tax brackets even if their real incomes are unchanged. This problem could be avoided through **indexation** of tax brackets so that they also rise with inflation.

The **budget deficit** is the difference between outlays and receipts. It is equal to government **purchases** plus **transfers** plus **interest on the government debt** minus **taxes**. The **structural** or **full-employment deficit** is the one that would occur, given the current fiscal policies, if the economy were at full employment. The **cyclical deficit** is the difference between the actual deficit and the structural deficit. It measures the impact of the current state of the economy on the deficit.

The relation between the deficit and interest rates was one of the most important issues of the 1984 presidential election. Over the past thirty years, the empirical evidence suggests that the relation of deficits to high real interest rates is weak. The period 1982–84 seems to be an exception, as both real interest rates and budget deficit reached all-time highs.

Government debt at the start of next year equals debt at the start of this year plus this year's deficit (or minus the surplus). This relationship is called the **intertemporal government budget constraint:**

$$D_{t+1} = D_t + G_t + F_t + RD_t - T_t, \tag{11-1}$$

where D is government debt, G is purchases, F is transfers, R is the interest rate (so RD is interest payments on the debt), and T is taxes. The government budget is balanced when the stock of government debt is not growing.

Combining the forward-looking theory of consumption with the intertemporal government budget deficit raises some interesting questions. When the government lowers taxes in order to raise disposable income, it must borrow. Eventually, this borrowing must be paid back through tax increases. If families are rational and very forward looking, they will anticipate these tax increases and not change their consumption.

If consumption does not change, there is no reason for interest rates to change. The proposition that government budget deficits will not affect consumption, and therefore do not affect interest rates, is called **Ricardian Equivalence**, after the nineteenth-century British economist David Ricardo. Even if these tax increases will not occur until the next generation, it has been argued by Robert Barro of Harvard University

158

that consumption will not increase because the family should be viewed as a dynasty in which future generations are as important as the current generation.

Fiscal policy shifts the IS curve directly through government purchases, and indirectly through the effect of taxes and transfers on consumption. The experience of the last 30 years is that government purchases rarely offset fluctuations in aggregate demand, leading to the conclusion that government purchases should be thought of as a disturbance, rather than as an instrument to control aggregate demand. The magnitude of the effect of tax cuts, both because of uncertainty about whether the cut will be permanent or temporary and because of the possibility that people increase saving in anticipation of future tax increases, is highly uncertain.

Government reaction functions are descriptions of the systematic response of fiscal policy to economic fluctuations. They are examples of **policy rules** discussed in Chapter 7. For instance, we have seen that transfer payments rise and fall in relation to the departures of output from potential GNP. An algebraic government reaction function for transfer payments might be

$$F = 350 - .25(Y - Y^*), \tag{11-2}$$

where F is transfer payments, Y is GNP, and Y^* is potential GNP. Transfer payments are automatic stabilizers because, when income rises above potential, transfer payments automatically fall. This reduces the multiplier and makes the IS curve steeper.

Self-Test

Fill in the Blank

1. Federal government purchases of goods and services and transfers are called _____ .

2. Most federal government purchases of goods and services are for

   _____ .

3. The largest single purchase item for state and local governments is

   _____ .

4. Government transfer programs that respond to the state of the economy are _____ .

5. The elasticity of changes in real tax receipts with respect to changes in real GNP is _____ 1.

6. The tax system is _____ when an increase in inflation raises the tax brackets by the same amount.

7. The government budget deficit is the difference between government _____ and _____ .

8. The _____ or _____ deficit is the deficit that would occur if the economy were at potential GNP.

9. The _____ deficit is the difference between the actual deficit and the structural deficit.

10. The relation between the deficit and the accumulation of debt is the_____ .

11. The proposition that government budget deficits do not affect consumption is called _____ .

12. _____ are descriptions of the systematic response of fiscal policy to economic fluctuations.

True-False

13. Most federal government outlays are purchases of goods and services.

14. The federal and state and local governments raise revenue from similar sources.

15. Like the federal government, state and local governments usually run deficits.

16. Programs to increase federal purchases of goods and services have been a major force toward ending recessions.

17. Automatic stabilizers help mitigate recessions.

18. Tax receipts fluctuate more than real GNP.

19. There has been a strong empirical relation between deficits and high real interest rates during the past thirty years.

20. During the past few years, it seems that the relation between deficits and high real interest rates has gotten stronger.

21. The intertemporal budget constraint says that the government budget must be balanced each year.

22. Automatic stabilizers make the IS curve steeper.

23. If tax cuts do not affect consumption, they will not affect interest rates.

24. Ricardian Equivalence is the only explanation for tax cuts not affecting consumption.

Review Questions

25. What are the government transfer programs that constitute automatic stabilizers?

26. If the tax system is not indexed, why does inflation raise tax receipts?

27. Aside from automatic stabilizers, how are taxes lowered during recessions?

28. Why do deficits increase during recessions?

29. What is the difference between structural and cyclical deficits?

30. What is the intertemporal government budget constraint?

31. If families are very forward looking, why might a tax cut not affect consumption at all?

32. How can fiscal policy shift the IS curve?

33. Why are transfer payments automatic stabilizers?

34. How do automatic stabilizers affect the slope of the IS curve?

35. What is Ricardian Equivalence?

36. Why should government purchases be thought of as disturbances to aggregate demand?

Problem Set

Worked Problems

1. Suppose that federal government purchases $G = \$500$ billion, taxes $T = .4Y$, and transfers $F = .2Y$, with the price level $P = 1$. The

federal debt D is $1000 billion with the interest rate $R = .1$ (10 percent).

a. If real output $Y = $2000 billion, what is the deficit?

b. Calculate the structural deficit if potential output $Y^* = $2500 billion.

c. What is the cyclical deficit in Part b?

a. *The deficit* $= G + F + RD - T$
$= G + .2Y + .1(1000) - .4Y$
$= 500 + 400 + 100 - 800$
$= 200 *billion.*

b. *The structural deficit* $= G + .2Y^* + .1(1000) - .4Y^*$
$= 500 + 500 + 100 - 1000$
$= 100 *billion.*

c. *The cyclical deficit* $=$ *Actual deficit - Structural deficit*
$= 200 - 100 = 100 *billion.*

2. Suppose that transfer payments are given by

$$F = 180 - .2(Y - Y^*)$$

with potential output $Y^* = $1600 billion. Add this reaction function to the IS-LM model given by Problem 1 of Chapter 5:

$$
\begin{aligned}
Y &= C + I + G + X & \text{(Income identity)} \\
C &= 100 + .9Y_d & \text{(Consumption)} \\
I &= 200 - 500R & \text{(Investment)} \\
X &= 100 - .12Y - 500R & \text{(Net exports)} \\
M &= (.8Y - 200R)P & \text{(Money demand)}
\end{aligned}
$$

with government spending $G = $200 billion, the tax rate $t = .2$, the nominal money supply $M = $800 billion, and the predetermined-price level $P = 1$.

a. What is the IS curve? Compare it with the IS curve in Problem 1 of Chapter 5.

b. Derive the aggregate demand curve and calculate the effect of increases in government spending or real money on GNP. Compare your answer with Problem 2 of Chapter 5.

a. *As in Chapter 5, the IS curve is derived by substituting consumption, investment, net exports, and government spending into the income identity. It is important to remember that disposable income* $Y_d =$ *income Y + transfers F − taxes T.*

162

$$Y = 100 + .9[Y + 180 - .2(Y - 1600) - .2Y] + 200 - 500R$$
$$+ 200 + 100 - .12Y - 500R$$
$$= 1050 + .42Y - 1000R$$
$$= 1810 - 1724R.$$

It is steeper than the IS curve in Chapter 5 because the multiplier is smaller.

b. *The aggregate demand curve is calculated as in Chapter 5. From the LM curve,*

$$Y = 1.25(M/P) + 2500R.$$

From the condition for spending balance,

$$2500R = 2125 - 1.45Y + 2.5G.$$

Substituting the spending balance condition into the LM curve, we derive the aggregate demand curve,

$$Y = .51(M/P) + 867 + 1.02G.$$

Both monetary and fiscal policies are less effective than in Chapter 5 because the automatic stabilizers decrease the multiplier.

Review Problems

3. Suppose that federal government purchases $G = \$200$, taxes $T = .3Y$, and transfers $F = .1Y$, with the price level $P = 1$. The federal debt D is \$750 with the interest rate $R = .08$ (8 percent).

   a. If real output $Y = \$1000$, what is the deficit?

   b. Calculate the structural deficit if potential output $Y^* = \$1300$.

   c. What is the cyclical deficit in Part b?

4. Suppose that federal government purchases $G = \$400$, taxes $T = .4Y$, and transfers $F = .1Y$, with the price level $P = 1$. The federal debt D is \$1000 with the interest rate $R = .12$ (12 percent).

   a. If real output $Y = \$1500$ billion, what is the deficit?

   b. Calculate the structural deficit if potential output $Y^* = \$2000$.

   c. What is the cyclical deficit in Part b?

5. Suppose that transfer payments are given by

$$F = 2000 - .2(Y - Y^*)$$

with potential output $Y^* = \$1000$. Add this reaction function to the IS-LM model given by Problem 3 of Chapter 5:

$$Y = C + I + G + X \quad \text{(Income identity)}$$
$$C = 300 + .8Y_d \quad \text{(Consumption)}$$
$$I = 200 - 1500R \quad \text{(Investment)}$$
$$X = 100 - .04Y - 500R \quad \text{(Net exports)}$$
$$M = (.5Y - 2000R)P \quad \text{(Money demand)}$$

with government spending $G = \$200$, the tax rate $t = .2$, the nominal money supply $M = \$550$, and the predetermined-price level $P = 1$.

a. What is the IS curve? Compare it with the IS curve in Problem 3 of Chapter 5.

b. Derive the aggregate demand curve and calculate the effect of increases in government spending or real money on GNP. Compare your answer with Problem 4 of Chapter 5.

6. Suppose that transfer payments are given by

$$F = 120 - .1(Y - Y^*)$$

with potential output $Y^* = \$800$. Add this reaction function to the IS-LM model given by Problem 5 of Chapter 5:

$$Y = C + I + G + X \quad \text{(Income identity)}$$
$$C = 400 + .9Y_d \quad \text{(Consumption)}$$
$$I = 300 - 2000R \quad \text{(Investment)}$$
$$X = 100 - .05Y - 1000R \quad \text{(Net exports)}$$
$$M = (.4Y - 1000R)P \quad \text{(Money demand)}$$

with government spending $G = \$100$, the tax rate $t = .5$, the nominal money supply $M = \$180$, and the predetermined-price level $P = 1$.

a. What is the IS curve? Compare it with the IS curve in Problem 5 of Chapter 5.

b. Derive the aggregate demand curve and calculate the effect of increases in government spending or real money on GNP. Compare your answer with Problem 6 of Chapter 5.

7. Suppose that transfer payments are given by

$$F = 300 - .3333(Y - Y^*)$$

with potential output $Y^* = \$2100$. Add this reaction function to the IS-LM model given by Problem 7 of Chapter 5:

$$Y = C + I + G + X \quad \text{(Income identity)}$$
$$C = 400 + .9Y_d \quad \text{(Consumption)}$$
$$I = 200 - 1800R \quad \text{(Investment)}$$
$$X = 200 - .1Y - 200R \quad \text{(Net exports)}$$
$$M = (.8Y - 3000R)P \quad \text{(Money demand)}$$

with government spending $G = \$200$, the tax rate $t = .3333$, the nominal money supply $M = \$1104$, and the predetermined-price level $P = 1$.

a. What is the IS curve? Compare it with the IS curve in Problem 7 of Chapter 5.

b. Derive the aggregate demand curve and calculate the effect of increases in government spending or real money on GNP. Compare your answer with Problem 8 of Chapter 5.

MacroSolve Exercises

1. Plot the government deficit as a percentage of GNP against time using annual data.

    a. Have there been previous periods when the government deficit was as large a fraction of GNP as it is now?

    b. What happened to interest rates in those periods? Were they particularly high (in nominal or real terms)? Do the models that you have studied generally imply that high deficits should be accompanied by high real interest rates? Explain why it might be possible that some of the high deficit periods were not associated with high interest rates.

    c. Graph the real interest rate against the government deficit. On the basis of this, could you agree with the current public sentiment that high deficits cause high interest rates? Why might the statement not make sense, in any case? (Hint, consider what is exogenous and what is endogenous in macroeconomic models.)

2. Plot quarterly values of the unemployment rate and the ratio of the government deficit to GNP. Do the results demonstrate that high government deficits are bad because they cause high unemployment?

3. Plot the quarterly values of the ratios of net exports and the government deficit to GNP for the period 1981.1 to 1983.4. Do you see a positive or negative relationship between the two? (You may also want to graph one series against the other for the same period to help you answer the question.) Does your finding suggest that high government deficits cause high trade deficits? Repeat the analysis for the period 1967.1 to 1980.4. Why do your findings change in this period?

4. Select the "ISLM, Closed Econ" model to answer this question:

   a. Increase government spending by $50 billion. What happens to the interest rate and the government deficit?

   b. Reset the change in government spending to zero. Decrease the money supply by $20 billion. What happens to the interest rate and the government deficit?

   c. Do your answers to parts (a) and (b) imply that "deficits cause high interest rates"? Explain your answer.

5. Select the "AD/PA, Closed Econ" model. Increase government expenditure by $100 billion.

   a. Explain why the government deficit is less than $100 billion in the second period.

   b. Explain why the government deficit tends towards exactly $100 billion in subsequent periods (becoming exactly $100 billion at the end of the simulation period). How is this consistent with your answer to (a), above?

   c. Compute the change in investment and savings to show "how the deficit is financed" in the second and last periods. Explain why the pattern of financing changes between the periods.

Answers to the Self-Test

1. Outlays
2. National defense
3. Education
4. Automatic stabilizers
5. Greater than
6. Indexed
7. Outlays and receipts
8. Structural or full-employment
9. Cyclical
10. Intertemporal budget constraint
11. Ricardian Equivalence
12. Government reaction functions
13. False. Transfer payments exceed government purchases.
14. False. The federal government raises almost all of its revenue from income and social security taxes. About 40 percent of state and local government receipts comes from property and sales taxes.
15. False. State and local governments usually run surpluses.
16. False. Because these spending programs have been small with long lags, they have not significantly contributed toward ending recessions.

17. True. By quickly raising disposable income, automatic stabilizers increase aggregate demand and help mitigate recessions.
18. True. Tax receipts fluctuate more than real income because tax rates rise with income.
19. False. The empirical relation between deficits and real interest rates is weak.
20. True. Both real interest rates and the budget deficit reached all-time highs during the 1982–84 period.
21. False. The intertemporal budget constraint describes the evolution of government debt over time. It does not require that the budget be balanced in any single year.
22. True. Automatic stabilizers lower the marginal propensity to consume, lower the multiplier, and make the IS curve steeper.
23. True. If consumption is unaffected, the IS curve will not shift and interest rates will not change.
24. False. Consumes may not react to tax cuts because of uncertainty regarding whether they are temporary or permanent.
25. Automatic stabilizers are social security, unemployment insurance, food stamps, welfare, and Medicaid.
26. With inflation, people move into higher tax brackets and pay more in taxes even if their real income is unchanged.
27. Discretionary changes in taxes, such as the 1964 and 1981 tax cuts, have lowered taxes during recessions.
28. Government outlays rise during recessions because of automatic stabilizers and receipts fall because of the progressive tax system, causing budget deficits.
29. The structural deficit is the deficit that would occur at potential GNP. The cyclical deficit is the difference between the actual deficit and the structural deficit.
30. The intertemporal budget constraint says that the change in the government debt is equal to the deficit.
31. Very forward-looking families, using the government intertemporal budget constraint, will anticipate future tax increases and not change their consumption.
32. Government purchases shift the IS curve directly and policies on taxes and transfers shift the IS curve through the consumption function.
33. Transfer payments are automatic stabilizers because they fall when income rises above potential.
34. Automatic stabilizers operating through taxes and transfers reduce the marginal propensity to consume, reduce the multiplier, and make the IS curve steeper.
35. Ricardian Equivalence is the proposition that government budget deficits will not affect consumption.
36. Government purchases should be thought of as disturbances to aggregate demand because, historically, they have rarely been timed to offset fluctuations in aggregate demand.

Solutions to Review Problems

3. a. The deficit = 200 + 100 + 60 – 300 = $60.
   b. The structural deficit = 200 + 130 + 60 – 390 = $0.
   c. The cyclical deficit = $60.
4. a. The deficit = $70.
   b. The structural deficit = -$80 (surplus of $80).
   c. The cyclical deficit = $150.
5. a. The IS curve is $Y = 2000 – 3571R$. It is steeper than the IS curve in Chapter 5.
   b. The aggregate demand curve is $Y = .99(M/P) + 911 + .99G$. Both monetary and fiscal policy are less effective than in Chapter 5 because the multiplier is smaller.
6. a. The IS curve is $Y = 1565 – 4348R$. It is steeper than the IS curve in Chapter 5.
   b. The aggregate demand curve is $Y = 1.59(M/P) + 519 + .53G$. Both monetary and fiscal policy are less effective than in Chapter 5 because the multiplier is smaller.
7. a. The IS curve is $Y = 2375 – 2500R$. It is steeper than the IS curve in Chapter 5.
   b. The aggregate demand curve is $Y = .5(M/P) + 1275 + .75G$. Both monetary and fiscal policy are less effective than in Chapter 5 because the multiplier is smaller.

Solutions to MacroSolve Exercises

1. a. The Second World War stands out as a high deficit period; on a number of other occasions (in recessions) the deficit has been as high as now, but generally for a short period.
   b. There is little evidence that high deficits have been associated with high real interest rates. This may be attributable to the stance of monetary policy in those periods—since they were generally recession periods when monetary policy was attempting to stimulate the economy. During the war, monetary policy was particularly expansionary at the same time that fiscal policy was (as you can see from plotting the growth rate of the money supply).
   c. There is little reason to conclude that the two are positively related. Since both are endogenous variables in our model, and are both affected by a variety of exogenous factors, we should not be very surprised by this lack of a relationship.
2. There is a positive relationship between high deficits and high unemployment, but it is unlikely to be for the reason stated in the question. In a recession, when unemployment is high, tax revenues shrink and government expenditures rise (for example, unemployment insurance payouts), so high deficits often coexist with high

168

unemployment. One does not cause the other, however. Both are endogenous variables.

3. After 1981, there was a clear negative relationship between net exports and the government deficit. This is consistent with the belief that high government spending may cause high trade deficits. However, it is by no means clear that such a relationship existed before 1981. While high government spending may sometimes cause the deficit to increase, one should be wary of using the results of one time period to generalize about the behavior of the economy.

4. a. The interest rate is 6.2 percent and the deficit is $37 billion.
   b. The interest rate is 6.1 percent and the deficit is $11 billion.
   c. What has jointly led to the interest rate and deficit outcomes is the behavior of these variables in response to changes in either the money supply or government spending. There is no sense in which either endogenous variable can be said to have caused the other to change.

5. a. The deficit rises by less than $100 billion because the increase in GNP increases tax revenues (by 18.75 percent of the increase in GNP—$27 billion).
   b. The stimulus to GNP is only temporary, however, so tax revenues decline as GNP reverts back to $4000 billion.
   c. In the short run, savings increase as income increases, and finance 36 percent of the deficit. But as GNP returns to equilibrium, so do savings. This leaves only a decline in investment to finance the deficit.

CHAPTER 12   The Monetary System

Main Objectives

In the basic model presented in Chapters 5 and 6, we saw how changes in the money supply and shocks to money demand play a central role in economic fluctuations. Now in Chapter 12 we examine these factors more closely, and focus on the Federal Reserve, a powerful force in macroeconomic policy-making. We look at the selection of policy rules available to the Fed, and see how the Fed's choice among these rules influences the effectiveness of both monetary and fiscal policy. After reading the chapter, you should know what the Fed can and cannot do.

Key Terms and Concepts

The **monetary system** specifies how people pay each other when they conduct transactions (the means of payment) and the meaning of the prices put on goods (the unit of account). Although these are conceptually two separate functions, the dollar performs both in the United States.

The **money supply** consists of **currency**, the government's paper money and coins, plus **deposits** that individuals and firms hold at banks. The **monetary base** is currency plus **reserves** that banks hold at the Fed. The monetary base is also called **high-powered money**.

The Fed changes the money supply through **open-market operations**, purchases or sales of government bonds from the public with money. The money supply is increased by an open-market purchase and decreased by an open-market sale. The Fed directly controls the monetary base. The money supply is also influenced by the **reserve ratio, (r),** the percentage of checking deposits that banks are required to hold on reserve at the Fed, and the **currency deposit ratio, (c),** the amount of currency people hold as a ratio of their checking deposits.

The relation between the monetary base (M_B) and the money supply (M) is given by

$$M = mM_B \qquad (12\text{-}1)$$

where $m = (1 + c)/(r + c)$ is the **monetary base multiplier**. Because the reserve ratio r is less than one, the monetary base multiplier, which measures how much the money supply changes as a result of an open-market operation, is greater than one.

Banks, in their intermediation role, receive deposits from and make loans to the private sector. **Required reserves** are the amount, currently 12 percent, of their deposits that banks have to hold. **Excess reserves** are banks' actual reserves minus required reserves. The Fed can lend reserves to banks, and this lending, by increasing the amount of reserves held by banks, increases the monetary base just as an open-market operation does. The **discount rate** is the interest rate on these borrowings.

The **government budget identity** says that government spending (G) plus transfers (F) plus interest on the government debt (RD) minus taxes (T) equals the change in the monetary base (ΔM_B) plus the change in bonds (ΔB):

$$G + F + RD - T = \Delta M_B + \Delta B . \qquad (12\text{-}2)$$

We can use the government budget identity to be more precise in our definitions of monetary and fiscal policy. Fiscal policy is bond-financed changes in government spending, transfers, and taxes. Suppose government spending is increased. The monetary base and money supply remain unchanged ($\Delta M_B = 0$) while $\Delta G = \Delta B$. Monetary policy is an increase in the monetary base matched by a decrease in government bonds ($\Delta M_B = -\Delta B$). The government budget deficit, $G + F - T$, remains unchanged.

The **Federal Open-Market Committee (FOMC)** makes decisions about monetary policy. It sets target ranges (maximum and minimum growth rates) for the major monetary aggregates twice a year. It also gives specific instructions to the trading desk at the New York Fed about how to conduct week-by-week policy. These instructions usually tell the trading desk to buy and sell government securities to keep the interest rate at values consistent with the monetary targets. However, in late 1979, the Fed changed it procedures and began to tell the trading desk to keep reserves or the monetary base at levels consistent with the monetary targets, allowing interest rates to move as necessary. This procedure ended in mid-1982, when the Fed essentially returned to the operating procedure using interest rates.

The demand for money, as we saw in Chapter 5, depends positively on income and negatively on interest rates. One classification of the demand for money, originated by Keynes, distinguishes among three motives: the **transactions motive**, or the desire to hold money to facilitate day-to-day transactions; the **precautionary motive**, or the desire to hold money in case of unexpected expense; and the **speculative motive**, or the desire to hold money because of an expected decrease in the future price of bonds. **Liquidity preference** summarizes the fact that money, as the most liquid of all assets, can be sold readily if the need arises.

The transactions demand for money can be analyzed by using inventory theory. The **square-root rule** says that the value of average money holdings M that minimizes the total costs of holding money is given by

$$M = \sqrt{kW/2R_0}, \qquad (11\text{-}1)$$

where k is the cost of making each transaction, W is income for the period, and R_0 is the opportunity cost of holding money rather than another asset.

The demand for money as a store of wealth encompasses the precautionary and speculative demands. Money is riskless but pays relatively low interest, while bonds are risky but have a higher expected return. In general, people who are averse to risk hold a diversified portfolio and balance their wealth between money and bonds.

An additional motive for holding checking account balances is to pay for banking services. Service charges on most checking accounts can be eliminated by keeping a high enough balance. When you do this, the return on your wealth is paid in services rather than in cash.

Combing all of the motives for holding money, the **demand for currency** depends negatively on the interest rate and positively on income and the price level. The **demand for checking deposits** depends negatively on the difference between the market interest rate and the rate on checking deposits, and positively on income and the price level.

The **velocity** of money is defined as the ratio of nominal GNP to the money stock. It is a measure of the number of final goods transactions performed by the money stock during the year. Velocity is inversely related to money demand.

We have seen how the Fed, using open-market operations, can change the level of the monetary base. In conducting monetary policy, the Fed must choose among a set of targets:

Target the Money Supply (M_1). The Fed sets the monetary base to keep the money supply at a specified level. This produces the upward-sloping LM curve discussed in Chapter 5. Expansionary fiscal policy, as we have seen earlier, increases income and increases interest rates. If banks held only required reserves and the currency deposit ratio did not depend on the interest rate, so that the monetary base multiplier was

172

constant, the money supply could be targeted exactly. Since the monetary base multiplier is not constant, the money supply can be targeted only approximately.

Target the Interest Rate. The Fed varies the monetary base, by conducting daily open-market operations, to keep the interest rate constant. The LM curve is a horizontal line at the prescribed interest rate. Expansionary fiscal policy raises income without raising interest rates in the short run. There is no crowding out. Monetary policy that keeps interest rates constant when fiscal policy changes is called accommodative.

Target the Level of GNP. The Fed increases or decreases the monetary base to keep GNP constant. The LM curve is a vertical line at the prescribed level of GNP. Expansionary fiscal policy raises the interest rate without changing GNP. There is complete crowding out.

Shocks to the IS and LM curves also influence the Fed's choice among policy rules. Suppose, for example, that investment demand is erratic, causing the IS curve to shift a lot. Then the best policy for the Fed is to keep the LM curve steep. This mitigates the effect on GNP of the fluctuating IS curve. If, on the other hand, erratic money demand causes the LM curve to shift repeatedly, the best policy for the Fed is to keep the LM curve flat. By changing the money supply in response to fluctuating money demand, the effect on GNP can be minimized.

Lags in the effect of monetary policy greatly complicate the Fed's choices among various policies. These lags are the lag in the investment process and the lag in the response of net exports to dollar depreciation. At first, monetary expansion decreases interest rates without much effect on GNP. The peak effect on GNP takes about one to two years, after investment and net exports respond to the lower interest rates.

Coordination of monetary and fiscal policy can bring any desired combination of changes in GNP and the interest rate in the short run. For example, expansionary monetary and fiscal policy can raise GNP and keep the interest rate constant, while expansionary fiscal and contractionary monetary policy could raise the interest rate and keep GNP constant. The choice of the proper mix of monetary and fiscal policy is also influenced by concern about the international value of the dollar and the current account.

Self-Test

Fill in the Blank

1. A monetary system specifies the _____ and the

   _____.

2. Banks accept deposits and make loans in their _____ role.

3. The amount of reserves that banks hold above their required reserves is called _____ reserves.

4. The interest rate on borrowing by banks from the Fed is the _____ rate.

5. The desired maximum and minimum growth rates for the monetary aggregates over the upcoming year are called _____.

6. According to Keynes, the three motives in people's demands for money are the _____ , _____ and _____ motives.

7. A financial asset, such as money, is _____ if it can be sold readily.

8. The ration of nominal GNP to the money stock is called _____.

9. The money supply is equal to the monetary base times the _____.

10. A monetary policy that keeps interest rates constant when fiscal policy changes is said to _____ the new policy.

11. The monetary base is _____ plus _____.

12. The monetary base is also called _____.

True-False

13. Required reserves account for most banks' holding of reserves.

14. Money is the most liquid of all assets.

15. The opportunity cost of holding currency is the market interest rate.

16. The opportunity cost of holding checking deposits is the market interest rate.

17. If the Fed targets the interest rate, the LM curve will be horizontal.

18. If the Fed targets GNP, the LM curve will be horizontal.

19. If the Fed targets the interest rate, fiscal policy will be very effective.

20. If the Fed targets the interest rate, shocks to investment will produce large fluctuations in GNP.

21. The peak effect of monetary policy on GNP occurs very quickly.

22. In the short run, GNP cannot be increased without changing the interest rate.

23. The monetary base multiplier is constant.

24. The velocity of money is constant.

Review Questions

25. According to the square-root rule, what are the determinants of people's average money balances?

26. Why, according to Keynes's speculative motive, does the demand for money decrease with the interest rate?

27. What determines the demand for currency?

28. What determines the demand for checking deposits?

29. Describe the three policy rules available to the Fed.

30. If the Fed wishes to target a monetary aggregate such as M_1, describe the two operating procedures it can use to attain its target.

31. How does the policy rule adopted by the Fed influence the effectiveness of fiscal policy?

32. If the Fed wishes to minimize the effects of shocks on GNP, what policy rule should it follow?

33. What are the two lags in the effect of monetary policy?

34. Why does concern about the international value of the dollar make decisions regarding the fiscal and monetary policy mix more difficult?

35. What is the government budget identity?

36. How do monetary and fiscal policy differ in their effects on the monetary base?

Problem Set

1. a. According to the square-root rule, what is the average money balance M if income $W = \$1000$ billion, the cost of making a transaction $k = 4$, and the opportunity cost of holding money $R_o = .05$ (5 percent)?

   b. What happens to the average money balance M if income increases to $2000 billion?

   a. *The square-root rule says that the average money balance*

   $$M = \sqrt{kW/2R_o}$$

   $$= \sqrt{4(1000)/2(.05)}$$

   $$= \sqrt{40{,}000}$$

   $$= \$200 \text{ billion.}$$

   b. *The average money balance*

   $$= \sqrt{4(2000)/2(.05)}$$

   $$= \sqrt{80{,}000}$$

   $$= \$283 \text{ billion.}$$

   The average money balance is higher because the demand for money increases when income rises.

2. Suppose that the money supply is given by

$$M = 800 - .2(Y - Y^*)$$

with potential output $Y^* = \$1250$ billion. Add this monetary policy rule to the equations in Problem 1 of Chapter 5:

$$
\begin{aligned}
Y &= C + I + G + X && \text{(Income identity)} \\
C &= 100 + .9Y_d && \text{(Consumption)} \\
I &= 200 - 500R && \text{(Investment)} \\
X &= 100 - .12Y - 500R && \text{(Net exports)} \\
M &= (.8Y - 2000R)P && \text{(Money demand)}
\end{aligned}
$$

with government spending $G = \$200$ billion, the tax rate $t = .2$, and the predetermined-price level $P = 1$.

   a. What is the LM curve? Compare it with the LM curve in Problem 1 of Chapter 5.

b. Derive the aggregate demand curve and calculate the effect of an increase in government spending on GNP. Compare your answer with Problem 2 of Chapter 5.

a. *The LM curve is derived by equating the supply of money with the demand for money:*

$$800 - .2(Y - 1250) = .8Y - 2000R$$
$$Y = 1050 + 2000R.$$

It is steeper than the LM curve of Chapter 5 because of the Fed's "leaning against the wind" policy of decreasing the money supply when output rises above potential.

b. *The LM curve is*

$$Y = 1050 + 2000R.$$

From the condition for spending balance,

$$2000R = 800 - .8Y + 2G$$

Substituting the spending balance condition into the LM curve, we derive the aggregate demand curve:

$$Y = 1028 + 1.11G.$$

An increase in government spending has less effect on GNP than in Chapter 5 because the LM curve is steeper.

Review Problems

3. a. According to the square-root rule, what is the average money balance M if income $W = \$6000$, the cost of making a transaction $k = 3$, and the opportunity cost of holding money $R_o = .1$ (10 percent)?

   b. What happens to the average money balance M if the opportunity cost of holding money R_o increases to .15?

4. a. According to the square-root rule, what is the average money balance M if income $W = \$2000$, the cost of making a transaction $k = 5$, and the opportunity cost of holding money $R_o = .08$ (8 percent)?

   b. What happens to the average money balance M if the cost of making a transaction k rises to 6?

5. Suppose that the money supply is given by

$$M = 550 - .3(Y - Y^*)$$

with potential output $Y^* = \$1500$. Add this monetary policy rule to the equations in Problem 3 of Chapter 5:

$$
\begin{aligned}
Y &= C + I + G + X && \text{(Income identity)} \\
C &= 300 + .8Y_d && \text{(Consumption)} \\
I &= 200 - 1500R && \text{(Investment)} \\
X &= 100 - .04Y - 500R && \text{(Net exports)} \\
M &= (.5Y - 2000R)P && \text{(Money demand)}
\end{aligned}
$$

with government spending $G = \$200$, the tax rate $t = .2$, and the predetermined-price level $P = 1$.

a. What is the LM curve? Compare it with the LM curve in Problem 3 of Chapter 5.

b. Derive the aggregate demand curve and calculate the effect of an increase in government spending on GNP. Compare your answer with Problem 4 of Chapter 5.

6. Suppose that the money supply is given by

$$M = 180 - .6(Y - Y^*)$$

with potential output $Y^* = \$800$. Add this monetary policy rule to the equations in Problem 5 of Chapter 5:

$$
\begin{aligned}
Y &= C + I + G + X && \text{(Income identity)} \\
C &= 400 + .9Y_d && \text{(Consumption)} \\
I &= 300 - 2000R && \text{(Investment)} \\
X &= 100 - .05Y - 1000R && \text{(Net exports)} \\
M &= (.4Y - 1000R)P && \text{(Money demand)}
\end{aligned}
$$

with government spending $G = \$100$, the tax rate $t = .5$, and the predetermined-price level $P = 1$.

a. What is the LM curve? Compare it with the LM curve in Problem 5 of Chapter 5.

b. Derive the aggregate demand curve and calculate the effect of an increase in government spending on GNP. Compare your answer with Problem 6 of Chapter 5.

7. Suppose that the money supply is given by

$$M = 1104 - .2(Y - Y^*)$$

with potential output $Y^* = \$1680$. Add this monetary policy rule to the equations in Problem 7 of Chapter 5:

$$Y = C + I + G + X \qquad \text{(Income identity)}$$
$$C = 400 + .9Y_d \qquad \text{(Consumption)}$$
$$I = 200 - 1800R \qquad \text{(Investment)}$$
$$X = 200 - .1Y - 200R \qquad \text{(Net exports)}$$
$$M = (.8Y - 3000R)P \qquad \text{(Money demand)}$$

with government spending $G = \$200$, the tax rate $t = .3333$, and the predetermined-price level $P = 1$.

a. What is the LM curve? Compare it with the LM curve in Problem 7 of Chapter 5.

b. Derive the aggregate demand curve and calculate the effect of an increase in government spending on GNP. Compare your answer with Problem 8 of Chapter 5.

MacroSolve Exercises

1. Plot the behavior of the velocity of M1 using quarterly data. Is velocity procyclical or countercyclical? Why do you think this is? Do you find the same result using annual data?

2. Graph velocity against the short-term interest rate using quarterly data. What relation do you see between them?

   a. Is this relationship consistent with the money demand theory that you have learned?

   b. Do you see the same relationship in the annual data?

   c. Will this type of velocity movement make the effects of monetary policy on GNP greater or smaller than they would be if velocity were constant? Explain why.

   d. Will this type of velocity movement make the effects of fiscal policy on GNP greater or smaller than they would be if velocity were constant? Explain why.

3. Use the "ISLM, Closed Econ" model to show whether an increase in government spending causes a larger or smaller increase in GNP when the money supply is manipulated to keep interest rates constant than when the money supply is fixed.

4. If the income elasticity of money demand increases, does the LM curve become flatter or steeper? Is the government spending multiplier larger or smaller? (Hint: find out how large the multiplier is in the basic "ISLM, Closed Econ" model, then use the

Change Params option to increase the income elasticity of money demand.)

5. If the interest elasticity of money demand increases, is the government spending multiplier larger or smaller? Explain in words why your answer to the last question is different from your answer to this question.

Answers to the Self-Test

1. Means of payment and unit of account
2. Intermediation
3. Excess
4. Discount
5. Target ranges
6. Transactions, precautionary, and speculative
7. Liquid
8. Velocity
9. Monetary base multiplier
10. Accommodate
11. Currency plus reserves
12. High-powered money
13. True. Excess reserves are small.
14. True. It can be sold most readily.
15. True. The market interest rate is the foregone return on currency.
16. False. The opportunity cost of holding checking deposits is the market interest rate minus the interest rate paid on checking deposits minus the avoided service charges.
17. True. A constant interest rate is a horizontal LM curve.
18. False. If the Fed targets GNP, the LM curve will be vertical.
19. True. There would be no crowding out.
20. True. Because the LM curve would be horizontal, shocks to investment would produce large fluctuations in GNP.
21. False. The peak effect of monetary policy on GNP occurs between one and two years.
22. False. Coordinated expansionary fiscal and monetary policy can increase GNP in the short run without changing the interest rate.
23. False. The monetary base multiplier depends on the reserve ratio and the currency deposit ratio, neither of which are constant.
24. False. Velocity changes when the demand for money changes.
25. The average money balance depends positively on income and the cost of making transactions, and negatively on the opportunity cost of holding money.
26. When interest rates were high people would expect them to fall and bond prices to rise in the future, and would therefore want to hold more bonds and less money.

27. The demand for currency depends negatively on the interest rate and positively on income and the price level.
28. The demand for checking deposits depends negatively on the difference between the market interest rate and the rate on checking deposits, and positively on income and the price level.
29. The Fed can target the level of the money supply, interest rate, or GNP.
30. The Fed can buy and sell government bonds to keep either the interest rate or the monetary base at levels consistent with the monetary targets.
31. The policy rule adopted by the Fed determines the slope of the LM curve, which influences the effectiveness of fiscal policy.
32. If the IS curve is erratic, say, because of shifts in investment demand, the Fed should maintain a steep LM curve. If the LM curve is erratic, say, because of shifts in money demand, the Fed should maintain a flat LM curve.
33. The two lags in the effect of monetary policy are the response of investment to changes in the interest rate and the response of net exports to changes in the exchange rate.
34. In a closed economy, the government can use two instruments, fiscal and monetary policy, to attain two goals, the level of GNP and the interest rate. Concern about the exchange rate adds another goal without adding another instrument, making it likely that all three goals cannot be attained.
35. The government budget identity is that government spending plus transfers plus interest on the government debt minus taxes equals the change in the monetary base plus the change in bonds.
36. Monetary policy increases the monetary base, while fiscal policy leaves it unchanged.

Solutions to Review Problems

3. a. The average money balance $M = \$300$.
    b. $M = \$245$. The demand for money falls when the opportunity cost of holding money rises.
4. a. The average money balance $M = \$250$.
    b. $M = \$274$. The demand for money falls when the cost of making a transaction rises.
5. a. The LM curve is $Y = 1250 + 2500R$. It is steeper than the LM curve in Chapter 5.
    b. The aggregate demand curve is $Y = 1333 + .83G$. Because the LM curve is steeper, increases in government spending have less effect on GNP than in Chapter 5.
6. a. The LM curve is $Y = 660 + 1000R$. It is steeper than the LM curve in Chapter 5.
    b. The aggregate demand curve is $Y = 733 + .28G$. Because the LM curve is steeper, increases in government spending have less effect on GNP than in Chapter 5.

7. a. The LM curve is $Y = 1440 + 3000R$. It is steeper than the LM curve in Chapter 5.
    b. The aggregate demand curve is $Y = 1509 + .86G$. Because the LM curve is steeper, increases in government spending have less effect on GNP than in Chapter 5.

Solutions to MacroSolve Exercises.

1. It is not obvious that velocity is either pro- or countercyclical.
2. a. Two things are clear. First, velocity has increased over time; and second, it increases as interest rates increase. The latter is consistent with increased interest rates decreasing the quantity of money demanded and hence increasing the ratio of nominal income to money (i.e., increasing velocity).
    b. The relationship is even more pronounced in annual data.
    c. If velocity increases as interest rates rise, then monetary policy will have smaller effects than if velocity were constant. You can check this by comparing the response of output to a change in the money supply in the ISLM model section of MacroSolve when the interest elasticity of money demand is increased and decreased.
    d. If velocity increases as interest rates increase, then fiscal policy will have larger effects on output than if velocity were constant.
3. The government spending multiplier is larger when the interest rate is kept constant, because the increase in government spending does not lead to any crowding out of investment expenditures when the interest rate does not rise.
4. If the income elasticity of money demand increases (the quantity of money demanded responds more to changes in income), the LM curve will be steeper, so the multiplier will be smaller.
5. If the interest elasticity of money demand increases (the quantity of money demanded responds more to changes in interest rates), the spending multiplier will be larger. As income rises following an increase in government spending, the quantity of money demanded increases. If money demand is more interest elastic, a smaller increase in interest rates will keep the quantity of money demanded equal to its fixed supply than would be the case for less elastic money demand.

    In the previous question, a higher income elasticity of money demand causes the quantity of money demanded to increase more when GNP rises, hence requiring a larger increase in interest rates to clear the money market. This increase in interest rates reduces investment, making the spending multiplier smaller.

PART III

The Micro Foundations of Aggregate Supply and Price Adjustment

CHAPTER 13   Aggregate Supply and Economic Growth

Main Objectives

We have seen how models with sticky prices can explain economic fluctuations and have analyzed the effects of monetary and fiscal policy in both the short and long run. However, we have not yet examined the growth process underlying the fluctuations. Chapter 13 focuses on the problems of long-term growth of potential output. It simplifies away the short-run fluctuations by looking at an economy that is always in full employment because prices and wages are perfectly flexible. The lesson here is that monetary policy determines the price level and the inflation rate, while fiscal policy determines the division of output between consumption, investment, government purchases, and net exports.

Key Terms and Concepts

The **classical model** is the name given to macroeconomic models that assume flexible prices and wages, first proposed in the nineteenth century. In the classical model, the economy is always at full employment because wages and prices can adjust instantaneously to offset the effect of disturbances.

The **aggregate supply** of productive factors—labor and capital—determines total output in the full-employment economy. Aggregate supply can be described by a production function that relates total output to total labor and capital inputs:

$$Y = F(N, K), \tag{13-1}$$

where Y is output, N is employment, and K is the stock of capital.

The stock of capital, as we saw in Chapter 9, is predetermined by past investment and savings decisions. The **marginal product of labor,** the additional output that is produced by one additional unit of work, declines as the amount of employment increases. Firms choose the level of employment so that the marginal product of labor equals the real wage. The **demand for labor** is a negative function of the real wage because the marginal product of labor declines with increased labor input.

The **supply of labor** depends on the real wage in two contrasting ways. The **substitution effect** is that, at higher real wages, the incentive to work is stronger and people will want to work more. This increases the labor supply. The **income effect** is that higher real wages, by increasing people's income, make them better off. People who are better off choose to spend more time at home and less time in the labor market, which increases the labor supply. Research indicates that these two effects offset each other. The net effect of the real wage on labor supply is approximately zero.

Employment is determined in the labor market at the intersection of the supply and demand schedules, as shown in Figure 13-1. Because the capital stock is predetermined by past investment decisions, the level of output in any one year, as calculated from the production function, is determined solely by the labor market.

The **natural rate of unemployment** is the amount of unemployment when the labor market is in equilibrium. The natural rate is positive

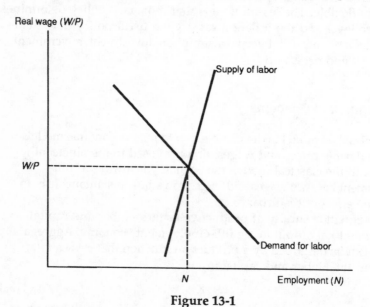

Figure 13-1

for three reasons. Frictional unemployment occurs when people leave one job to look for another, finish school and look for employment, or look for a job after having been out of the labor force. Another reason is that there may be unemployment in some sectors even when the economy as a whole is at full employment. A third reason is that some disadvantaged groups—young people, members of racial minorities, and the unskilled—spend a large fraction of each year out of work. Economists differ on numerical estimates of the natural rate, but 6 percent seems to be a good approximation.

Potential output grows rather steadily from year to year. We can model the sources of growth of potential output using the following production function:

$$Y_t = A_t F(N_t, K_t),$$ (13-2)

where A_t is a measure of total factor productivity. A modification of this production function says that the rate of growth of output equals the rate of growth of productivity plus the weighted rates of growth of labor and capital:

$$\Delta Y/Y = \Delta A/A + .7\Delta N/N + .3\Delta K/K,$$ (13-3)

where .7 is the share of labor and .3 is the share of capital in national income..

Policies to stimulate growth can be directed toward productivity, capital formation, or labor input. Policies to increase productivity include tax incentives, such as those passed in 1981 to encourage research and development. Since the process of productivity growth is not well understood by economists, it is hard to evaluate these policies. Investment tax credits give firms tax breaks for investment. They are an example of policies to stimulate capital formation. The investment tax credit appears to increase output growth for a few years, after which investment declines to more normal levels. The Tax Reform Act of 1986 repealed the investment tax credit, which is expected to reduce capital formation.

Policies to increase labor supply have focused on tax cuts and tax reform. Tax cuts, such as President Reagan's 1981 tax cut, have both substitution and income effects. If, as the evidence suggests, the labor supply schedule is steep, the effect on labor supply of tax cuts will be quite small. Tax reforms that are revenue neutral, such as the Tax Reform Act of 1986, do not have income effects. The labor supply schedule should shift by the full amount of the substitution effect, and the impact on the growth of output is potentially quite substantial.

It is possible, although far from certain, that the Tax Reform Act of 1986 will raise economic growth. This will occur if the stimulus to growth through increased labor supply is greater than the decrement to growth through lower capital formation.

Monetary and fiscal policy in a full-employment economy can be
analyzed using the IS-LM model of Chapter 5, but with perfectly
flexible instead of sticky prices. With perfectly flexible prices, the
long-run results of Chapter 6 apply to the short run. Output is
determined by aggregate supply. The price level, the interest rate, the
exchange rate, and the allocation of output between consumption,
investment, government spending, and net exports is determined by
aggregate demand.

Expansionary fiscal policy, as illustrated in Figure 13-2, shifts the
IS curve to the right, increasing the price level and the interest rate.
The rise in prices shifts the LM curve to the left, returning the economy
to potential GNP. Unless the policy change alters incentives in such a
way as to change potential GNP, output is unaffected: an increase in
government purchases decreases consumption, investment, and net
exports because interest rates rise; and tax cuts raise consumption and
lower investment and net exports.

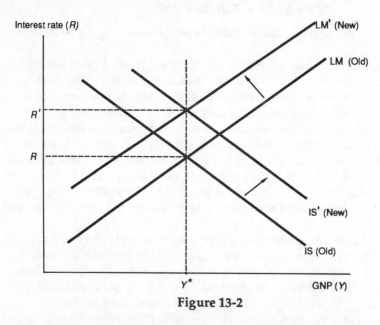

Figure 13-2

Expansionary monetary policy, as illustrated in Figure 13-3, shifts
the LM curve to the right, raising the price level and lowering the
interest rate. The rise in prices shifts the LM curve back to the left,
returning the interest rate to its original level at a higher price level.
Expansionary monetary policy—an increase in the money supply—
increases the price level. All other variables remain unchanged. This
property is called **monetary neutrality**.

188

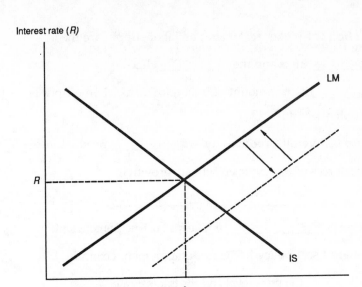

Figure 13-3

Superneutrality of money is the property of the classical model that all real variables are unaffected by changes in the rate of growth of the money supply. There are several reasons why superneutrality may not hold in the real world—even in the long run: the tax system may not be superneutral, higher inflation makes holding real capital more attractive, fluctuations in inflation could lead to inefficiencies in the production process, and inflation creates inefficiencies in the monetary system by making currency and reserves more costly.

Self-Test

Fill in the Blank

1. Macroeconomic models that assume flexible prices and wages are called _____ .

2. The _____ of productive factors determines total output in the full-employment economy.

3. The _____ relates total output to total labor and capital inputs.

4. The additional output that is produced by one additional unit of work is the _____

189

5. The two effects of higher real wages on labor supply are the

   _____ effect and the _____ effect.

6. The _____ is the amount of unemployment when output is
   equal to potential GNP.

7. A measure of overall productivity is _____ productivity.

8. The three sources of economic growth are growth in

   _____ , _____ , and _____ .

9. A tax reform is _____ if it keeps tax receipts constant.

10. Expansionary fiscal policy in the full-employment economy

    _____ the price level and the interest rate.

11. The property of the classical model that a change in the level of
    the money supply leaves all real variables unaffected is called

    _____ .

12. The property of the classical model that a change in the rate of
    growth of the money supply leaves all real variables unaffected is
    called _____ .

True-False

13. An economy in which wages and prices are perfectly flexible is
    always exactly at full employment.

14. Higher real wages unambiguously increase the supply of labor.

15. With perfectly flexible prices and wages, the level of output in any
    one year is determined solely by the labor market.

16. Unemployment is zero when the labor market is in equilibrium.

17. The natural rate of unemployment is constant.

18. Tax cuts unambiguously increase the supply of labor.

19. The Tax Reform Act of 1986 increased capital formation.

20. The Tax Reform Act of 1986 increased labor supply.

21. Monetary policy is neutral in the classical model.

22. Fiscal policy is neutral in the classical model.

23. Fiscal policy has no effect on output in the classical model.

24. Increases in the rate of growth of the money supply leave output unaffected in the classical model.

25. What determines output in the full-employment economy?

26. Why is the demand for labor a negative function of the real wage?

27. Describe the empirical evidence regarding the effect of the real wage on labor supply.

28. Why is the natural rate of unemployment not equal to zero?

29. What types of policies can the government use to stimulate economic growth?

30. Why can a tax cut and a tax reform have different effects on labor supply?

31. How has the Tax Reform Act of 1986 affected economic growth?

32. What are the effects of an increase in the level of the money supply in the classical model?

33. What are the demand-side effects of expansionary fiscal policy in the classical model?

34. Under what circumstances do tax cuts increase potential output?

35. State the reasons why superneutrality of money may not hold in the real world.

36. How do the long-run effects of monetary and fiscal policy with sticky prices compare to the short-run effects of the same policies with perfectly flexible prices?

Problem Set

Worked Problems

1. a. Suppose that the growth rate of total factor productivity is 5 percent, the growth rate of employment is 8 percent, and the growth rate of capital is 4 percent. What is the growth rate of real output?

b. If the growth rate of productivity increases by 2 percentage points, what happens to the growth rate of real output?

a. *According to Equation 13-3, the growth rate of real output equals the growth rate of productivity plus the weighted growth rates of labor and capital:*

$$\Delta Y/Y = .05 + .7(.08) + .3(.04)$$
$$= .118(11.8 \text{ percent}).$$

b. *The growth rate of real output will also increase by 2 percentage points to 13.8 percent.*

2. Consider the following flexible-price IS-LM model:

$Y = Y^*$		(Aggregate supply)
$Y = C + I + G + X$		(Income identity)
$C = 100 + .9Y_d$		(Consumption)
$I = 200 - 500R$		(Investment)
$X = 100 - .12Y - 500R$		(Net exports)
$M = (.8Y - 2000R)P$		(Money demand)

with potential output $Y^* = \$1250$ billion, government spending $G = \$200$ billion, the tax rate $t = .2$, and the nominal money supply $M = \$800$ billion.

a. What is the interest rate R?

b. What is the price level P?

c. If government spending G increases to $300 billion, what happens to the interest rate and to the price level?

a. *With output always equal to potential GNP, we solve for the interest rate by using the same technique that we used to find the IS curve in Chapter 5.*

$$Y^* = C + I + G + X$$
$$1250 = 100 + .9[1250 - .2(1250)] +$$
$$200 - 500R + 200 + 100 - .12(1250) - 500R$$
$$1250 = 1350 - 1000R$$
$$R = .1(10 \text{ percent})$$

b. *The price level is determined by substituting the interest rate into the LM curve.*

$$M = (.8Y^* - 2000R)P$$
$$800 = [.8(1250) - 2000(.1)]P$$
$$800 = 800P$$
$$P = 1.$$

c. The interest rate is determined as in Part a.

$$1250 = 100 + .8[1250 - .25(1250)] + 300 - 1000R + 300$$
$$R = .2(20 \ percent).$$

The price level is determined as in Part b.

$$800 = [.8(1250) - 2000(.2)]/P$$
$$P = 1.33.$$

The increase in government spending raises both the interest rate and the price level.

Review Problems

3. a. Suppose that the growth rate of total factor productivity is 5 percent, the growth rate of employment is 4 percent, and the growth rate of capital is 3 percent. What is the growth rate of real output?

    b. If the growth rate of employment increases by 2 percentage points, what happens to the growth rate of real output?

4. a. Suppose that the growth rate of total factor productivity is 3 percent, the growth rate of employment is 6 percent, and the growth rate of capital is 6 percent. What is the growth rate of real output?

    b. If the growth rate of capital increases by 3 percentage points, what happens to the growth rate of real output?

5. Consider the following flexible-price IS-LM model:

$Y = Y^*$	(Aggregate supply)
$Y = C + I + G + X$	(Income identity)
$C = 300 + .8Y_d$	(Consumption)
$I = 200 - 1500R$	(Investment)
$X = 100 - .04Y - 500R$	(Net exports)
$M = (.5Y - 2000R)P$	(Money demand)

    with potential output $Y^* = \$1750$, government spending $G = \$200$, the tax rate $t = .2$, and the nominal money supply $M = \$550$.

    a. What is the interest rate R?

    b. What is the price level P?

    c. If government spending G increases to $300, what happens to the interest rate and to the price level?

193

6. Consider the following flexible-price IS-LM model:

$$Y = Y^*$$ (Aggregate supply)
$$Y = C + I + G + X$$ (Income identity)
$$C = 400 + .9Y_d$$ (Consumption)
$$I = 300 - 2000R$$ (Investment)
$$X = 100 - .05Y - 1000R$$ (Net exports)
$$M = (.4Y - 1000R)P$$ (Money demand)

with potential output $Y^* = \$1000$, government spending $G = \$100$, the tax rate $t = .5$, and the nominal money supply $M = \$180$.

a. What is the interest rate R?

b. What is the price level P?

c. If the nominal money supply M increases by 50 percent to $270, what happens to the interest rate and to the price level?

7. Consider the following flexible-price IS-LM model:

$$Y = Y^*$$ (Aggregate supply)
$$Y = C + I + G + X$$ (Income identity)
$$C = 470 + .9Y_d$$ (Consumption)
$$I = 600 - 3000R$$ (Investment)
$$X = 400 - .09Y - 1000R$$ (Net exports)
$$M = (.8Y - 7000R)P$$ (Money demand)

with potential output $Y^* = \$5000$, government spending $G = \$700$, the tax rate $t = .2$, and the money supply $M = \$2580$.

a. What is the interest rate R?

b. What is the price level P?

c. If government spending G falls to $620, what happens to the interest rate and to the price level?

d. If, in addition, the money supply M falls by 1/3 to $1720, what happens to R and P?

Answers to the Self-Test

1. Classical
2. Aggregate supply
3. Production function
4. Marginal product of labor
5. Substitution and income
6. Natural rate of unemployment
7. Total factor

8. Labor, capital, and productivity
9. Revenue-neutral
10. Raises
11. Monetary neutrality
12. Superneutrality of money
13. True. Wages and prices can adjust instantaneously to offset the effect of disturbances.
14. False. The supply of labor increases because of the substitution effect but decreases because of the income effect.
15. True. With the stock of capital predetermined, the level of output in any one year depends only on employment, which is determined in the labor market.
16. False. It is equal to the natural rate.
17. False. It has increased slowly since the 1950s.
18. False. Tax cuts have both substitution and income effects.
19. False. The Tax Reform Act of 1986 eliminated the investment tax credit, lowering capital formation.
20. True. The Tax Reform Act of 1986 lowered marginal tax rates and was revenue neutral, which should increase labor supply.
21. True. An increase in the money supply affects only the price level.
22. False. Even if fiscal policy does not affect output, it changes the composition of output between consumption, investment, government purchases, and net exports.
23. False. While the demand-side effects of fiscal policy do not affect output, changes in fiscal policy can alter incentives so as to change potential GNP.
24. True. This is superneutrality of money.
25. Output in the full-employment economy is determined by aggregate supply of productive factors, as described by the production function.
26. The demand for labor is a negative function of the real wage because the marginal product of labor declines with increased labor input.
27. Research indicates that the substitution and income effects offset each other, making the net effect approximately zero.
28. The natural rate is positive because of frictional unemployment, sector-specific unemployment, and high unemployment among disadvantaged groups.
29, The government can use policies designed to increase productivity, capital formation, or labor input.
30. A tax cut has both substitution and income effects, while a revenue-neutral tax reform has only substitution effects.
31. The Tax Reform Act of 1986 has had an ambiguous affect on economic growth because, while labor supply has increased, capital formation has decreased.
32. An increase in the level of the money supply increases the price level while leaving all other variables unchanged.
33. Expansionary fiscal policy leaves real output unchanged while altering its composition. Increases in government purchases decrease consumption, investment, and net exports, while tax cuts increase consumption at the expense of investment and net exports.

34. If substitution effects were larger than income effects, tax cuts would increase labor supply and potential output.
35. The tax system may not be superneutral, higher inflation makes holding real capital more attractive, fluctuations in inflation could lead to inefficiencies in the production process, and inflation creates inefficiencies in the monetary system by making holding currency and reserves more costly.
36. The long-run effects with sticky prices are identical to the short-run effects with perfectly flexible prices.

Solutions to Review Problems

3. a. The growth rate of real output $\Delta Y/Y = 8.7$ percent.
   b. $\Delta Y/Y$ increases to 10.1 percent.
4. a. $\Delta Y/Y = 9$ percent.
   b. $\Delta Y/Y$ increases to 9.9 percent.
5. a. The interest rate $R = .05$.
   b. The price level $P = .71$.
   c. If government spending increases to $300, R increases to .1 and P rises to .81.
6. a. The interest rate $R = 1$.
   b. The price level $P = .6$.
   c. If the nominal money supply increases by 50 percent to $270, the interest rate is unchanged and the price level rises by 50 percent to .9.
7. a. The interest rate $R = .08$.
   b. The price level $P = .75$.
   c. If government spending falls to $620, R falls to .06 and P falls to .72.
   d. If, in addition, the money supply falls to $1720, R is unchanged and P falls to .48.

CHAPTER 14　　New Classical Theory

Main Objectives

The classical model with flexible prices and wages presented in Chapter 13 appears to provide a good description of how the economy works in the long run. But it cannot explain short-run fluctuations of output from potential GNP. Chapters 14 and 15 take up two rival explanations of the short-run departures: new classical theory and the theory of wage and price rigidities. In Chapter 14, you should learn how the new classical theories maintain the flexible wage-price assumption of the classical model but incorporate information problems to explain short-run fluctuations.

Key Terms and Concepts

The classical model of Chapter 13 can explain fluctuations in output only through fluctuations in potential GNP. Since potential output in any one year is determined solely by employment, it can change only if the demand for labor or supply of labor shifts. Theories that attempt to explain economic fluctuations by changes in potential GNP are called **real business cycle theories**. It does not appear that shifts in labor supply and demand are sufficient to explain economic fluctuations. We need something more than the strict classical model if we want to explain the business cycle using flexible prices and wages.

The **new classical theory** combines flexible prices with **incomplete information** to explain fluctuations. Incomplete information refers to the possibility that firms may not play their classical role because they lack essential information. Information-based models use the microeconomic theory of firm supply to explain the departures of output from potential GNP.

Microeconomic theory tells us that a firm produces up to the point where the price of its good equals its marginal cost (the extra cost of producing one more unit of the good), which depends on the price of the firm's inputs to production. If the price of the firm's output rises relative to the price of other goods, including the price of its inputs, the firm will produce more. If the general price level rises, so that all prices rise, the relative price of the firm's output is unchanged and it will not increase its production.

Firms do not have complete information on the general price level in the economy. The **representative firm's supply curve** when the firm has to estimate the general price level is given by

$$Y_i = h(P_i - P^e) + Y_i^*,$$ (14-1)

where Y_i is the firm's production, P_i is the firm's price, P^e is the estimate of the general price level, and Y_i^* is the firm's potential or normal production. The firm's output, Y_i, is greater than normal, Y_i^*, by an amount equal to a constant h times the difference between the firm's price P_i and its estimate of the general price level P^e.

The **best-guess line** describes the firm's estimate of the general price level:

$$P^e = \hat{P} + b(P_i - \hat{P}),$$ (14-2)

where $\hat{P}$ is the forecast, made at the start of the year, of the general price level. The firm's guess of the general price level, P^e, is greater than what was forecast at the start of the year, $\hat{P}$, by an amount equal to a constant b times the difference between the firm's own price P_i and the forecast of the general price $\hat{P}$. The coefficient b represents the influence of the firm's own price on its estimate of the general price level, and is between zero and 1.

The **Lucas supply curve** is derived by substituting the best-guess line into the representative firm's supply curve, and then adding up across the n firms in the economy. It is named for Robert Lucas of the University of Chicago, who did the original research on the information-based model:

$$Y = nh(1 - b)(P - \hat{P}) + Y^*.$$ (14-3)

The Lucas supply curve says that output Y is greater than potential output Y^* if the price level P is greater than what was forecast $\hat{P}$. An unexpected general price rise causes firms, who cannot perfectly distinguish general and relative price changes, to raise their output above potential.

Combining the Lucas supply curve with **rational expectations**, the assumption that people in the economy make the most of the information that is available when making forecasts, produces several striking policy results. Suppose that the Fed, starting at potential output Y^*, increases the money supply M and that the increase is anticipated. From the aggregate demand curve,

$$Y = k_0 + k_1(M/P), \tag{14-4}$$

people know that either output Y or the price level P must rise. If their expectations are rational, they will forecast the price increase. From the Lucas supply curve (Equation 14-3), price increases that are forecast have no effect on output. Returning the the aggregate demand curve (Equation 14-4), since output does not change the price level must rise by as much as the money supply.

The result that anticipated monetary policy is ineffective—having no effect on real GNP—also has striking implications for the problem of disinflation. The Fed can reduce the rate of inflation without causing a recession simply by lowering the rate of money supply growth. As long as the Fed announces its policy, people will expect inflation to decrease. Since the lower inflation is forecast, output never falls below potential GNP.

Unanticipated changes in the money supply have real effects in the new classical model. If the Fed increases the money supply unexpectedly, prices will rise above their forecasted level. According to the Lucas supply curve, firms will respond by increasing their production, causing output to rise above potential. Over time, people will realize that the money supply has been increased, price forecasts will adjust, and output will return to potential. Another possibility for effective monetary policy arises if expectations are not rational. If expectations adjust slowly, even anticipated money supply increases will create departures of output from potential.

The new classical theory can in principle explain fluctuations of output around potential GNP. The mechanism is that unexpected changes in the money supply create price surprises that cause output to differ from potential. Empirical work completed over the last ten years, however, casts doubt over how well the theory works in practice. First, statistical studies have shown that there is a very weak relation between price surprises and the departures of output from potential GNP. Second, while early research by Robert Barro seemed to indicate that money surprises were important and actual money unimportant, later research indicates that actual money is also a factor in the departures of actual GNP from potential GNP.

Three other problems with the new classical theory should be mentioned. First, the information-based models—without some additional changes—are not capable of explaining the persistence of the departures of actual GNP from potential GNP. Second, the informational restriction placed on firms—the assumption that firms know the price of goods they are selling but not the price of goods they are buying—does not seem plausible for most firms. Finally, the assumption of perfectly flexible prices does not appear to describe how most markets work.

Self-Test

Fill in the Blank

1. Theories that revise the classical model by incorporating information problems are called _____.

2. _____ theories rely on shifts in potential GNP to explain economic fluctuations.

3. New classical theory combines _____ prices and _____ information.

4. The assumption that people make the most of available information when making forecasts is called _____.

5. The positive relationship between prices and output in information-based models is the _____.

6. A firm will supply more output than normal if the firm's price is greater than the _____.

7. The _____ represents the firm's best estimate of the general price level.

8. According to the Lucas supply curve, output can only exceed potential if the price level is greater than the _____ price level.

9. A _____ is the difference between the actual and the forecasted price level.

10. According to the new classical theory, an _____ increase in the money supply will have no effect on real GNP.

11. _____ changes in the money supply, on the other hand, cause departures of real GNP from potential GNP according to the new classical theory.

12. The information-based model with rational expectations predicts that inflation can be brought down without causing a

_____.

13. In the classical model, fluctuations of output can only be caused by shifts in labor supply or demand.

14. In the new classical model, fluctuations of output can only be caused by shifts of labor supply or demand.

15. The new classical model differs from the classical model by assuming perfectly flexible prices and wages.

16. Real business cycle theories emphasize monetary factors to explain economic fluctuations.

17. According to the information-based model, firms do not know the general price level.

18. The Lucas supply curve says that output will only exceed potential if there is a price surprise.

19. According to the Lucas supply curve, there would be no departures of output from potential if the firm's best guess of the general price level was its own price.

20. The Lucas supply curve says that prices adjust without any lag when output differs from potential.

21. Changes in the money supply have no effect on real GNP in the classical model.

22. Changes in the money supply have no effect on real GNP in the information-based model.

23. Anticipated monetary policy can be effective in the information-based model if people's expectations adjust slowly.

24. Empirical evidence indicates that money surprises are the only important factor in the relationship between the money supply and departures of output from potential GNP.

25. How do real business cycle theories explain economic fluctuations?

26. Why do we need to go beyond the classical model to explain short-run economic fluctuations?

27. According to the representative firm's supply curve, when will a firm increase its production above normal?

28. How do firms estimate the general price level?

29. What determines the size of the coefficient b in the best-guess line?

30. According to the Lucas supply curve, why do positive price surprises cause firms to increase output above potential?

31. What is the major difference between the Lucas supply curve and the price-adjustment curve of Part I?

32. What are the two crucial assumptions behind the policy ineffectiveness and instantaneous disinflation results of the new classical model?

33. Why does unanticipated monetary policy have real effects in the information-based model?

34. Why does anticipated monetary policy have no real effects in the information-based model?

35. What are the costs of reducing inflation in the information-based model?

36. How well does the new classical theory explain the departures of actual GNP from potential GNP?

Problem Set

Worked Problems

1. Suppose that each firm has the supply schedule

$$Y_i = 10(P_i - P^e) + 5$$

and the best-guess line

$$P^e = \hat{P} + .4(P_i - \hat{P}).$$

a. What is the Lucas supply schedule if there are 100 firms in the economy?

b. Suppose there is a price surprise so that the actual price level P = 1.1 while the forecasted price level $\hat{P}$ = 1. What is the effect on output?

c. How would the effect of the price surprise change if the coefficient in the best-guess line was .1 instead of .4?

a. *The representative firm's output*

$$Y_i = 10[P_i - \hat{P} - .4(P_i - \hat{P})] + 5$$
$$= 10(1 - .4)(P_i - \hat{P}) + 5$$
$$= 6(P_i - \hat{P}) + 5.$$

Adding up across 100 firms,

$$Y = 600(P - \hat{P}) + 500,$$

which is the Lucas supply curve.

b. *From the Lucas supply curve,*

$$Y = 600(1.1 - 1) + 500$$
$$= \$560 \ billion.$$

The price surprise raises output \$60 billion above potential.

c. *The Lucas supply curve would be*

$$Y = 900(P - \hat{P}) + 500$$

and the price surprise would raise output to \$590 billion. Because the firm's own price has less influence on its estimate of the general price level, price surprises have more effect on output.

2. Suppose that the Lucas supply curve is

$$Y = 475(P - \hat{P}) + 1250$$

and the aggregate demand curve is

$$Y = 750 + .625(M/P)$$

with the money supply $M = \$800$ billion.

a. What is the price level P if output Y is equal to potential output Y^* with no expected changes in policy?

b. Suppose that the Fed announces that it will increase the money supply to \$880 billion and then enacts that policy. What are the new levels of output and the price level?

c. Suppose that the increase in the money supply is unanticipated. What are the new levels of output and the price level?

a. From the aggregate demand curve with output equal to potential output:

$$1250 = 750 + .625(800)/P$$
$$P = 1.$$

b. Since the increase in the money supply is anticipated, people forecast the new higher price level. With no price surprises, $Y = Y^* = \$1250$ billion. The price level can be calculated from the aggregate demand curve:

$$1250 = 750 + .625(880)/P$$
$$P = 1.1.$$

The price level rises in proportion to the anticipated increase in the money supply. Output is unchanged.

c. Because the increase in the money supply is unanticipated, the forecasted price does not adjust. From the Lucas supply curve,

$$Y = 475(P - 1) + 1250.$$

From the aggregate demand curve,

$$Y = 750 + .625(880)/P.$$

Solving for P:

$$475(P - 1) + 1250 = 750 + 550/P$$
$$475P^2 + 25P - 550 = 0.$$

Using the quadratic formula:

$$P = \frac{(-25) \pm \sqrt{(25)^2 - 4(475)(-550)}}{2(475)}$$

The only economically sensible solution is for the price level to be positive:

$$P = 1.05.$$

Solving for Y using the Lucas supply curve:

$$Y = 475(1.05 - 1) + 1250$$
$$= \$1273.75 \text{ billion.}$$

The unanticipated increase in the money supply increases prices less than proportionately and raises output above potential.

3. Suppose that each firm has the supply schedule

$$Y_i = 20(P_i - P^e) + 8$$

and the best-guess line

$$P^e = \hat{P} + .3(P_i - \hat{P}).$$

a. What is the Lucas supply schedule if there are 200 firms in the economy?

b. Suppose there is a price surprise so that the actual price level P = 1.2 while the forecasted price level $\hat{P}$ = 1. What is the effect on output?

c. How would the effect of the price surprise change if the coefficient in the best-guess line was .9 instead of .3?

4. Suppose that each firm has the supply schedule

$$Y_i = 10(P_i - P^e) + 10$$

and the best-guess line

$$P^e = \hat{P} + .5(P_i - \hat{P}).$$

a. What is the Lucas supply schedule if there are 100 firms in the economy?

b. Suppose there is a price surprise so that the actual price level P = .8 while the forecasted price level $\hat{P}$ = 1. What is the effect on output?

c. How would the effect of the price surprise change if the coefficient in the best-guess line was 15 instead of 10?

5. Suppose that the Lucas supply curve is

$$Y = 43.3(P - \hat{P}) + 1000$$

and the aggregate demand curve is

$$Y = 700 + 1.5(M/P)$$

with the money supply M = $400.

a. What is the price level P if output Y is equal to potential output Y^* with no expected changes in policy?

b. Suppose that the Fed announces that it will increase the money supply to $480 and then enacts that policy. What are the new levels of output and the price level?

c. Suppose that the increase in the money supply is unanticipated. What are the new levels of output and the price level?

6. Suppose that the Lucas supply curve is

$$Y = 560(P - \hat{P}) + 1500$$

and the aggregate demand curve is

$$Y = 1000 + 1.25(M/P)$$

with the money supply $M = \$400$.

a. What is the price level P if output Y is equal to potential output Y^* with no expected changes in policy?

b. Suppose that the Fed announces that it will decrease the money supply to $320 and then enacts that policy. What are the new levels of output and the price level?

c. Suppose that the decrease in the money supply is unanticipated. What are the new levels of output and the price level?

7. Suppose that the Lucas supply curve is

$$Y = 556(P - \hat{P}) + 2500$$

and the aggregate demand curve is

$$Y = 1582 + .90(M/P)$$

with the money supply $M = \$1275$.

a. What is the price level P if output Y is equal to potential output Y^* with no expected changes in policy?

b. Suppose that the Fed announces that it will decrease the money supply to $1020 and then enacts that policy. What are the new levels of output and the price level?

c. Suppose that the decrease in the money supply is unanticipated. What are the new levels of output and the price level?

Answers to the Self-Test

1. New classical
2. Real business cycle

206

3. Flexible and imperfect
4. Rational expectations
5. Lucas supply curve
6. General price level
7. Best-guess line
8. Forecasted
9. Price surprise
10. Anticipated
11. Unanticipated
12. Recession
13. True. Output can fluctuate only if potential GNP changes.
14. False. Unanticipated changes in the money supply will also cause fluctuations.
15. False. New classical theory differs by incorporating information problems.
16. False. Real business cycle theories emphasize changes in potential GNP.
17. True. Firms estimate the general price level using the best-guess line.
18. True. Output can only exceed potential if actual prices are greater than forecasted prices.
19. True. The coefficient b in the best-guess line would be equal to 1, and there would be no price surprises.
20. True. Prices are perfectly flexible.
21. True. Changes in the money supply only affect prices in the classical model.
22. False. Unanticipated changes in the money supply affect real GNP.
23. True. If expectations adjust slowly, even anticipated increases in the money supply can raise actual prices above forecasted prices.
24. False. Actual money also helps explain the departures of output from potential GNP.
25. Real business cycle theories rely on changes in aggregate supply to explain economic fluctuations.
26. In the classical model, economic fluctuations can only be caused by shifts in potential GNP. These changes are not sufficient to explain the observed business cycle.
27. A firm will increase its production above normal when the firm's price exceeds the general price level.
28. Firms begin the year with a forecast of the general price level. This can be an explicit forecast, maybe done by an economic consulting firm, or simply an unstated belief in what prices will be. During the year, they revise this forecast using the price of their own product.
29. The coefficient b in the best-guess line represents the influence of the firm's own price on its estimate of the general price level.
30. Positive price surprises cause firms to think that their relative price has increased, and so they raise output above normal.
31. The Lucas supply curve, with perfectly flexible prices, says that prices rise immediately if output is above potential. The price-adjustment curve, with sticky prices, says that the rise in prices occurs with a lag.
32. The assumptions are that prices are perfectly flexible and that expectations are rational.

33. Unanticipated changes in the money supply create price surprises, causing firms to change production and output to diverge from potential GNP.
34. Anticipated monetary policy has no real effects in the information-based model because it cannot create price surprises.
35. According to the information-based model, inflation can be lowered without causing a recession. There are no costs.
36. While the new classical theory can in principle explain economic fluctuations, research over the last ten years indicates that price surprises are neither of sufficient magnitude nor timed appropriately to explain the departures of output from potential.

Solutions to Review Problems

3. a. The Lucas supply curve is $Y = 2800(P - \hat{P}) + 1600$.
   b. Output increases above potential by $560 to $2160.
   c. Output increases by $80 to $1680. Price surprises have less effect because the firm's own price has more influence on its estimate of the general price level.

4. a. The Lucas supply curve is $Y = 500(P - \hat{P}) + 1000$.
   b. Output decreases below potential by $100 to $900.
   c. Output decreases by $150 to $850. Price surprises have more effect.

5. a. The price level $P = 2$.
   b. The price level $P = 2.4$. Output is unchanged.
   c. The price level $P = 2.3$. Output $Y = \$1013$.

6. a. The price level $P = 1$.
   b. The price level $P = .8$. Output is unchanged.
   c. The price level $P = .9$. Output Y is $1444.

7. a. The price level $P = 1.25$.
   b. The price level $P = 1$. Output is unchanged.
   c. The price level $P = 1.1$. Output $Y = \$2417$.

CHAPTER 15   The Theory of Wage and Price Rigidities

Main Objectives

We saw in Chapter 14 that, although the new classical and real business cycle models are in principle able to explain economic fluctuations, they have not stood up well to empirical tests. A theory that seeks to explain short-run departures without giving up the long-run classical outlook is that, in the short run, wages and prices do not adjust. They are "sticky," heading where the classical model predicts they will be, but arriving there with a lag. Chapter 15 looks at the staggered wage setting model to explain the microeconomics of the wage and price rigidities that form the basis of the model with sticky prices. We see how these rigidities are temporary, enabling us to explain both short-run fluctuations from and long-run steady growth of potential output.

Key Terms and Concepts

Wage determination in the United States differs between the union and the non-union sectors. Most wage contracts negotiated under major collective-bargaining agreements last three years. In about half of these contracts, the nominal wage is set in advance for all three years. In the other half, the wage is partially indexed to inflation. The indexing provisions are usually less than 100 percent. The government sometimes attempts to influence wage setting directly through **incomes policies**, in which corporations and unions are either told or encouraged to restrain price and pay increases.

Wage setting in the union sector is not synchronized. At any one time, only a small fraction of workers are signing contracts. The others have either recently signed contracts or will sign contracts in the near future. Wage contracts are said to be **staggered** because the period in which one contract is in force overlaps the period in which other contracts are in force.

There are three major factors that influence the outcome of wage bargaining in the union sector. The first factor is the state of the labor market. If unemployment is high, labor will be in a relatively weak bargaining position and wage settlements ought to be low. Conversely, wage settlements ought to be high if unemployment is low. The second factor is the wage paid to comparable workers in other industries. Because of the staggering of wage contracts, this includes both the wage settlements of workers who have recently signed contracts and the expected wage settlements of workers who will be signing their contracts in the near future. The third factor is the expected rate of inflation. If inflation is expected to be high, workers will ask for larger wage increases. Firms will be willing to pay them because their own prices are expected to rise.

In the non-union sector, it is typical for wages to be adjusted once each year. Like union contracts, these adjustments are not synchronized. The same factors that influence wage bargaining in the union sector—the state of the labor market, the wage paid to comparable workers, and expected inflation—also influence wage bargaining in the non-union sector.

Whether we consider the union or the non-union sector, it is clear that a worker and his employer do not negotiate new wages on a daily, or even a weekly, basis in response to changes in labor demand. This is where the rigidity of the wage rate begins. The **adjustment cost**, which is the cost of renegotiating a contract, makes long-term wage contracts desirable.

Indexing provisions in wage contracts could insure workers against unexpected inflation. The primary reason that indexing is not more widespread, and why it is not 100 percent when it occurs, is that indexing to the cost of living can be harmful if prices rise because of supply-side disturbances. With such disturbances, the real wage must eventually decline so that it equals the marginal product of labor. With 100 percent indexation, the real wage cannot adjust. This can be harmful to both workers and firms because, if the real wage cannot decrease to equal the marginal product of labor, firms will reduce employment. If prices rise because of expansionary monetary policy, these problems do not occur. It is not possible, however, to tell in advance what might cause prices to rise. Indexing also adds complexity to wage negotiations and uncertainty about the wage that the workers will actually receive, both of which may be considered undesirable.

The chapter here turns from wages to prices. Basic microeconomic theory explains how prices of individual products are determined in **auction markets**, where prices fluctuate day by day to keep demand and supply equal. According to the standard auction market model, an increase in demand for a product will raise its price. Direct observation of many markets, however, indicates that the prediction of price fluctuations in response to demand fluctuations does not hold. When prices change, it is usually because costs change.

The **markup equation** is an algebraic relation that incorporates the above ideas:

$$P = W + Q, \tag{15-1}$$

where P is the price, W is the wage, and Q is an index of other costs of production. It says that prices rise fully when costs rise but do not respond at all to demand. When demand changes, firms, at least in the short run, hold prices fixed to try to keep their profit margins constant. The markup equation is consistent with the fact that, in the United States, the real wage does not fluctuate much during business cycles.

Markup pricing seems to be a plausible model for real-world pricing systems: firms know more about their costs than about demand for their products on a day-to-day basis; pricing decisions made through markups over cost are easy to explain to customers; markups are easy for managers to implement; markups are easy to write into long-term price contracts; and, finally, most markets are not as competitive as simple demand and supply analysis requires.

A simple algebraic model of staggered wage setting and price determination can be used to express these ideas. Suppose all wage contracts last 2 years, that all wage adjustment occurs at the beginning of the contract, and there is no indexation. Let the subscript "–1" represent the previous period and "+1" represent expectations of the next period. The average wage is given by

$$W = 1/2(X + X_{-1}), \tag{15-2}$$

where this period's wage W is the simple average of last period's contract wage X_{-1} and this period's contract wage X. The contract wage X is set each period according to

$$X = 1/2(W + W_{+1}) - c/2[(U - U^*) + (U_{+1} - U^*)], \tag{15-3}$$

where U is the unemployment rate, U^* is the natural rate of unemployment, and c is a coefficient describing the response of wages to unemployment. The contract wage depends on the expected average wage and expected labor market conditions over the life of the contract. Using Equations 15-2 and 15-3, we can solve for the contract wage X to get

$$X = 1/2(X_{-1} + X_{+1}) - c[(U - U^*) + (U_{+1} - U^*)]. \tag{15-4}$$

The contract wage depends on the past and expected future contract wages as well as on labor market conditions. Wage determination has a backward-looking component X_{-1} and a forward-looking component X_{+1}.

The problem of disinflation can be examined using the staggered wage-setting model. If the Fed decreases the rate of growth of the money supply, the contract wage will not fully adjust immediately because it is partly dependent on the past contract wage and current labor market conditions. There will be a recession until enough time has elapsed so that all contracts come up for renewal. The Fed can mitigate, but not eliminate, the recession by announcing the money supply reduction in advance and by "**gradualism**," reducing the growth rate slowly, rather than "**cold turkey**," reducing the growth rate immediately.

The issue of the effectiveness of monetary policy when expectations are rational is closely related to the problem of disinflation. With staggered wage contracts, even anticipated monetary policy can increase output over potential until all contracts come up for renewal. Since these effects may last for several years, the staggered wage contract model, unlike the new classical theory, has the potential to explain the observed persistence in economic fluctuations.

The long-run trade-off between inflation and unemployment is the same in the staggered wage-setting model as in the classical and new classical models. there is no trade-off between inflation and unemployment in the long run. Regardless of the rate of inflation, as long as it is steady and anticipated the unemployment rate is always equal to the natural rate.

Contract theory is a modification of the standard auction market model, designed to explain wage rigidities in labor markets. We know from microeconomics that employment determined in auction markets would be efficient, with both the marginal product of labor and the marginal rate of substitution between income and leisure equal to the real wage. But labor markets are not auction markets—they are governed by either explicit or implicit contracts.

The **optimal contract model** shows that, if contracts are written to cover all contingencies, the outcome of the contract is just as efficient as the outcome of the auction market. These contracts specify the real wage and level of employment for different states of productivity. If workers are assumed to be risk averse while firms are assumed to be risk neutral, the optimal contract smooths workers' incomes to reduce uncertainty. Unlike the auction market model, the real wage may be lower during states of high productivity than during states of low productivity.

Contracts that incorporate **asymmetric information**, so that firms know more than the workers do about whether a shock to productivity has occurred, provide a more realistic portrayal of what we know about labor contracts. These contracts specify compensation schedules for different levels of employment, such as time-and-a-half for overtime, rather than specifying different levels of employment in different states.

212

Self-Test

Fill in the Blank

1. In an _____ contract wages automatically increase if there is inflation.

2. Government policies that attempt to influence wage setting directly are called _____ policies.

3. Most wage contracts negotiated under major collective-bargaining agreements last _____ .

4. In the non-union sector, wages are typically set for _____ .

5. Wage contracts are said to be _____ because the period in which one contract is in force overlaps the period in which other contracts are in force.

6. Indexing could insure workers against _____ inflation.

7. Wages are set for long period of time because of _____.

8. The relationship between prices and costs is described by the _____ equation.

9. When the Fed lowers inflation by slowly reducing the rate of growth of the money supply, it is called _____ .

10. _____ refers to an immediate reduction in the rate of the money supply in order to bring down inflation.

11. Standard microeconomic theory treats the labor market as an _____ market.

12. _____ is an attempt to extend economic theory beyond auction markets in order to explain rigidities in labor markets.

13. Most of the workers in the United states are unionized.

14. Most major union contracts are 100 percent indexed.

15. Most indexed contracts are contingent on the state of the economy.

16. Wage setting in Japan is staggered much as it is in the United States.

17. The real wage in the United States does not fluctuate much during business cycles.

18. Wage determination is purely forward-looking.

19. The disinflation policies of gradualism and cold turkey both cause recessions.

20. Staggered wage setting makes it more difficult for the Fed to bring down inflation.

21. The staggered wage-setting and new classical models have the same implications regarding the effectiveness of monetary policy when expectations are rational.

22. The staggered wage-setting and new classical models have the same implications regarding the long-run trade-off between inflation and unemployment.

23. The labor market can be well described by the auction market model.

24. According to the optimal contract model, the real wage may be lower during states of high productivity than during states of low productivity.

Review Questions

25. What are the three major factors that influence the outcome of wage bargaining?

26. What are the major similarities and differences between wage setting in the union and the non-union sectors?

27. Why are wages in union contracts generally predetermined for three years?

28. Why is indexing not more widespread?

29. What are some of the explanations for markup pricing?

30. Why is wage determination both backward- and forward-looking?

31. Compare the effects of the disinflation policies of gradualism and cold turkey.

32. According to the staggered wage-setting model, how should the Fed conduct disinflation policy in order to mitigate the resultant recession?

33. How can anticipated monetary policy increase output above potential if wage contracts are staggered?

34. Why is there no long-run trade-off between inflation and unemployment in the staggered wage-setting model?

35. According to the optimal contract model, how can the outcome of a contract be just as efficient as the outcome of the auction market?

36. According to contract theory, how does asymmetric information affect the design of contracts?

Problem Set

Worked Problems

1. Suppose the marginal product of labor is $20 - .25H$ and the marginal rate of substitution between income and leisure is $1.5H - 50$, where H is the number of hours worked. According to the auction market model, what are the number of hours worked and the real wage?

   The number of hours worked will adjust so that the marginal product of labor and the marginal rate of substitution equal the real wage. In this example, the number of hours worked = 40 and the real wage = $10.

2. Suppose that the contract wage is given by

   $$X = 1/2(X_{-1} + X_{+1}) - 2[(U - .06) + (U_{+1} - .06)],$$

   where last period's contract wage $X_{-1} = 1$ and the unemployment rate $U = .06$ (6 percent).

   a. If neither the contract wage nor the unemployment rate is expected to change next period, what is the contract wage X?

   b. What is the effect on X if next period's unemployment rate is expected to be .08 (8 percent)?

a. *The contract wage X = 1/2(1 + 1) = 1.*

b. *The contract wage X = 1/2(1 + 1) − 2(.08 − .06) = .96. It decreases because the expected unemployment rate increases.*

Review Problems

3. Suppose that the marginal product of labor is $23 - .3H$ and the marginal rate of substitution between income and leisure is $.8H - 32$, where H is the number of hours worked. According to the auction market model, what are the number of hours worked and the real wage?

4. Suppose that the marginal product of labor is $32 - .4H$ and the marginal rate of substitution between income and leisure is $1.5H - 25$, where H is the number of hours worked. According to the auction market model, what are the number of hours worked and the real wage?

5. Suppose that the contract wage is given by

$$X = 1/2(X_{-1} + X_{+1}) - 2[(U - .06) + (U_{+1} - .06)],$$

where last period's contract wage $X_{-1} = 1$ and the unemployment rate $U = .09$ (9 percent).

a. If neither the contract wage nor the unemployment rate is expected to change next period, what is the contract wage X?

b. What is the effect on X if next period's contract wage is expected to be .9?

6. Suppose that the contract wage is given by

$$X = 1/2(X_{-1} + X_{+1}) - 1.5[(U - .06) + (U_{+1} - .06)],$$

where last period's contract wage $X_{-1} = 1$ and the unemployment rate $U = .04$ (4 percent).

a. If neither the contract wage nor the unemployment rate is expected to change next period, what is the contract wage X?

b. What is the effect on X if next period's unemployment rate is expected to be .06 and next period's contract wage is expected to be 1.06?

Answers to the Self-Test

1. Indexed
2. Incomes

3. Three years
4. One year
5. Staggered
6. Unanticipated
7. Adjustment costs
8. Markup
9. Gradualism
10. Cold turkey
11. Auction
12. Contract theory
13. False. Only about 20 percent of the workers in the United States are unionized.
14. False. While about 50 percent of major union contracts are indexed, most of these contracts have less than 100 percent indexation.
15. False. Those contracts that are indexed are contingent on the cost of living.
16. False. Wage setting in Japan is more synchronized than in the United States.
17. True. There is no noticeable cyclical movement of the real wage.
18. False. Wage determination also has a backward-looking component.
19. True. With staggered wage setting, all disinflation policies cause recessions.
20. True. Staggered wage setting makes it impossible to bring down inflation without causing a recession.
21. False. Monetary policy is more effective in the staggered wage-setting model.
22. True. There is no long-run trade-off in either model.
23. False. Labor markets are governed by either implicit or explicit contracts.
24. True. Because optimal contracts smooth workers' incomes, the real wage may be lower in states where there is high productivity and high employment.
25. Wage bargaining is influenced by the state of the labor market, the wage paid to comparable workers in other industries, and the expected rate of inflation.
26. Wage setting in the non-union sector is governed by the same factors as in the union sector. The major difference is that, while most union contracts last for three years, wages in the non-union sector are typically adjusted once each year.
27. Wages in the union sector are generally predetermined for three years because of adjustment costs.
28. Indexing is not more widespread because it can be harmful if prices rise because of supply-side disturbances.
29. Information limitations, customer relations, managerial rules of thumb, long-term price contracts, and oligopoly or monopolistic competition are some of the explanations for markup pricing.
30. Because wage setting is staggered, previous wage decisions and expectations of future wage settlements both enter into the wage determination process.

31. Cold turkey brings down inflation faster than gradualism, but at the cost of a larger recession.
32. The Fed should bring down inflation by announcing the money supply reduction in advance and by reducing the growth rate gradually.
33. Anticipated monetary policy can increase output above potential until all contracts come up for renewal.
34. Since the rate of inflation in the long run is steady and anticipated, the staggering of contracts is irrelevant.
35. If contracts are written to cover all contingencies, the outcome of the contract is just as efficient as the outcome of the auction market.
36. With asymmetric information, contracts specify compensation schedules for different levels of employment rather than specifying different levels of employment in different states.

Solutions to Review Problems

3. The number of hours worked = 50. The real wage = $8.
4. The number of hours worked = 30. The real wage = $20.
5. a. The contract wage $X = .88$.
   b. The contract wage X decreases to .83 because the expected contract wage falls.
6. a. The contract wage $X = 1.06$.
   b. The contract wage is unchanged. It increases because the expected contract wage rises and decreases because the expected unemployment rate rises.

CHAPTER 16   Aggregate Dynamics and Price Adjustment

Main Objectives

Chapter 16 is like Chapter 7 in that it integrates the analysis from all the previous chapters and tests its ability to analyze the major issues. Our model now incorporates wage-price rigidities and rational expectations. With this chapter, you should understand how it can be used to analyze the dynamic response of inflation and output to various disturbances. (The empirical texts of the model using data from several countries provide evidence in support of the theory.) You should also be able to explain how changes in policy or the economic environment affect the coefficients of the model of price adjustment and of expected inflation.

Key Terms and Concepts

The Phillips curve, introduced in Chapter 6, is our basic model of price adjustment:

$$\pi = f(Y_{-1} - Y^*)/Y^* + \pi^e + Z, \qquad (16\text{-}1)$$

where π is inflation, π^e is expected inflation, Y^* is potential output, Y_{-1} is last period's output, Z is a price or supply shock that reflects changes in the price of raw materials, and f is a coefficient. Inflation depends on **market conditions** (represented by the output gap), expected inflation, and price shocks. Equation 16-1 has a number of important properties.

1. Prices are set as a markup over the costs of production. The first two terms in Equation 16-1 reflect the influence of the rate of change in wages. The last term reflects changes in the price of raw materials.

2. Wages respond with a lag to unemployment. Since wage contracts are staggered, the average wage cannot fully respond immediately to departures from the natural rate of unemployment. The first term of Equation 16-1 also incorporates Okun's law to relate deviations of output from potential to departures of unemployment from the natural rate.

219

3. Wages respond to expected inflation. When workers expect higher inflation, they incorporate these expectations into their wage negotiations. One reason that workers might expect higher inflation is if workers in other industries have recently signed three-year contracts with large raises for the second and third years.

4. There is no long-run trade-off between inflation and output. In the long run, the average effect of supply shocks will be zero and, regardless of the level of inflation, actual and expected inflation will be equal. Thus the market conditions term must be zero and so output must equal potential GNP. We have earlier called the lack of a long-run trade-off the natural rate property or the accelerationist property.

The coefficients of the price-adjustment model respond to changes in economic conditions. The indexing of labor contracts means that wages are affected by current as well as by lagged inflation. This can create a wage-price spiral as higher prices and wages reinforce each other, driving each other higher. Indexing makes nominal wages more responsive to market conditionings, raising the value of f, and to supply shocks, raising the value of Z. If the average length of the business cycle decreases, inflation will be less responsive to departures of output from potential and f will be smaller.

Modeling expected inflation is one of the most difficult issues in understanding the price-adjustment process. One factor to consider is forward-looking forecasts. Wage negotiations are influenced by people's expectations of future wage setting. Another factor is staggered contracts and backward-looking wage behavior. Wage negotiations are influenced by contracts signed in the recent past because they have an effect on future inflation. Both factors need to be included in any realistic model of expected inflation.

Another difficulty in modeling expected inflation is that the model itself will change when economic conditions are altered. For example, when the Fed announces a change in monetary policy that puts more weight on controlling inflation, the model of expected inflation will change if people believe the announcement. If the announcement is not believed, the model will not change until an actual change in inflation convinces people that the new policy is real.

A simple algebraic model that relates expected inflation to actual inflation in the previous two years is

$$\pi^e = .4\pi_{-1} + .2\pi_{-2}. \tag{16-2}$$

Using this model and the price-adjustment equation, with $f = .25$ and $Z = 2.5$, we can look at the effects of several policies.

1. A stimulus that pushes output 3 percent above potential for one year will raise inflation by .75 percent in the second year. Over time, inflation will decrease and will gradually approach zero.

2. A materials price shock of 1 percent for one year which, because of indexing, produces a contribution to the price adjustment equation, Z, of 2.5 percent. Combined with an accommodative aggregate demand policy so that output does not change, this raises inflation by 2.5 percent in the first year. Over time, inflation slowly falls to zero.

3. A monetary policy that creates a one-year inflation raises output above normal in the first year. Output falls below normal in the second year to bring inflation down, and then gradually rises back to potential.

4. A stimulus that pushes output 3 percent above normal indefinitely cannot be analyzed by this model. Because the sum of the coefficients of lagged inflation, .4 and .2, is less than 1, inflation will not accelerate. If the government enacted such a policy, the coefficients might change to

$$\pi^e = .5\pi_{-1} + .5\pi_{-2}, \tag{16-3}$$

where, since expected inflation equals actual inflation after two years, inflation will accelerate over time. More generally, no mechanical model of expected inflation (one that can be written as a single algebraic expression) is applicable to all situations. When the economic environment changes, so will the process of expectations formation.

The equations for price adjustment (16-1) and expectations formation (16-2) can be combined with the aggregate demand curve to produce a complete macroeconomic model. A numerical example of an aggregate demand curve might be

$$Y = 2067 + 3.22(M/P) \tag{16-4}$$

where the money supply M = \$750 billion. We look at several examples:

1. A recovery from a demand-deficient recession describes how an economy, starting below full employment with zero expected inflation, returns to full employment and stable prices. The initial level of output is below potential, causing prices to fall according to the price-adjustment curve. As prices fall, the aggregate demand curve shows that output rises. Eventually, the economy reaches potential output with a lower price level. There is very little overshooting in this example.

2. A **stagflation** is a situation of both high unemployment (caused by deficient aggregate demand) and positive expected inflation (caused by past inflation). A recovery from stagflation describes how an economy, again starting below full employment but now with positive expected inflation, returns to full employment and stable prices. At the beginning of a recovery from stagflation, inflation will be negative if the influence of below-potential output dominates and will be positive if the influence of expected inflation dominates. Even if inflation is

initially positive, expected inflation will decline over time and inflation will turn negative. The remainder of the recovery is as described above. The main effect of starting at a point of positive expected inflation instead of zero expected inflation is to delay the recovery.

3. A boom is set off by an expansion of aggregate demand. There is higher output at first followed later by inflation. Over time, output falls back to potential at a higher price level. In the numerical example, there is very little overshooting.

4. An oil price shock is an example of a supply shock Z. The economy is initially thrown into stagflation with output below potential and positive expected inflation. The recovery from stagflation proceeds as explained above.

All of the cases considered above display **counterclockwise loops**: the economy tends to spiral back to equilibrium in a counterclockwise fashion. Following a boom, inflation rises and output falls, whereas, following a recession, inflation falls and output rises. Indeed, the combinations of inflation and output for the United States, the United Kingdom, and Germany for the 1970s and 1980s provide evidence supporting the existence of counterclockwise loops.

Self-Test

Fill in the Blank

1. The basic model of price adjustment used in the text is the

   _____.

2. According to the Phillips curve, prices are set as a

   _____ over the costs of production.

3. _____ relates deviations of output from potential to departures of unemployment from the natural rate.

4. Because contracts are staggered, wages respond with a

   _____ to unemployment.

5. Wages are also influenced by _____ inflation.

6. The proposition that there is no long-run trade-off between inflation and unemployment is called the _____ or the

   _____ property.

7. Indexing of labor contracts can create a _____ as higher prices and wages reinforce each other.

8. Expected inflation is influenced by forward-looking _____ and backward-looking _____.

9. A _____ describes how an economy, starting below full employment with zero expected inflation, returns to full employment and stable prices.

10. A _____ is a situation where output is below potential and there is positive expected inflation.

11. A _____ is an expansion of real GNP above potential output.

12. Inflation and output display _____ loops.

True-False

13. Prices are set as a markup over the costs of production in the Phillips curve.

14. Wages respond immediately to unemployment.

15. There is no long-run trade-off between inflation and unemployment.

16. If labor contracts are indexed, wages are affected only by lagged inflation.

17. A stimulus that increases output above potential for one year will permanently raise the inflation rate.

18. A stimulus that increases output above potential for one year will permanently raise the price level.

19. A stimulus that increases output above potential indefinitely will raise inflation without bound.

20. A recovery begins with unemployment below the natural rate.

21. There is a stagflation if output is below potential and prices are expected to fall.

22. An oil price increase throws the economy into stagflation.

23. Following a boom, inflation rises and output falls.

24. Empirical evidence for the 1970s and 1980s supports the existence of counterclockwise loops.

25. According to the expectations-augmented Phillips curve, what are the three influences on inflation?

26. What does the coefficient f of the price-adjustment model measure?

27. How is Okun's law incorporated into the expectations-augmented Phillips curve?

28. How does indexing change the coefficients of the price-adjustment model?

29. Why are expectations of inflation both forward and backward looking?

30. Why is no mechanical model of inflation applicable to all situations?

31. What causes prices to fall and output to rise during a recovery?

32. What causes prices to rise and output to fall after a boom?

33. Why can inflation be either positive or negative at the beginning of a recovery from stagflation?

34. What is the main effect on a recovery of starting at a point of positive expected inflation?

35. What causes a boom?

36. What are several examples of the movements of inflation and output that are described by counterclockwise loops?

Problem Set

Worked Problems

1. Suppose that price adjustment is given by

$$\pi = .2[(Y_{-1} - Y^*)/Y^*] + \pi^e + Z$$

and expected inflation is

$$\pi^e = .5\pi_{-1} + .1\pi_{-2}.$$

a. What are the effects on inflation if, starting from potential output with zero expected inflation, policy-makers increase output by 10 percent for one year?

b. What are the effects on inflation, again starting from potential output with zero expected inflation, of a 3 percent materials price shock that lasts one year if aggregate demand policy keeps output equal to potential.

a. *There is no inflation in the first year because, with no materials price shock, inflation depends only on lagged output and inflation. Inflation is 2 percent in the second year because of the output gap and continues because of the influence of expected inflation. Over time, the inflation rate decreases until it reaches zero.*

Year	π
1	.000 (0 percent)
2	.020 (2 percent)
3	.010 (1 percent)
4	.007 (.7 percent)
5	.005 (.5 percent)

b. *In the first year, inflation is 3 percent because of the shock. Thereafter, it is determined by expected inflation and slowly decreases to zero.*

Year	π
1	.030 (3 percent)
2	.015 (1.5 percent)
3	.011(1.1 percent)
4	.007 (.7 percent)
5	.004 (.4 percent)

2. Consider the following macroeconomic model:

$$Y = 750 + 1.5(M/P) \qquad \text{(Aggregate demand)}$$
$$\pi = .25[(Y_{-1} - Y^*)/Y^*] + \pi^e + Z \qquad \text{(Price adjustment)}$$
$$\pi^e = .4\pi_{-1} + .2\pi_{-2} \qquad \text{(Expected inflation)}$$

with potential output $Y^* = \$1500$ billion and the money supply $M = \$500$ billion.

a. Suppose the economy starts out at a position with the price level $P = 1.25$, but with zero actual expected inflation. Describe the path of the recovery to full employment and stable prices.

b. How is the recovery affected if the economy starts out at a position of stagflation, with inflation equal to 25 percent.

a. *In the first year, output is below potential at $1350 billion. The output gap causes deflation of 2.5 percent, which lowers prices to 1.22 and raises output to $1365 billion in the second year.*

Starting in the third year, expected deflation begins to contribute toward lower prices, and prices fall while output rises until employment with stable prices is attained.

Year	π	P	Y
1	.000 (0 percent)	1.25	$1350
2	−.025 (−2.5 percent)	1.22	1365
3	−.033 (−3.3 percent)	1.18	1386
4	−.037 (−3.7 percent)	1.14	1410
5	−.036 (−3.6 percent)	1.10	1432
6	−.033 (−3.3 percent)	1.06	1455
7	−.028 (−2.8 percent)	1.03	1478
8	−.022 (−2.2 percent)	1.01	1495

b. The main difference between the recoveries is that, at the beginning, the influence of expected inflation is greater than the influence of market conditions, so that inflation is positive. Output falls at first and the recovery takes longer. The first eight years are presented below.

Year	π	P	Y
1	.250 (25 percent)	1.25	$1350
2	.075 (7.5 percent)	1.34	1308
3	.048 (4.8 percent)	1.40	1284
4	−.002 (−.2 percent)	1.40	1285
5	−.027 (−2.7 percent)	1.36	1301
6	−.044 (−4.4 percent)	1.30	1327
7	−.052 (−5.2 percent)	1.23	1360
8	−.053 (−5.3 percent)	1.16	1394

Review Problems

3. Suppose that price adjustment is given by

$$\pi = .25[(Y_{-1} - Y^*)/Y^*] + \pi^e + Z$$

and expected inflation is

$$\pi^e = .4\pi_{-1} + .2\pi_{-2}.$$

a. What are the effects on inflation if, starting from potential output with zero expected inflation, policy-makers increase output by 20 percent for one year?

b. What are the effects on inflation, again starting from potential output with zero expected inflation, of a 4 percent materials price shock that lasts one year if aggregate demand policy keeps output equal to potential.

226

4. Suppose price adjustment is the same as in Problem 1 but expected inflation is

$$\pi^e = .6\pi_{-1} + .4\pi_{-2}.$$

What are the effects on inflation if, starting from potential output with zero expected inflation, policy-makers increase output by 10 percent indefinitely?

5. Consider the following macroeconomic model:

$$Y = 1000 + 2(M/P) \qquad \text{(Aggregate demand)}$$
$$\pi = .25[(Y_{-1} - Y^*)/Y^*] + \pi^e + Z \qquad \text{(Price adjustment)}$$
$$\pi^e = .5\pi_{-1} + .1\pi_{-2} \qquad \text{(Expected inflation)}$$

with potential output $Y^* = \$2000$ and the money supply $M = \$500$.
   Suppose the economy starts out at potential output with the price level $P = 1$, and with zero actual or expected inflation. If the Fed increases the money supply to $550, describe the path of the boom.

6. Consider the following macroeconomic model:

$$Y = 400 + 1.5(M/P) \qquad \text{(Aggregate demand)}$$
$$\pi = .25[(Y_{-1} - Y^*)/Y^*] + \pi^e + Z \qquad \text{(Price adjustment)}$$
$$\pi^e = .6\pi_{-1} + .2\pi_{-2} \qquad \text{(Expected inflation)}$$

with potential output $Y^* = \$1000$ and the money supply $M = \$500$.
   Suppose the economy starts out at potential output with the price level $P = 1$, and with zero actual or expected inflation. Describe the path of the economy following a materials price shock of 10 percent.

7. Consider the following macroeconomic model:

$$Y = 1582 + .90(M/P) \qquad \text{(Aggregate demand)}$$
$$\pi = .25[(Y_{-1} - Y^*)/Y^*] + \pi^e + Z \qquad \text{(Price adjustment)}$$
$$\pi^e = .6\pi_{-1} + .2\pi_{-2} \qquad \text{(Expected inflation)}$$

with potential output $Y^* = \$2500$ and the money supply $M = \$1275$.
   Suppose the economy starts out at potential output with the price level $P = 1.25$, and with zero actual or expected inflation. If the Fed decreases the money supply to $1020, describe the path of the recession and recovery.

MacroSolve Exercises

1. Using annual data, graph the GNP gap on the horizontal axis against the inflation rate on the vertical axis. You will get inflation-output loops such as those shown in Chapter 16 of the textbook. The loop between 1930 and 1935 is clockwise, while most of the postwar loops observed in the data are counter-clockwise. (It will be easier to see this if you slow down the display—remember that you can then stop the display by pressing any key.) What might explain the difference in the directions of the loops in the different periods?

2. If prices were very flexible, would you expect to see flatter or steeper inflation-output loops following an increase in demand? Would the same be true for the loops following a price shock?

3. a. Simulate the "AD/PA, Closed Econ" model in response to a 10 percent price shock. Tabulate the results, and draw on a sheet of paper the implied inflation-output loop. (Hint: calculate the inflation rate as the percentage growth rate of the price index, and the GNP gap as the difference between GNP and 4000.)

   b. Do the same for the "AD/PA zero exp π" case (where the expected inflation rate is zero). Is the inflation-output loop flatter or steeper than in part (a)? Explain both why this is, and the policy implications of the changed slope.

   c. Do the loops become flatter or steeper when the responsiveness of prices to output increases?

Answers to the Self-Test

1. Phillips curve
2. Markup
3. Okun's law
4. Lag
5. Expected
6. Natural rate or the accelerationist
7. Wage-price spiral
8. Forecasts and wage behavior
9. Recovery
10. Stagflation
11. Boom
12. Counterclockwise
13. True. These include wage costs and the cost of materials.

14. False. They respond to unemployment with a lag.
15. True. The long-run unemployment rate will be the natural rate regardless of the rate of inflation.
16. False. Indexing means that wages are also affected by current inflation.
17. False. Inflation will eventually return to its original level.
18. True. Inflation will first rise and then fall to its original level, permanently increasing the price level.
19. True. This is the accelerationist property.
20. False. A recovery begins with output below potential and unemployment above the natural rate.
21. False. A stagflation involves output below potential and positive expected inflation.
22. True. It lowers output below potential and causes positive expected inflation.
23. True. This is an example of a counterclockwise loop.
24. True. They characterize inflation and output movements for the United States, the United Kingdom, and Germany.
25. Market conditions, expected inflation, and price shocks are the three influences on inflation.
26. The coefficient f measures the sensitivity of inflation to market conditions.
27. Okun's law is used to represent the pressure of labor market conditions on wage inflation by the output gap.
28. Indexing makes nominal wages more responsive both to market conditions and to supply shocks, raising the values of f and Z.
29. Expectations of inflation are forward looking because they are influenced by people's expectations of future wage setting. They are backward looking because they are influenced by contracts signed in the recent past.
30. No mechanical model of inflation is applicable to all situations because the model itself will change when economic conditions are altered.
31. Prices fall first because of market conditions and then because of expected deflation. Output rises because prices fall.
32. Prices rise first because of market conditions and then because of expected inflation. Output falls because prices rise.
33. Inflation can be either positive or negative because market conditions and expected inflation exert opposite influences.
34. The main effect of starting at a point of positive expected inflation is to delay the recovery.
35. A boom is caused by an expansion of aggregate demand.
36. Examples of counterclockwise loops are that, following a boom, inflation rises and output falls, whereas, following a recession, inflation falls and output rises.

Solutions to Review Problems

3. a. There is no inflation in the first year and 5 percent inflation in the second year. Over time, the inflation rate decreases until it reaches zero.

Year	π
1	.000 (0 percent)
2	.050 (5 percent)
3	.020 (2 percent)
4	.018 (1.8 percent)

b. In the first year, inflation is 4 percent because of the shock. Thereafter, it slowly decreases to zero.

Year	π
1	.040 (4 percent)
2	.016 (1.6 percent)
3	.014 (1.4 percent)
4	.009 (.9 percent)
5	.007 (.7 percent)

4. The policy of keeping output at 10 percent above potential indefinitely raises inflation without bound.

Year	π
1	.000 (0 percent)
2	.025 (2.5 percent)
3	.040 (4 percent)
4	.059 (5.9 percent)
5	.076 (7.6 percent)
6	.094 (9.4 percent)
7	.112 (11.2 percent)
8	.130 (13 percent)

5. In the first year, output rises to $2100 with the price level unchanged. First market conditions and then expected inflation begin to cause inflation, and prices rise while output falls to potential.

Year	π	P	Y
1	.000 (0 percent)	1.00	$2100
2	.013 (1.3 percent)	1.01	2086
3	.017 (1.7 percent)	1.03	2068
4	.018 (1.8 percent)	1.05	2049
5	.017 (1.7 percent)	1.07	2030
6	.013 (1.3 percent)	1.08	2015
7	.010 (1 percent)	1.09	2008
8	.006 (.6 percent)	1.10	2003

6. In the first year, inflation is 10 percent, the price level rises to 1.1, and output falls to $945. This causes a stagflation. The first eight years of the recovery are presented below.

Year	π	P	Y
1	.100 (10 percent)	1.10	$945
2	.046 (4.6 percent)	1.15	921
3	.028 (2.8 percent)	1.18	908
4	.003 (.3 percent)	1.18	908
5	−.016 (−1.6 percent)	1.16	917
6	−.030 (−3 percent)	1.13	933
7	−.038 (−3.8 percent)	1.09	952
8	−.041 (−4.1 percent)	1.05	974

7. In the first year, output falls to $2316 with the price level unchanged. First market conditions and then expected deflation begin to cause deflation, and prices fall while output rises to potential.

Year	π	P	Y
1	.000 (0 percent)	1.25	$2316
2	−.018 (−1.8 percent)	1.23	2330
3	−.028 (−2.8 percent)	1.20	2350
4	−.035 (−3.5 percent)	1.16	2375
5	−.039 (−3.9 percent)	1.11	2406
6	−.040 (−4 percent)	1.07	2443
7	−.014 (−1.4 percent)	1.06	2452

Solutions to MacroSolve Exercises

1. One explanation for the 1930s behavior is that there were negative shocks to aggregate demand, pushing the economy down and to the left in the graph. Then, in 1934, there was a burst of inflation as prices began to recover (a supply shock–perhaps due to changes in government regulations). This caused inflation to increase, moving the economy up and to the right as demand was being stimulated too.

2. More flexible prices would lead to thinner loops, with greater price and less output movement.

3. a. Plot output on the horizontal axis, and the inflation rate on the vertical axis.

   b. The loops are thinner when the expected price level is always 0, as this leads prices to adjust faster, without being tied down to their previous values. Thinner loops imply more rapid adjustment of the economy to exogenous changes.

   c. A stronger response of prices to output causes faster price adjustment and hence thinner loops.

PART IV

Macroeconomic Policy Evaluation

CHAPTER 17   Designing and Maintaining a Good Macro Policy

Main Objectives

The government is run by politicians, not by economists. That may or not be for the best. Nevertheless, economic analysis can be useful in thinking about policy options. In this chapter we move beyond the macroeconomic model and how it describes the economy's response to disturbances. We look at the policy options that have already been outlined, and think about how they can be mixed optimally. You should learn the trade-offs along the policy frontier between inflation and unemployment stability, and consider how the frontier can be improved.

Key Terms and Concepts

In analyzing macroeconomic policy, economists rely on the following five propositions.

1. People look forward into the future, and their expectations can be modeled by assuming that they have a sense of economic fluctuations and that they use their information to make unbiased (but not error-free) forecasts.

This is the premise of rational expectations. People know that many features of economic fluctuations characterize each business cycle and use their knowledge to form expectations of the future.

2. Macroeconomic policy can be usefully described and evaluated as a policy rule, rather than by treating the policy instruments as exogenous and looking only at one-time changes in these instruments.

This is a consequence of the rational expectations approach. If the government follows a particular policy, people will incorporate their knowledge of the policy into their expectations. Thus the policy instruments become an integral part of the model. For policy evaluation, we can stipulate policy as a rule. These rules can be activist, and thus incorporate feedback from the state of the economy to the policy instruments or **passive**, as, for instance, the fixed growth rate rule for the money supply.

3. In order for a particular policy rule to work well, it is necessary to establish a commitment to that rule.

This follows from the problem of **time inconsistency**. When people are forward looking, there is incentive for policy-makers to deviate from an announced policy rule—they can make things better by being inconsistent. However, once people realize that policy is inconsistent, the policy-makers lose credibility and the outcome becomes inferior to the original plan. Research on time inconsistency suggests that the scope for discretionary policy should be limited.

4. The economy is basically stable; after a shock the economy will eventually return to its normal trend paths of output and employment. However, because of rigidities in the structure of the economy, the return could be slow.

Demand and price shocks move output and employment away from their long-run, or potential, growth paths. Because wage and price setting have both forward- and backward-looking components, there are wage-price rigidities. These rigidities prevent the economy from quickly returning to equilibrium following a shock.

5. The objective of macroeconomic policy is to reduce the size (or the duration) of the fluctuations from normal levels of output, employment, and inflation after shocks hit the economy.

Macroeconomic policy rules that respond to shocks in a systematic manner exert considerable influence on the size and duration of the fluctuations caused by the shocks. How these rules should be constructed is the main concern of this chapter.

The **targets** of macro policy are the variables, such as inflation and unemployment, that we care about, while the **instruments** are the variables, such as the monetary base and tax rate, that are used to carry out the policy. The **social welfare function** summarizes the costs of having the target variables deviate from their desired levels. It reflects value judgments regarding the relative importance of the targets.

Whenever the number of instruments is less than the number of targets there is a trade-off between the different target variables. Equality of instruments and targets is not sufficient to avoid a trade-off unless the instruments affect the targets independently. For example, since monetary and fiscal policy both affect the aggregate demand curve, the two are not sufficient to avoid a trade-off between inflation and unemployment variability.

The **policy frontier** describes the set of different combinations of employment and price stability that can be achieved. The **squared error** is a simple measure of the loss from having a variable not equal its target value. One example is the **inflation loss**—the average of the squared deviation of the inflation rate from its target, near zero. (If inflation is 3 percent and target inflation is zero, the inflation loss is 9.) Another example is the **unemployment loss**—the average squared departure of unemployment from the natural rate. (If unemployment is 10 percent and the natural rate of unemployment is 6 percent, the unemployment loss is 16.)

The costs of inflation are hard to quantify. They include "shoe-leather" costs of conserving money holdings, distortions because much of the tax system is not indexed, capricious gains and losses by debtors and creditors, and problems caused by the failure of private pension plans to be indexed. Other, probably more important, reasons why people dislike inflation are that they see inflation as a breakdown of the basic government responsibility to provide a stable unit of purchasing power and that some people view inflation as a decrease in their wages relative to prices, rather than as a general increase in both.

The costs of unemployment are clearer. The direct costs of lost GNP, as measured by Okun's law, are very high in a typical recession. In addition, there are indirect costs such as the loss of training when a young worker becomes unemployed and the social costs from the experience of unemployment itself.

The policy frontier, or trade-off, between inflation loss and unemployment loss can be described in terms of a policy rule. The price-adjustment equation with expected inflation equal to last period's inflation is

$$\pi = f(Y_{-1} - Y^*)/Y^* + \pi_{-1} + Z. \tag{17-1}$$

Aggregate demand shifts can be offset through a policy that moves aggregate demand back to its original level. The choice of a rule to counter price shocks is more complicated. The policy response function is

$$(Y_{-1} - Y^*)/Y^* = -g\pi_{-1}, \tag{17-2}$$

where g is the **coefficient of response**. If g is zero, the policy response keeps output at potential and fully accommodates inflation. If g is greater than zero, the policy response lowers output in order to stabilize inflation. The effects of different values of g on inflation can be seen by substituting Equation 17-2 into Equation 17-1:

$$\pi = (1 - fg)\,\pi_{-1} + Z. \tag{17-3}$$

If g is zero so that $k = (1 - fg) = 1$, then the price shock Z permanently raises the inflation rate by Z. If k is zero, the effect of the price shock disappears after only one year. If k is between zero and 1, the effect of the price shock gradually disappears.

A policy of **strict price stability** ($k = 0$) involves a large amount of unemployment loss. A policy of **strict unemployment stability** ($k = 1$) involves a large amount of inflation loss. The best policy will achieve a compromise between the two types of losses, and will have k between zero and 1.

In terms of the empirical evidence presented in Chapter 16, the United Kingdom followed an accommodative policy during the early 1970s that became less accommodative during the late 1970s and early 1980s. Germany followed a less accommodative policy throughout the period. The United States was more accommodative than Germany but less accommodative than the United Kingdom before the advent of the Thatcher administration in 1979.

Nominal GNP targeting is an example of a compromise policy that is easy to express. Since aggregate demand disturbances do not initially affect the price level, nominal GNP targeting correctly offsets them. For price shocks, nominal GNP targeting, which sets $g = 1$, favors unemployment stability over price stability. Since a reasonable value for f is .2, $k = .8$. This means that 80 percent of a price shock is tolerated as a continued increase in inflation the year after it occurs.

We have focused on how to conduct macroeconomic policy in order to choose the best point on the policy frontier. These choices always involve a trade-off between output and price stability. If we could move the frontier towards the origin, we could improve the trade-off.

Streamlining the labor market, or making wages more responsive to price shocks, would move the policy frontier closer to the origin. Some proposals to increase the speed of adjustment of wages include better job matching, eliminating government price and wage fixing, reforming unemployment compensation, and legislating the share economy. It is not clear that any of these proposals would be effective or that their benefits would outweigh their costs.

Other proposals to move the frontier towards the origin include improving indexation so that price increases arising from imports and other materials costs would be excluded, avoiding government price shocks, and using controls and incentives, such as tax-based incomes policies, which reward businesses and workers who follow government guidelines for price and wage increases. As with the proposals to streamline the labor market, it is not clear how effective these would be.

Protectionist trade measures, such as tariffs and quotas, raise inflation when they are imposed and lower inflation when they are removed. Avoiding these prices shocks keeps the policy frontier as close to the origin as possible.

Self-Test

1. Policy rules are _____ if they involve feedback from the state of the economy.

2. _____ policy is formulated on a case-by-case basis.

3. With wage and price rigidities there is a _____ between output and inflation variability.

4. The _____ of macro policy are the variables that we care about.

5. The _____ of macro policy are the variables that are used to carry out the policy.

6. The _____ summarizes the costs of having the target variables deviate from their desired levels.

7. The _____ describes the set of different combinations of employment and price stability that can be achieved.

8. The _____ is the average of the squared deviation of the inflation rate from its target.

9. The unemployment loss is the _____ of unemployment from the natural rate.

10. Two extreme policies are _____ and _____ stability.

11. An example of a compromise policy is _____ targeting.

12. Tax-based _____ reward businesses and workers who follow government guidelines for wage and price increases.

True-False

13. People use the information available to them to make unbiased forecasts.

14. A fixed growth rate rule for the money supply is an activist policy rule.

15. The economy returns quickly to equilibrium following a shock.

16. Equality of instruments and targets is not sufficient to avoid a trade-off between the different target variables.

17. The target level of unemployment should be zero.

18. The costs of unemployment are not very large.

19. Aggregate demand shifts can be offset through a policy that moves the aggregate demand curve back to its original level.

20. If policy is fully accommodative, a price shock permanently raises the inflation rate.

21. The best policy is normally one of either strict price stability or strict unemployment stability.

22. Nominal GNP targeting is not optimal if there are demand shocks.

23. Moving the policy frontier towards the origin could improve both output and price stability.

24. Tariffs and quotas are examples of demand disturbances.

Review Questions

25. What is the premise of rational expectations?

26. Why does rational expectations lead to consideration of policy rules?

27. What is the difference between activist and passive policy rules?

28. What does research on time inconsistency indicate about the conduct of economic policy?

29. Why can monetary and fiscal policy not be used to avoid a trade-off between inflation and unemployment variability?

30. Why is it difficult to compare the costs of inflation with the costs of unemployment?

31. What is the relation between the degree that policy is accommodative and the persistence of price shocks?

32. Why does the best policy normally involve a compromise between inflation and unemployment losses?

33. How did the policies followed by the United States in the 1970s and early 1980s compare with the policies followed by Germany and the United Kingdom?

34. What are the implications of nominal GNP targeting for the response to price shocks?

35. What types of policies could potentially improve the trade-off between output and price stability?

36. Why do protectionist measures worsen the policy frontier?

Problem Set

Worked Problems

1. Suppose that price adjustment is given by

$$\pi = .2[(Y_{-1} - Y^*)/Y^*] + \pi_{-1} + Z$$

and the policy response function is

$$(Y_{-1} - Y^*)/Y^* = -1\pi_{-1}.$$

a. What is the equation that describes inflation?

b. What type of policy response function is this? Does it favor unemployment or price stability?

c. Suppose that the policy response function is

$$(Y_{-1} - Y^*)/Y^* = -4\pi_{-1}.$$

What is the equation that describes inflation? How is the balance between unemployment and price stability affected?

a. *Substituting the policy response function into the price-adjustment equation,*

$$\begin{aligned} \pi &= .2(-1)\pi_{-1} + \pi_{-1} + Z \\ &= (1 - .2)\pi_{-1} + Z \\ &= .8\pi_{-1} + Z. \end{aligned}$$

b. *Since g = 1, the policy response function targets nominal GNP. It favors unemployment stability since k = .8.*

c. *The equation that describes inflation is*

$$\pi = .2\pi_{-1} + Z.$$

This less accommodative policy favors inflation stability since k = .2.

2. Suppose that price adjustment is given by

$$\pi = .25[(Y_{-1} - Y^*)/Y^*] + \pi_{-1} + Z$$

and the policy response function is

$$(Y_{-1} - Y^*)/Y^* = -1\pi_{-1},$$

with potential output $Y^* = \$1500$ billion.

a. Suppose the economy starts out at potential output with zero actual or expected inflation. Describe the path of the economy for 5 years following a materials price shock of 10 percent.

b. Suppose that the policy response function is

$$(Y_{-1} - Y^*)/Y^* = -2\pi_{-1}.$$

Describe the path of the economy following the same shock, and compare it with the path in Part a.

a. *Inflation is determined by substituting the policy response function into the price-adjustment equation,*

$$\pi = .75\pi_{-1} + Z.$$

Inflation is 10 percent in the first year and 7.5 percent (.75 time .1) in the second. Output, which is calculated from the policy response function, is $1350 billion in the first year ($1500 billion minus the output gap of $150 billion) and $1388 billion in the second. The first 5 years are presented below.

Year	π	Y
1	.100 (10 percent)	$1350
2	.075 (7.5 percent)	1388
3	.056 (5.6 percent)	1416
4	.042 (4.2 percent)	1437
5	.032 (3.2 percent)	1452

b. *The inflation equation for the less accommodative policy response function is*

$$\pi = .5\pi_{-1} + Z.$$

Inflation is brought down more quickly but the decrease in output is larger:

Year	π	Y
1	.100 (10 percent)	$1200
2	.050 (5 percent)	1350
3	.025 (2.5 percent)	1425
4	.013 (1.3 percent)	1462
5	.006 (.6 percent)	1481

3. Suppose that price adjustment is given by

$$\pi = .25[(Y_{-1} - Y^*)/Y^*] + \pi_{-1} + Z$$

and the policy response function is

$$(Y_{-1} - Y^*)/Y^* = -2\pi_{-1}.$$

a. What is the equation that describes inflation?

b. What type of policy response function is this? Does it favor unemployment or price stability?

c. Suppose that the policy response function is

$$(Y_{-1} - Y^*)/Y^* = -4\pi_{-1}.$$

What is the equation that describes inflation? How is the balance between unemployment and price stability affected?

4. Suppose that price adjustment is given by

$$\pi = .2[(Y_{-1} - Y^*)/Y^*] + \pi_{-1} + Z$$

and the policy response function is

$$(Y_{-1} - Y^*)/Y^* = -3\pi_{-1}.$$

a. What is the equation that describes inflation?

b. What type of policy response function is this? Does it favor unemployment or price stability?

c. Suppose that the policy response function is

$$(Y_{-1} - Y^*)/Y^* = 0.$$

What is the equation that describes inflation? How is the balance between unemployment and price stability affected?

5. Suppose that price adjustment is given by

$$\pi = .2[(Y_{-1} - Y^*)/Y^*] + \pi_{-1} + Z$$

and the policy response function is

$$(Y_{-1} - Y^*)/Y^* = -2\pi_{-1},$$

with potential output $Y^* = \$1500$.

a. Suppose the economy starts out at potential output with zero actual or expected inflation. Describe the path of the economy for 5 years following a materials price shock of 6 percent.

b. Suppose that the policy response function is

$$(Y_{-1} - Y^*)/Y^* = -5\pi_{-1}.$$

Describe the path of the economy following the same shock, and compare it with the path in Part a.

6. Suppose that price adjustment is given by

$$\pi = .2[(Y_{-1} - Y^*)/Y^*] + \pi_{-1} + Z$$

and the policy response function is

$$(Y_{-1} - Y^*)/Y^* = -1.5\pi_{-1},$$

with potential output $Y^* = \$1500$.

a. Suppose the economy starts out at potential output with zero actual or expected inflation. Describe the path of the economy for 5 years following a materials price shock of 10 percent.

b. Suppose that the policy response function is

$$(Y_{-1} - Y^*)/Y^* = 0.$$

Describe the path of the economy following the same shock, and compare it with the path in Part a.

7. Suppose that price adjustment is given by

$$\pi = .25[(Y_{-1} - Y^*)/Y^*] + \pi_{-1} + Z$$

and the policy response function is

$$(Y_{-1} - Y^*)/Y^* = -2\pi_{-1},$$

with potential output $Y^* = \$2500$.

a. Suppose the economy starts out at potential output with zero actual or expected inflation. Describe the path of the economy for 5 years following a materials price shock of 15 percent.

b. Suppose that the policy response function is

$$(Y_{-1} - Y^*)/Y^* = -3\pi_{-1}.$$

Describe the path of the economy following the same shock, and compare it with the path in Part a.

MacroSolve Exercises

1. Suppose that your welfare function is the sum over five years of the square of the inflation rate and the square of the GNP gap (the per-

centage deviation of real GNP from 4000). Use the "AD/PA, Closed Econ" model to answer the following questions, assuming that there is a price shock of 10 percent.

a. Suppose that neither the money supply nor government spending is changed. What is the value of your welfare function?

b. Suppose that the money supply is increased by $60 billion. What is the value of the welfare function now? By this criterion, is the economy better off or worse off after this policy of accommodation?

c. Suppose, instead, that the government followed an extinguishing policy of decreasing the money supply by $60 billion. Is this policy preferred by the welfare criterion to the policy of accommodation?

2. An alternative index of welfare that is often discussed during presidential elections is the so-called "Misery Index," the sum of the inflation rate and the unemployment rate. Recall that the unemployment rate is related to the GNP gap by Okun's Law (Chapter 3). If the natural unemployment rate is 6 percent, then the unemployment rate is generated by the following equation:

$$U = 6 - GNPGAP/3.$$

Use this equation to calculate the "Misery Index" corresponding to the situation in cases (a), (b), and (c) of question 1. Comment on the differences between the relative desirability of the alternative policies between the two welfare functions.

Answers to the Self-Test

1. Activist
2. Discretionary
3. Trade-off
4. Targets
5. Instruments
6. Social welfare function
7. Policy frontier
8. Inflation loss
9. Average squared departure
10. Strict price and strict unemployment
11. Nominal GNP
12. Incomes policies
13. True. This is the rational expectations assumption.
14. False. It is a passive rule.

15. False. Because of rigidities, the economy returns slowly to equilibrium.
16. True. The instruments must have independent effects on the target variables.
17. False. It should be the natural rate.
18. False. The costs of lost GNP are very high in a typical recession.
19. True. Aggregate demand shifts can be completely offset.
20. True. Fully accommodative policy never lowers output to stabilize inflation.
21. False. The best policy is normally a compromise between price and unemployment stability.
22. False. Nominal GNP targeting completely offsets demand shocks.
23. True. Moving the policy frontier towards the origin improves the trade-off between output and price stability.
24. False. Tariffs and quotas are price shocks.
25. The premise of rational expectations is that people, in making forecasts, use their knowledge of economic fluctuations.
26. Rational expectations leads to consideration of policy rules because people use their knowledge of these rules to form their expectations of future events.
27. Activist policy rules involve feedback from the state of the economy to the policy instruments, while passive rules do not.
28. Research on time inconsistency indicates that, in order for a particular policy rule to work well, it is necessary to establish a commitment to that rule.
29. Since monetary and fiscal policy both affect the aggregate demand curve, they cannot be used independently to avoid a trade-off.
30. The direct costs of lost GNP from high unemployment can be measured by Okun's law. The costs of inflation, such as the cost of conserving money holdings, are harder to quantify.
31. The higher the degree of accommodation, the more persistent are price shocks.
32. Policies of strict price or strict output stability normally involve such large unemployment or inflation losses that compromise policies are better.
33. The policies followed by the United States were more accommodative than those followed by Germany but less accommodative than those of the United Kingdom before the Thatcher administration.
34. Nominal GNP targeting favors unemployment stability over price stability in response to price shocks.
35. Policies to streamline the labor market, improve indexation, and avoid government price shocks, as well as the use of controls and incentives, could potentially improve the trade-off.
36. Protectionist measures impose price shocks, worsening the trade-off between output and price stability.

Solutions to Review Problems

3. a. Inflation $\pi = .5\pi_{-1} + Z$.
   b. The policy response function is moderately accommodative. It favors neither employment nor price stability.

c. Inflation $\pi = Z$. The policy rule is completely nonaccommodative. The effects of the price shock on inflation disappear after one year.

4. a. Inflation $\pi = .4\pi_{-1} + Z$.
   b. The policy response function is moderately accommodative. It slightly favors price stability since $k = .4$.
   c. Inflation $\pi = \pi_{-1} + Z$. The policy rule is fully accommodative. The price shock permanently raises inflation by Z.

5. a. Inflation $\pi = .6\pi_{-1} + Z$. The policy rule is somewhat accommodative.

Year	π	Y
1	.060 (6 percent)	$1320
2	.036 (3.6 percent)	1392
3	.022 (2.2 percent)	1432
4	.013 (1.3 percent)	1461
5	.008 (.8 percent)	1476

   b. Inflation $\pi = Z$. The policy rule is completely nonaccommodative. The effect of the price shock on inflation disappears after one year but the decrease in output is much greater.

Year	π	Y
1	.060 (6 percent)	$1050
2	.000 (0 percent)	1500

6. a. Inflation $\pi = .7\pi_{-1} + Z$. The policy rule is not very accommodative.

Year	π	Y
1	.100 (10 percent)	$1275
2	.070 (7 percent)	1343
3	.049 (4.9 percent)	1390
4	.034 (3.4 percent)	1424
5	.024 (2.4 percent)	1446

   b. Inflation $\pi = \pi_{-1} + Z$. The policy rule is fully accommodative. The price permanently raises inflation by 10 percent but has no effect on output.

Year	π	Y
1	.100 (10 percent)	$1500
2	.100 (10 percent)	1500

7. a. Inflation $\pi = .5\pi_{-1} + Z$. The policy rule is moderately accommodative.

Year	π	Y
1	.150 (15 percent)	$1750
2	.075 (7.5 percent)	2125
3	.038 (3.8 percent)	2313
4	.019 (1.9 percent)	2405
5	.010 (1 percent)	2453

b. Inflation $\pi = .25\pi_{-1} + Z$. The policy rule is less accommodative. Inflation is brought down more quickly but the initial decrease in output is larger.

Year	π	Y
1	.150 (15 percent)	$1375
2	.038 (3.8 percent)	2219
3	.010 (1 percent)	2429

Solutions to MacroSolve Exercises

1. a. The welfare index is 184. Recall that if output were constant and inflation were zero, the index would be 0—which would be preferable to this outcome.
    b. In this case, the welfare index is 141, which is preferable to the index in the previous case. The contributions of both the GNP gap and inflation are smaller. Note, however, that the price level is higher in this case—if the welfare index included the price level, this policy might be inferior.
    c. The index is worse than either case, at 341. This is because there is both a deep recession, and a decrease in the price level from 110 towards 90. Since the index is equally increased by either inflation or deflation, this deflation worsens the index.
2. a. The Misery Index is 37.8.
    b. The Misery Index is 47.2. This is even worse than the "no policy" case, because the inflation that is accommodated boosts the index more than the milder recession diminishes it.
    c. The Misery Index is 29.6. Despite the very deep recession, the negative inflation each year after the first reduces the index. Notice that this is exactly opposite to the previous equation. The choice of index clearly leads to very different indications of which policies are desirable.

CHAPTER 18   Macroeconomic Policy in the World Economy

Main Objectives

Chapter 18 extends the review of optimal macroeconomic policy to the world economy. You should be able to compare the advantages of fixed exchange rate systems with those of flexible exchange rates, and understand how monetary and fiscal policy work under both systems. You should also understand how the exchange rate question has different answers depending on whether the country you live in is large or small.

Key Terms and Concepts

An **international monetary system** is a set of rules for each country's monetary authority that stipulates how exchange rates are to be determined. Exchange rates can be **fixed** (set by agreement among governments), **floating** (determined by market forces), or **managed** (influenced by policy-makers attempting to smooth out exchange rate fluctuations).

The **Bretton Woods System** was the international monetary system from the end of World War II until 1971. Each of the participating countries agreed to **intervene** in currency markets to keep the value of its currency against the dollar within a narrow range, called the **intervention band**, around its fixed exchange rate, called the **par value**.

A **reserve inflow** or **balance of payments surplus** occurred when a central bank prevented an appreciation of its currency by purchasing dollar securities. When a country defended its currency by selling dollar securities, there was a **reserve outflow** or **balance of payments deficit**.

The **International Monetary Fund (IMF)** was created to provide relatively short-term loans to countries to help them support their currencies during temporary periods of balance of payments difficulty, and the **World Bank** was created to make longer-term loans to developing countries. Today, both the IMF and the World Bank are involved in lending to developing countries that have gotten deeply into debt.

According to purchasing power parity, if inflation is higher in one country than in another the exchange rate should appreciate by the difference between the foreign inflation rate and the domestic inflation rate. The Bretton Woods System allowed for the par values of exchange rates to be lowered, called a **devaluation**, or raised, a **revaluation**, but such changes did not occur very frequently. The Bretton Woods System was abandoned in 1971 after inflation worsened for several years in the United States.

The current system is an amalgam of the various systems. Eleven countries, including the United States, Canada, Japan, and the United Kingdom, let their currencies float independently with relatively little intervention and several others, including Argentina and Israel, float with more managed intervention. Another eight countries belong to the European Monetary System, which fixes exchange rates among the member countries but jointly floats against the dollar. Several countries, including Brazil and Chile, have a crawling peg system under which the currency is indexed to an indicator, such as the domestic price index. Most developing countries fix their exchange rate to a single currency, usually the dollar, but some peg to a composite of currencies.

Consider a sticky-price economy with a fixed exchange rate. With high capital mobility, we showed in Chapter 10 that, in order to hold the exchange rate at the prescribed level, the central bank must adopt a monetary policy to hold the domestic interest rate at the world rate. If the country is small relative to the rest of the world, so that it cannot affect the world interest rate, then it has no control over its domestic interest rate.

The central bank of an open economy can hold domestic securities, called **domestic credit**, or foreign securities, called **foreign reserves**. The balance sheet of the central bank requires that the monetary base equal the domestic credit plus foreign reserves. If the central bank tries to increase the money supply by raising domestic credit through an open-market operation, it puts pressure on the interest rate to fall. With high capital mobility, investors demand foreign exchange so that they can receive the higher foreign return. This puts pressure on the currency to depreciate, which the central bank resists by selling its foreign reserves for domestic currency at the fixed exchange rate. The net result is that the monetary base is unchanged. Thus, under fixed exchange rates, the central bank of a small country does not have control of its own money supply.

Sterilized intervention occurs when a central bank sells foreign reserves and buys domestic credit (or vice versa) at the same time in the same amount. This eliminates the effect of intervention on the money supply. With high capital mobility, sterilized intervention does not have much effect on the exchange rate. Many small countries impose

capital controls, such as restrictions on the amount of currency that domestic residents can purchase, in an attempt to gain some control over
their money supplies.

Fiscal policy is enhanced in an economy with fixed exchange rates
because, since the domestic interest rate is unaffected by domestic
policy, there is no crowding out. These results need to be qualified if the
country, like the United States, is large enough to have some effect on
the world interest rate. Monetary policy can be effective to the extent
that the country can lower its interest rate, and there will be some
crowding out with fiscal policy if the interest rate can be raised.

To consider long-term prospects, the text takes up the classical
economy with perfectly flexible wages and prices. For a small country
with a fixed exchange rate, the world price level P_w is unaffected by
domestic monetary policy. According to purchasing power parity,

$$PE = P_w, \tag{18-1}$$

where P is the domestic price level and E is the exchange rate. Assume
that monetary policy abroad is not changing and that P_w is constant.
Since P_w is determined abroad and E is fixed, the domestic price level P
is independent of monetary policy. If the central bank increases
domestic credit, upward pressure on prices will force it to sell foreign
reserves in order to maintain the exchange rate. The central bank has
lost control of the money supply just as in the fixed-price model.

If the foreign price level increases, so must the domestic price level.
By pegging the exchange rate, the central bank will automatically
increase the money supply to accommodate the increase in domestic
prices. If there is steady foreign inflation the domestic inflation rate
must adjust to equal the world inflation rate.

A large classical economy with a fixed exchange rate has some
control over its money supply because it has some effect on the world
price level. An increase in the money supply for a small classical
economy with a floating exchange rate will increase the domestic price
level and depreciate the exchange rate in order to maintain purchasing
power parity. Monetary policy will have the same effects in a large
classical economy as in a small classical economy if exchange rates
float perfectly.

A floating exchange rate system permits different countries to have
different inflation rates, even in the long run, as long as the rate of
depreciation of the currency is equal to the difference between the home
inflation rate and the foreign inflation rate. The behavior of actual
inflation rates and exchange rates for the decade following the
breakdown of the Bretton Woods System comes very close to this
theoretical prediction.

Macroeconomic policy-making in the world economy can be thought
of as a game where each country, having a social welfare function that

251

includes both price and output stability, chooses their instruments to minimize a combination of each type of loss. With a **noncooperative policy choice** each country conducts policy without regard for the other. With a **cooperative policy choice** each country agrees to use a policy rule that doesn't have an adverse effect on the other countries.

An appreciation of the dollar, or equivalently a depreciation of other currencies, has two effects. The depreciation is like an aggregate demand shock that increases net exports in the rest of the world. The appropriate response by policy-makers in the rest of the world is to offset this demand disturbance by tighter fiscal or monetary policy. There is no loss of world welfare on this account.

The second effect of the appreciation of the dollar is to raise the price of imported products, to create a materials price shock, in the rest of the world. Since either inflation, unemployment, or both must rise, the appreciation of the dollar results in a loss of welfare in the rest of the world. A cooperative policy would be one in which both the United States and other countries are more accommodative to inflation than they would be under a noncooperative policy. There is little empirical evidence, however, about the size of the difference between the policies.

Self-Test

Fill in the Blank

1. An _____ is a set of rules for each country's monetary authority that stipulates how exchange rates are to be determined.

2. The _____ was the international monetary system from the end of World War II until 1971.

3. The _____ was created to provide relatively short-term loans to countries to help them support their currencies during temporary periods of balance of payments difficulty.

4. The _____ was created to make longer-term loans to developing countries.

5. With fixed exchange rates, countries _____ to keep currencies close to their par values.

6. With fixed exchange rates, the narrow range around the par value within which countries keep their exchange rates is called the

_____ .

7. Changes in par values of exchange rates are _____ or

_____ .

8. The _____ fixes exchange rates among member countries but jointly floats against the dollar.

9. In a _____ system the currency is indexed to an indicator, such as the domestic price index.

10. _____ is when the central bank offsets the effects on the money supply of keeping the exchange rate fixed.

11. Many small countries impose _____ in an attempt to gain some control over their money supply.

12. A _____ policy choice is when each country agrees to use a policy rule that doesn't adversely affect the other countries.

True-False

13. Today's international monetary system is called the Bretton Woods System.

14. Under the Bretton Woods System, devaluations and revaluations occurred frequently.

15. Most major industrialized countries today are independently or jointly floating.

16. With fixed exchange rates and high capital mobility, domestic and foreign interest rates are equalized.

17. The money supply of a small country is endogenous under fixed exchange rates.

18. Sterilized intervention does not affect the money supply.

19. Fiscal policy is ineffective in a small country with a fixed exchange rate.

20. According to the classical model, a small country with a fixed exchange rate cannot affect its prices level.

21. The money supply of a small classical economy with a fixed exchange rate will increase if the foreign price level rises.

22. Monetary policy will have the same effects in a large classical economy as in a small classical economy if the exchange rate is fixed.

23. Monetary policy will have the same effects in a large classical economy as in a small classical economy if exchange rates float perfectly.

24. In the classical model with fixed exchange rates, inflation rates are the same in all countries.

Review Questions

25. What are the three basic ways that exchange rates can be determined?

26. Under the Bretton Woods System, when did reserve inflows and outflows occur?

27. What is the difference between the lending policies of the International Monetary Fund and those of the World Bank?

28. Describe the balance sheet of the central bank.

29. Why does a small country lose control of its money supply under fixed exchange rates and high capital mobility?

30. If capital is not perfectly mobile, how can the central bank regain some control over its money supply?

31. With high capital mobility, why does sterilized intervention not have much effect on the exchange rate?

32. What are the effects of an increase in the money supply for a small classical economy with a floating exchange rate?

33. Under what circumstances does a floating exchange rate system permit countries to have different inflation rates in the long run?

34. What is the difference between cooperative an noncooperative policy?

35. What are the two effects of an appreciation of the dollar on the rest of the world?

36. Why does an appreciation of the dollar lower welfare in the rest of the world?

Problem Set

1. Consider the following macro model of a small open economy:

$$Y = C + I + G + X \qquad \text{(Income identity)}$$
$$C = 100 + .8Y_d \qquad \text{(Consumption)}$$
$$I = 300 - 1000R \qquad \text{(Investment)}$$
$$X = 195 - .1Y - 100(EP/P_w) \qquad \text{(Net exports)}$$
$$M = (.8Y - 2000R)P \qquad \text{(Money demand)}$$
$$R = R_w \qquad \text{(Interest rate)}$$

with government spending $G = \$200$ billion, the tax rate $t = .25$, the world interest rate $R_w = .08$, the exchange rate fixed at $E = 1.15$, and the predetermined domestic P and foreign P_w price levels both equal to 1.

a. What are the values of Y and M predicted by this model?

b. Calculate the effect of an increase in government spending of $10 billion on Y and M.

c. Suppose that the equations refer to a small classical open economy in which the domestic price level P is flexible and output is always equal to potential output at $Y^* = \$1200$ billion. What is the effect on P and M of an increase in G of $10 billion?

a. From the income identity,

$$Y = 100 + .8(Y - .25Y) + 300 - 1000(.08) + 200$$
$$+ 195 - .1Y - 115$$
$$= 600 + .5Y$$
$$= \$1200 \text{ billion.}$$

From the money demand equation,

$$M = .8(1200) - 2000(.08) = \$800 \text{ billion.}$$

b. From the income identity,

$$Y = 400 + .5Y + G$$
$$= 800 + 2G.$$

An increase in G of $10 billion raises Y by $20 billion to $1220 billion. There is no crowding out.

From the money demand equation,

$$M = .8(1220) - 160 = \$816 \text{ billion.}$$

c. *From the income identity,*

$$Y^* = 100 + .6Y^* + 300 - 80 + 210 + 195 - .1Y^*$$
$$\quad - 100(1.15P)$$
$$Y^* = 1450 - 230P$$
$$1200 = 1450 - 230P$$
$$P = 1.09.$$

From the money demand equation,

$$M = [.8(1200) - 160] \, 1.09 = \$872 \text{ billion.}$$

2. Suppose that prices in Problem 1 adjust according to the price-adjustment equation,

$$\pi = .5(Y_{-1} - Y^*)/Y^* + \pi_{-1},$$

where π is the rate of inflation and potential output $Y^* = \$1200$ billion. As in Problem 1, increase government spending by $10 billion starting from potential GNP. Starting with a price level $P = 1$, calculate the paths of inflation, the price level, output, and the money supply for 5 years. Describe the long-run outcome of this policy.

In year 1, with the price level predetermined, Y and M are calculated as in Problem 1a. Over time, prices rise, output falls to potential, and the money supply rises. In the long run, the values are calculated as in Problem 1c.

Year	π	P	Y	M
1	.0000 (0 percent)	1.000	$1220	$816
2	.0083 (.83 percent)	1.008	1218	821
3	.0155 (1.55 percent)	1.024	1215	831
4	.0216 (2.16 percent)	1.046	1209	844
5	.0255 (2.55 percent)	1.073	1203	861

Review Problems

3. Consider the following macro model of a small open economy:

$$Y = C + I + G + X \qquad \text{(Income identity)}$$
$$C = 300 + .75Y_d \qquad \text{(Consumption)}$$
$$I = 300 - 2000R \qquad \text{(Investment)}$$
$$X = 500 - .2Y - 200(EP/P_w) \qquad \text{(Net exports)}$$
$$M = (.5Y - 2000R)P \qquad \text{(Money demand)}$$
$$R = R_w \qquad \text{(Interest rate)}$$

with government spending $G = \$200$, the tax rate $t = .2$, the world interest rate $R_w = .10$, the exchange rate fixed at $E = 1.0$, and the predetermined domestic P and foreign P_w price levels both equal to 1.

a. What are the values of Y and M predicted by this model?

b. Calculate the effect of an increase in government spending of $20 on Y and M.

c. Suppose that the equations refer to a small classical open economy in which the domestic price level P is flexible and output is always equal to potential output at $Y^* = \$1500$. What is the effect on P and M of an increase in G of $20?

4. Suppose that prices in Problem 3 adjust according to the price-adjustment equation,

$$\pi = .25(Y_{-1} - Y^*)/Y^* + \pi_{-1},$$

where π is the rate of inflation and potential output $Y^* = \$1500$. As in Problem 3, increase government spending by $20 starting from potential GNP. Starting with a price level $P = 1$, calculate the paths of inflation, the price level, output, and the money supply for 5 years. Describe the long-run outcome of this policy.

5. Consider the following macro model of a small open economy:

$Y = C + I + G + X$	(Income identity)
$C = 400 + .8Y_d$	(Consumption)
$I = 400 - 3000R$	(Investment)
$X = 114 - .2Y - 40(EP/P_w)$	(Net exports)
$M = (.4Y - 1000R)P$	(Money demand)
$R = R_w$	(Interest rate)

with government spending $G = \$100$, the tax rate $t = .5$, the world interest rate $R_w = .12$, the exchange rate fixed at $E = 1.35$, and the predetermined domestic P and foreign P_w price levels both equal to 1.

a. What are the values of Y and M predicted by this model?

b. Calculate the effect of an increase in government spending of $20 on Y and M.

c. Suppose that the equations refer to a small classical open economy in which the domestic price level P is flexible and output is always equal to potential output at $Y^* = \$750$. What is the effect on P and M of an increase in G of $20?

6. Suppose that prices in Problem 5 adjust according to the price-adjustment equation,

$$\pi = .25(Y_{-1} - Y^*)/Y^* + \pi_{-1},$$

where π is the rate of inflation and potential output $Y^* = \$750$. As in Problem 5, increase government spending by $20 starting from potential GNP. Starting with a price level $P = 1$, calculate the paths of inflation, the price level, output, and the money supply for 5 years. Describe the long-run outcome of this policy.

MacroSolve Exercises

1. The "ISLM, Open, Fixed E" model is a model of a large economy under fixed exchange rates (or a small economy with effective capital controls and fixed exchange rates).

   a. What central properties of the model are affected by the "large economy" or "effective capital controls" assumptions?

   b. Compare the results of a monetary expansion in this model and its floating exchange rate counterpart "ISLM, Open, Flex E." Explain exactly why monetary policy is more powerful in one case than the other.

   c. Compare the effectiveness of fiscal policy in the two models. Explain why the model with the most powerful monetary policy under fixed exchange rates is the model with the least powerful fiscal policy.

2. Repeat the above analysis for the equivalent open economy models ("AD/PA, Open, Fixed E" and "AD/PA, Open, Flex E"). Explain any differences in the long-run effects of fiscal and monetary policies.

3. Examine the effects of a price shock (assumed to affect only the home country—so that P_w remains constant) in the fixed and flexible rate dynamic models (assuming that the money supply and government spending remain constant). Explain why the severity of the recession is smaller in the fixed exchange rate case.

Answers to the Self-Test

1. International monetary system
2. Bretton Woods System

3. International Monetary Fund
4. World Bank
5. Intervene
6. Intervention band
7. Devaluations or revaluations
8. European Monetary Systems
9. Crawling peg
10. Sterilized intervention
11. Capital controls
12. Cooperative
13. False. The Bretton Woods System was the international monetary system from the end of World War II until 1971.
14. False. Changes in par values occurred infrequently.
15. True. They float either independently or in arrangements such as the European Monetary System.
16. True. This is an implication of interest rate parity.
17. True. The money supply is determined by the need to intervene in order to fix the exchange rate.
18. True. Sterilization involves offsetting open-market operations to keep the money supply constant.
19. False. The effectiveness of fiscal policy is enhanced because there is no crowding out.
20. True. Because of purchasing power parity, the domestic price level is determined by the fixed exchange rate and the exogenous foreign price level.
21. True. The money supply must be increased to keep the exchange rate from appreciating.
22. False. The large classical economy has some control over its money supply because it has some effect on the world price level.
23. True. The size of the economy makes no difference in this case.
24. True. This is an implication of purchasing power parity with fixed exchange rates.
25. Exchange rates can be fixed, floating, or managed.
26. Reserve inflows occurred when a central bank intervened to keep its currency from appreciating, outflows when it intervened to keep its currency from depreciating.
27. The International Monetary Fund makes relatively short-term balance of payments loans, while the World Bank makes longer-term development loans.
28. The balance sheet of the central bank requires that the monetary base equal domestic credit plus foreign reserves.
29. Because high capital mobility requires that the domestic and foreign interest rates be equal, the commitment to fix the exchange rate determines the level of the money supply.
30. The central bank can run sterilization operations to offset the effects on the money supply of keeping the exchange rate fixed.
31. Sterilized intervention does not affect the money supply. With high capital mobility, it does not have much effect on the exchange rate.

32. The domestic price level will increase and the exchange rate will depreciate in order to maintain purchasing power parity.
33. The rate of depreciation of the currency must be equal to the difference between the home inflation rate and the foreign inflation rate.
34. With cooperative policy, each country agrees to use a policy rule that does not have an adverse affect on the other countries. With noncooperative policy, each country conducts policy without regard for the others.
35. The appreciation of the dollar affects the rest of the world like an aggregate demand disturbance plus a materials price shock.
36. The aspect of the dollar appreciation that acts like a price shock requires that inflation, unemployment, or both must rise. This results in a loss of welfare for the rest of the world.

Solutions to Review Problems

3. a. Output Y = $1500. The money supply M = $550.
   b. Output increases by $33 to $1533. The money supply M = $567.
   c. The price level P = 1.1. The money supply M = $605.

4.

Year	π	P	Y	M
1	.0000 (0 percent)	1.000	$1533	$567
2	.0055 (.55 percent)	1.006	1532	569
3	.0109 (1.09 percent)	1.017	1528	574
4	.0156 (1.56 percent)	1.033	1523	580
5	.0194 (1.94 percent)	1.053	1516	589

5. a. Output Y = $750. The money supply M = $180.
   b. Output increases by $25 to $775. The money supply M = $190.
   c. The price level P = 1.37. The money supply M = $247.

6.

Year	π	P	Y	M
1	.0000 (0 percent)	1.000	$775	$190
2	.0083 (.83 percent)	1.008	774	191
3	.0164 (1.64 percent)	1.025	773	194
4	.0242 (2.42 percent)	1.049	772	198
5	.0314 (3.14 percent)	1.082	769	203

Solutions to MacroSolve Exercises

1. a. These assumptions help the government fix the exchange rate without losing all control over the money supply.
   b. Monetary policy is more powerful under flexible exchange rates, as the reduction in the interest rate that accompanies a monetary expansion leads the exchange rate to depreciate, reducing the decline in net exports that would exist were the exchange rate to be fixed.

c. Fiscal policy is weaker under flexible exchange rates, as a fiscal expansion is muted by a reduction in net exports. When the exchange rate is fixed, net exports do not fall as much as when the exchange rate is allowed to appreciate.

2. The effects of fiscal and monetary policies are similar in the two cases. In the long run, a fiscal expansion leads to a continued trade deficit in the flexible exchange rate case, because it leads to an appreciation of the exchange rate. A monetary expansion causes a long-run trade deficit in the fixed exchange rate case, but not when rates are allowed to float. This is because the monetary expansion increases the price level but not the nominal exchange rate; consequently it causes the real exchange rate to appreciate. In the flexible exchange rate regime, the nominal exchange rate depreciates, bringing the real exchange rate back to equilibrium.

3. The price shock affects the economy by reducing real money balances. For the same reason that monetary policy is more powerful under flexible exchange rates, the price shock has a larger effect under flexible exchange rates.